Jim Haynes is a first-generation Aussie whose mother migrated from the UK as a child during the Depression. His father arrived on a British warship at the end of World War II, met his mother and stayed. 'My parents always insisted we were Australian, not British,' says Jim.

Educated at Sydney Boys High School and Sydney Teachers' College, he taught for six years at Menindee, on the Darling River, and later at high schools in northern New South Wales and in London. Jim has also worked in radio and as a nurse, cleaner and sapphire salesman, and has two degrees in literature from the University of New England and a master's degree from the University of Wales in the UK.

Jim formed the Bandy Bill & Co Bush Band in Inverell in 1978. He also worked in commercial radio and on the popular ABC program *Australia All Over*. In 1988 he signed as a solo recording artist with Festival Records, began touring and had a minor hit with 'Mow Ya Lawn'. Other record deals followed, along with hits like 'Since Cheryl Went Feral' and 'Don't Call Wagga Wagga Wagga'.

Jim was awarded the Order of Australia Medal in 2016 'for service to the performing arts as an entertainer, author, broadcaster and historian'. He has written and compiled 29 books, released many albums of songs, verse and humour, and broadcast his weekly Australiana segment on Macquarie Radio for twenty years. He lives at Moore Park in Sydney with his wife, Robyn.

ALSO BY JIM HAYNES

Adventurers, Pioneers and Misfits
The Big Book of Australia's War Stories
Best Australian Drinking Stories
Great Australian Scams, Cons and Rorts
Australia's Most Unbelievable True Stories
The Big Book of Australian Racing Stories
The Best Gallipoli Yarns and Forgotten Stories
Australia's Best Unknown Stories
The Best Australian Yarns
The Best Australian Bush Stories
The Best Australian Sea Stories
The Best Australian Trucking Stories
The Great Australian Book of Limericks
The Best Australian Racing Stories
The Big Book of Verse for Aussie Kids

GREAT
FURPHIES
OF
AUSTRALIAN
HISTORY

WHAT YOU REALLY
NEED TO KNOW—
THE TRUTH BEHIND
THE MYTHS

JIM HAYNES

ALLEN&UNWIN
SYDNEY • MELBOURNE • AUCKLAND • LONDON

First published in 2021

Allen & Unwin
83 Alexander Street
Crows Nest NSW 2065
Australia
Phone: (61 2) 8425 0100
Email: info@allenandunwin.com
Web: www.allenandunwin.com

A catalogue record for this
book is available from the
National Library of Australia

ISBN 978 1 76087 981 5

Set in 12/15 pt Minion Pro by Midland Typesetters, Australia
Printed in Australia by McPherson's Printing Group

10 9 8 7 6 5 4 3 2

For Robyn

CONTENTS

'Australian history is almost always picturesque; indeed, it is so curious and strange, that it is itself the chiefest novelty the country has to offer, and so it pushes the other novelties into second and third place. It does not read like history, but like the most beautiful lies. And all of a fresh new sort, no mouldy old stale ones. It is full of surprises, and adventures, and incongruities, and contradictions, and incredibilities . . .'

Mark Twain, *Following the Equator*

INTRODUCTION

WHEN LIES BECOME LEGENDS

'. . . you should say what you mean,' the March Hare went on.

'I do,' Alice hastily replied, 'at least—at least I mean what I say—that's the same thing you know.'

'Not the same thing a bit!' said the Hatter.

Alice's Adventures in Wonderland, Lewis Carroll, 1865

One of the greatest of all Aussie myths, relating to our landscapes and characters and lifestyle, is that we inhabit a land of deserts, tough outback characters, rural pursuits and vast stretches of bushland.

Well, Australia does have vast bushland and vast deserts, and there are a few tough outback characters, though they are hard to find these days.

The truth is that Australia ranks in the top 5 per cent of the most urbanised nations in the world and our population hugs the coast. Only a tiny percentage of our population has ever lived in 'the outback' and it is as big a mystery to most Australians as it is to the rest of the world. The 'outback', for most Australians, is an exotic tourist destination.

The distinguishing factor that shaped our history and our national character is actually the fact that we are surrounded by ocean. Before the European invasion, the vast majority of Indigenous people lived on the coast or within easy reach of the sea. When Europeans arrived they had to cling to the coastal areas of the continent for obvious reasons.

Firstly, that's where much of the fertile land is and easy access to fresh water. Secondly, the sea was the primary means of transport until quite recently. It was the major link for Australians travelling to other parts of the country, and indeed it was Australia's only link to the rest of the world. We became a wealthy nation not because we produced wool, gold, beef, coal and iron in vast quantities from the inland, but because clipper ships and steamers carried our wool, gold, beef, coal and iron to the world.

The distinguishing characteristic of Australia's history and lifestyle is that we are 'girt by sea'.

Australians, along with all other human beings, believe many things that are not true. This is because we have been told about them by people we respect—teachers, those in the media, authors, religious leaders, family members—and the stories have been constantly repeated—in history books, textbooks, advertising material, trivia quizzes and by word of mouth.

Often, we believe them because we simply like the story that goes with the lie, and even enjoy passing it on, because it makes us seem well informed, knowledgeable and clever.

If the 'lie' seems a more interesting and colourful story than the truth, chances are that it will become generally accepted and passed around until it becomes the 'myth' that people choose to believe, without even challenging the story by applying any test of probability, credibility or 'common sense'—or testing its validity with any research.

Once the myth is accepted, it often becomes part of the collected information on Google and Wikipedia, and then there is a good chance it will become widely believed and disseminated as the 'truth'.

Often these stories become accepted and popularised in the form of an 'urban myth' and, although many of them are easily proven to be untrue by even the most cursory research, they continue to be believed.

———

With such things as bush folklore, mistaken word and name derivations, and sporting history furphies, these misconceptions that become myths are merely an annoyance to pedants and those with particular related academic or recreational interests.

Often, sentiment plays a part, and comforting lies are more palatable than uncomfortable truths. There is, however, a far more sinister side to myth creation.

There are times when the creation of myths can have the effect of perverting both our history and our culture, if we are not careful. The attempted demonisation of James Cook and the beatification of Edward Kelly are perfect examples of this.

Although much of the factual and circumstantial evidence shows that Kelly was a violent and egotistical career criminal, a pathological liar and a murderer, the myth of the brave rebel fighting for the rights of the underdog against harsh persecution has persisted, flourished and grown out of all proportion. Of all the Aussie myths, the story of the Kelly Gang is the easiest to debunk through research. Yet, the myth is so strong in Australian minds that it is virtually impossible to 'demythify'. You have to strain credibility, common sense and much of the written evidence to near breaking point in order to establish and validate the myth of Ned Kelly, but people keep doing it.

If this continues, who knows, we may one day see a biography that reads:

Edward Kelly was famous in Victoria during the late 1800s.

His business empire grew through livestock trading and the acquisition of valuable equestrian assets and innovative banking schemes.

Beginning in 1870, he devoted several years of his life to government service, finally taking leave to resume his dealings with the livestock industry. In the late 1870s, he was a key player in a vital investigation run by the Victoria Police Force.

In 1880, Mr Kelly passed away during an important civic function held in his honour when the platform upon which he was standing collapsed.

In the case of James Cook, a complete lack of any understanding of what the man was about and how much control he had over his own destiny has led to his place in our history being totally misrepresented in recent times. Here is a perfect example of the past being judged by those who have no concept of history and can only think of the past in terms of their own modern-day moral compass and sentiments, in an age of entitlement and individual rights.

Researching and writing these accounts has reinforced my belief that any understanding of the past requires the ability to shift the mind to other times and understand the social and political landscapes in which people then operated.

The reason several of the parts in this book are longer than others is that the *truth* is always in the *background* to the story—never in the events themselves. Understanding history is not about knowing *what* happened, it's about knowing *why* it happened.

To understand any event in any war or discovery or social conflict, it is essential to have some knowledge of the politics of the time, the diplomatic skulduggery of the period, the social forces at work within the population, and the accepted laws, conventions and spiritual ideas of the age.

I have attempted to expose some of these Australian myths and misconceptions by explaining the facts, as far as they can be discovered by research, and the social and political contexts in which the events occurred.

PART ONE

COMMONLY BELIEVED
AUSSIE FURPHIES

'Why, sometimes I've believed as many as six impossible things before breakfast.'

Through the Looking-Glass, Lewis Carroll, 1871

THE 'COMMON SENSE' TEST

O ccasionally, when I'm giving talks on Australian social history, I meet people who simply refuse to believe certain things in spite of the fact that the truth is often glaringly obvious and provable.

Some of the iconic Australian furphies and fallacies are so deeply embedded in our minds through repetition, and our desire to believe them, that accepting another truth is a very hard thing to manage. Challenging the version of events that people have always accepted as the truth and often feel quite comfortable with, and even proud of, sometimes meets with strong resistance. They have fond memories of the people who told them the furphy—parents, grandparents, teachers—and don't wish to believe that they were wrong.

After telling an audience about the truth behind the 'Ashes myth', for example, I have, on several occasions, had men tell me that, while they concede my version could be true, they will continue to believe what they were told as kids. One fellow even told me his great uncle knew someone who was there at The Oval in 1882 'when it happened and saw it', in spite of the fact that no one has ever claimed the supposed burning took place on the field immediately after the game.

I always invite an audience to 'step back' mentally from what they have been told and apply the 'common sense' test. How likely is it, for example, that cricketers in the moment of historic victory would suggest burning something? And, just how do you burn a hardwood cricket bail, a wooden stump or a leather-and-cork ball, and collect the ashes? Why would anyone walk a valuable racehorse to Melbourne when every other horse went by steamship? And so on.

The truth is that we believe what we want to believe. Not everyone wants to be confronted with a 'new' truth when they have believed the old one all their lives.

'THE ASHES' MYTH

The first cricket Test was played in 1877 between the touring Englishmen and a Combined Australian XI ... what is significant about that?

Well, there was no Australia in 1877. Cricket gave us an Aussie identity 24 years before we were a nation and it had a huge effect on national spirit, even though only three colonies were represented in the team: New South Wales, Victoria and Tasmania.

British teams had toured here from the 1850s but had always played against teams of seventeen or fifteen players from each separate colony and, in 1866, an Aboriginal team toured the UK, as much as a novelty as a sporting team, but they did quite well on the field, winning fourteen, losing fourteen, and drawing nineteen matches in six months.

New South Welshman Charles Bannerman set two records in the first Test ever played and one will never be beaten, although the other might be. He scored the first run in Test history, and scored 67 per cent of the runs in an innings—he made 165, retired hurt.

There was controversy right from the beginning. Due to the bitter intercolonial rivalry that existed at the time, the two best bowlers in the country refused to play. Victorian Frank Allan decided to go to the Warrnambool Show instead, and New South Wales bowler Fred Spofforth would not bowl to the Victorian wicketkeeper Jack Blackman and boycotted the match.

There's also an irony in our first Test team's make-up ... seven of the Australian team were born in Britain, including Bannerman!

The next year a combined team, including Spofforth, paid their own way to the UK and destroyed W.G. Grace's MCC side at Lords, bowling them out for 33 and 19! In this match Spofforth gained his nickname, 'The Demon Bowler'.

Sadly, this match was not given 'Test' status.

A total of eight Tests were played before 1882—seven in Australia and one in the UK. Australia won four Tests, England won two, and two were drawn.

In 1882 England lost at home for the first time and Spofforth won the Test for Australia, taking 7 for 44. He bowled his last 11 overs for 2 runs and 4 wickets, and Australia won by 8 runs.

After the match the following poem was published in *Punch* magazine:

> Well done, Cornstalks! Whipt us fair and square,
> Was it luck that tript us? Was it scare?
> Kangaroo Land's 'Demon', or our own
> Want of 'devil', coolness, nerve, backbone?

Also a mock obituary was famously inserted in the *Sporting Times*, which read:

> In Affectionate Remembrance of ENGLISH CRICKET, which died at the Oval on 29th AUGUST, 1882, Deeply lamented by a large circle of sorrowing friends and acquaintances R.I.P.
> N.B.—The body will be cremated and the ashes taken to Australia.

This was the beginning of 'The Ashes' myth, which is not really a cricket story at all—it's a love story.

When the man who would become the 8th Earl of Darnley, Ivo Bligh, led the English team to Australia in the following English winter, the English press joked that he was going to 'bring back the ashes'.

After his team won two of the three official Tests, in Sydney, they moved on to Melbourne where they were invited to stay at Rupertswood, the palatial home of Sir (later Lord) William and Lady Clarke, who had met Bligh when they travelled back home on the SS *Peshawar*, which was bringing the English cricket team to Australia in 1882.

During a party at Rupertswood, a group of ladies, including Ivo Bligh's future wife Florence Morphy of Beechworth, made a presentation to him of a terracotta scent bottle, which contained some ashes.

It was a continuation of the joke about the death of English cricket and the cremation of the body and the ashes being taken to Australia. The presentation was received with much amusement and, when the team was leaving for home, the presentation was repeated, after a small plaque had been added to the scent bottle.

Florence Rose Morphy was the youngest of seven children of an old friend of the Clarkes, a gold commissioner and police magistrate in Beechworth who had died in 1861. The family were living on a government pension at Hawthorn in Melbourne when, in 1881, Florence became the governess and music teacher to the Clarke children at Rupertswood, where she and Ivo Bligh met for the first time on 15 November 1882.

The story is more a love story than a cricket story. Bligh, who had injured his hand and could not play in many of the tour matches, spent much of his time at Rupertswood, courting Florence, and wrote home to his father, telling him that he had met 'the most delightful creature' whom he intended to marry.

In spite of some opposition from his family, due to the fact that she was a colonial lass and the Morphy family had become quite impoverished after the death of Florence's father, Ivo Bligh returned to Australia to marry Florence, in St Mary's Church, Sunbury, in 1884—not long after the team had arrived home in triumph (carrying 'The Ashes').

Back in Britain, Ivo inherited the Irish peerage as the Earl of Darnley, when his older brother, Edward, passed away in 1900. Florence became the Countess of Darnley and the couple lived as lord and lady of the manor at Cobden in Kent where, during World War I, they opened Cobden Hall as a military hospital. Florence worked as the matron, and more than 2000 Australian soldiers received treatment and recuperated there. In 1917, Prime Minister Billy Hughes spent Christmas at Cobden and, in 1919, Florence Bligh, Countess of Darnley, was made a dame of the British Empire in recognition of her efforts during the war.

When Ivo died in 1927 Florence presented the little trophy to the MCC and, consequently, its ownership resides with that organisation. It was, originally, a personal gift from a future wife to her future husband but has evolved into 'The Ashes', the coveted prize for the winner of cricket Tests between Australia and England. A replica and, since 1999, a Waterford crystal trophy are presented to the 'holders' of the symbolic ashes.

In 1998 the Darnleys' 82-year-old daughter-in-law wrote to the MCC and declared that the ashes in the terracotta scent bottle were the remains of her mother-in-law's hat veil. MCC officials are, however, '95 per cent certain' that the urn contains the ashes of a cricket bail, most likely one used in a social game between the English team and one chosen by Sir W.J. Clarke.

While 'bail' and 'veil' sound similar, and a misunderstanding is plausible, anyone understanding the nature of the 'joke' presentation (and how hard it is to actually cremate a cricket bail and recover the ashes) will realise that 'The Ashes' are, in all likelihood, derived from something much easier to incinerate than a wooden bail.

It is highly unlikely that cricketers, after an important win, would be bothered incinerating a hardwood bail, or stump, or cricket ball, and the joke death notice in the *Sporting Times* in 1882 and the letter to the MCC in 1998 make the truth fairly apparent.

There is even an uncorroborated apocryphal story that the little bottle fell from the mantel at Cobden Hall and the original ashes spilled out and were replaced by ashes from the fireplace.

The Countess of Darnley died in August 1944, aged 85.

THE GHAN

Ask any Aussie why the train that runs from Adelaide to Darwin is called 'The Ghan' and most will tell you it was named as a tribute to the Afghan cameleers who carried goods through the outback before there were trains or roads, and carried the materials to build the railway.

That is what the railway publicity tells you, it's in all the 'encyclopediae' and is a widely accepted 'fact'.

However, it is not true.

In the 1920s we had a White Australia Policy, and we were not given to naming things after ethnic minorities.

Although Western Australians had voted 'yes' to federating in the second referendum, after voting 'no' in the first one, the very hesitant Western Australian government had prevaricated until the last minute and finally agreed to join the other colonies when promised an east coast to west coast railway. In fact, the Western Australian government hesitated so long that Western Australia had no input at all into the drawing up of the Australian constitution. (This came back to haunt them in 1933, when they voted at a referendum to leave Australia, with 68 per cent agreeing, only to be told by a select committee of the British parliament that it was not possible to change the Australian constitution!)

By 1917 a line was built from Port Augusta in South Australia to Kalgoorlie in Western Australia and the Commonwealth Railways had at least built a section of a trans-continental line. The commissioner of Commonwealth Railways, Norris Bell, for reasons best known to himself, then decided to extend, at Commonwealth expense, a line that ran north from Port Augusta to Oodnadatta. It was to be extended into the middle of nowhere. The 'middle of nowhere' was a town called Stuart, later known as Alice Springs. The Commonwealth government completed the section from Rumbalara to Stuart.

The southern section of the 'Great Northern Railway' had been begun in 1877 by the South Australian government. The line ran from Port Augusta to Oodnadatta and the train was a 'limited mixed' that was given the official title of 'The Oodnadatta Night Train'. A 'limited mixed' is a goods train that has a passenger carriage attached and operates on lines where there is a 'limited' demand for a passenger service. After the route was extended, it became known as the 'limited mixed' once more. This meant that, due to very few passengers wanting to use it, it was not a passenger train, but a goods train with a pas-senger car tacked on.

In 1926 the Commonwealth Railways took over the South Australian line from Port Augusta to Oodnadatta, because it linked Adelaide to the South Australian East–West Express line, which ran from Terowie in the east of the state to Port Augusta via Peterborough and Quorn. This meant that, with many bewildering gauge changes, there was a service from Adelaide via Terowie to Melbourne, via Peterborough and Broken Hill to Sydney, and via Port Augusta and Kalgoorlie to Perth!

On 6 May 1929, a fellow from Prahran, in Melbourne, had taken over as commissioner of Commonwealth Railways when Norris Bell retired. His name was George Gahan (pronounced 'garn').

So, the legendary 'Ghan' came into existence on 4 August 1929 when the first passengers arrived in the town of Stuart (Alice Springs). The train was two and a half hours late and the name was adopted as a private staff joke at the expense of George Gahan, Commis-sioner of the Commonwealth Railways, who was on that first train. Most of those on the train were only going as far as Quorn, to access the East–West Express to Terowie or Peterborough, in order to reach the eastern states.

Commissioner Gahan had a special commissioner's carriage built. The carriage cost £7584 of the Commonwealth government's money and featured an observation saloon with curved glass, four sleeping compartments, a bathroom, a dining saloon, a kitchen and a compartment to accommodate the two male servants. The interior of the car was of the best Tasmanian oak.

The train was slow, the section from Quorn to Stuart regarded as unnecessary by many, including many in the South Australian Railways at the time. It was also regarded as an extravagant toy for the commissioner and a waste of federal money. Staff on the train often outnumbered passengers and there was no way the train could have ever covered its costs. The line was beset by problems with washaways and derailments, termites eating the sleepers and notoriously sloppy work practices, so much so that the Commonwealth Railways, which operated the service, was often referred to as the 'Comical Railways'.

As it was considered 'slow and useless' by railway staff, they took great delight in sarcastically christening the train 'Gahan's Express', as a derogatory joke at their commissioner's expense. It later became 'The Gahan' (pronounced garn).

So, the story of the derivation of the name 'Ghan' (pronounced 'gann'), which most people believe, because they are told it over and over, is another self-perpetuating myth—a furphy!

AUSTRALIA'S CAR

It has long been believed that the much-loved, legendary Holden was 'the first car specifically designed for Australian conditions'.

Well, that's not a legend, it's another myth.

During World War II the Australian government, along with both Ford and General Motors-Holden, explored the possibility of a locally produced affordable motorcar.

The Holden Company began in 1856 as saddle and harness makers. In 1908 the company moved into the automotive field, before becoming a subsidiary of USA company General Motors (GM) in 1931.

After World War II General Motors-Holden continued to pursue the idea of a locally produced vehicle. Managing director Laurence Hartnett wanted a local design, while General Motors preferred to see an American design.

The final design for 'Australia's Own Car' was based on a US-designed, but previously rejected, post-war Chevrolet.

Incidentally, the name 'Holden' was chosen in honour of Sir Edward Holden, the company's first chairman. Other names considered were 'GeM', 'Austral', 'Melba', 'Woomerah', 'Boomerang', 'Emu' and 'Canbra'.

WHO CROSSED THE BLUE MOUNTAINS?

History is so often simplified to the point where it becomes 'untrue'. We are told that 'a certain person' discovered something or achieved something or invented something, when the truth is it was a team effort, or the result of a series of explorations or developments or inventions.

There are many examples of this in our history, and, no doubt, in the history of all nations.

One example that is particularly annoying to Australian historians and aviation buffs is the credit given to the Wright brothers for 'inventing and pioneering powered flight'. Earlier pioneers, like George Cayley, Horatio Phillips and Percy Pilcher in Britain, the Voisin brothers in France, Brazilian Alberto Santos-Dumont, Australian Lawrence Hargrave and even American Octave Chanute, are rarely mentioned. Hargrave undoubtedly flew a powered aeroplane over Sydney Harbour before the Wright brothers efforts but never claimed it as a 'first'. What makes this even more galling is Hargrave, who did not believe in copyrights or patents, made his work known and freely available to others, while the Wright brothers used his ideas and inventions—and patented several of them!

This dumbing down of history is partly our fault for wanting things to be simple.

Who invented 'powered flight'?

Real answer: 'Octave Chanute, George Cayley, Horatio Phillips, Percy Pilcher, the Voisin brothers, Alberto Santos-Dumont, Lawrence Hargrave and the Wright brothers . . . and others.'

Too hard.

Simple answer: 'The Wright brothers.'

Sometimes it's about self-interest and who had the biggest ego or needed to be recognised.

Other times, as in the case of the 'first crossing', by Europeans, of the Blue Mountains, status and snobbery are also involved. The credit is given to three 'gentlemen' in 1813. Blaxland, Lawson and Wentworth: the names roll off the tongue and are easily remembered and often repeated. However, there were quite a few others lower down the social scale who went before them.

It is known that Lieutenant William Dawes of the marines made a three-day foray into the mountains directly west of the colony, with Lieutenant George Johnston and Assistant Surgeon Lowes, at Governor Phillip's request. They trekked into the mountains, as far as the present-day town of Linden, quite early in the colony's history, in December 1789.

Further to the north in 1795, ex-convicts Matthew Everingham and John Ramsay, accompanied by William Reid, a sailor from the First Fleet, explored well past the site of the present-day town of Bilpin and stood on top of Mount Wilson, just some 20 kilometres east of where Lithgow is today.

In 1797 George Bass set out with a party of strong, reliable fellows and provisions for two weeks. He had specially made ropes, scaling irons that fitted over boots and hooks that fastened to hands. The party made it as far as Pulpit Rock, near Blackheath!

John Wilson, an ex-convict, crossed the mountains further south, in January 1798, fifteen years before the famous trio Blaxland, Lawson and Wentworth, who get all the credit. Wilson was accompanied by Governor Hunter's servant John Price and a convict named Roe. They made the first recorded sightings of lyrebirds, koalas and wombats, and passed into the rich country west of the Great Dividing Range near the Wombeyan Caves. They had, in fact, gone over a very low part of the range, you might say 'around the mountains'.

The official records of the Blaxland, Lawson and Wentworth expedition, including the diaries of the explorers, make no mention of the names of the 'four servants' who accompanied them.

The Sydney Gazette only mentions the expedition briefly at the time and it is not until 100 years later that the three explorers are made heroes in history books for school kids.

So, that bit of our 'history' seems to have been invented at a time when the historians were looking for heroes, around the time of Australia's Federation. Convicts were unsuitable as role models, it seems, so the long-forgotten expedition by the three 'gentlemen' was dusted off and became a feat of great endeavour to inspire the new nation.

Five convicts were remunerated for their services in the first two expeditions across the mountains: the one with Blaxland, Wentworth and Lawson, and the next with surveyor George Evans.

It is possible that an ex-convict, James Byrne, was the first European to cross the mountains west of Sydney and later led the three famous 'gentlemen explorers' across.

Byrne is never mentioned by name in Blaxland's journal, being referred to only as 'a man who was used to shooting kangaroos in that country' and 'a servant'.

Byrne was born in 1769 in Wicklow, Ireland, and arrested for taking part in the Irish War of Independence in 1798. He was transported for life as an Irish rebel on the *Anne*, arriving in Port Jackson on 21 February 1801.

Records show he was paid from the Police Fund for services as a guide to the party who crossed the Blue Mountains and 'for services in making discoveries west of the Blue Mountains'.

Five other convicts or ex-convicts were paid from the Police Fund for services in 'making discoveries west of the Blue Mountains', in a document dated 30 April 1814, and received grants of land in December 1814 for 'crossing the Blue Mountains'.

The earlier date of 5 February 1814 for James Byrne, as well as other research, indicates that he was part of the first 'official' expedition over the Blue Mountains.

All five convicts accompanied George Evans on the second expedition.

James Byrne was granted a conditional pardon for his work as a guide to Blaxland, Lawson and Wentworth, and later a full pardon for his work with Evans. He was granted land at Appin, which he never took up, and later moved south with his family to settle at Collector, where he died in 1849.

MR GOCHER'S PROTEST

William Gocher is credited as being the man who enabled us all to enjoy swimming at the ocean beaches of Sydney in daylight hours, when, supposedly, he famously swam in defiance of the local government restrictions on bathing, which were enforced by local councils under the *Police Offences Act (No. 5) of 1901*.

Section 77 of the Act read:

> Whosoever bathes in any part of Sydney Cove, or in any waters exposed to view from any wharf, street, public place, or dwelling-house in or near the said city or towns between the hours of six o'clock in the morning and eight in the evening shall be liable to a penalty not exceeding one pound.

Gocher was an interesting character. Born in Ipswich in the UK in 1856, he and his siblings were all converted to Catholicism when young, and William and two brothers migrated to Australia. William arrived in 1872 and worked as an artist and journalist. He was a champion of the 'Bimetallic League' and published a pamphlet, *Australia the Light of the World*, challenging the use of the gold standard and promoting the state takeover of the banks. His ideas were derived from the 'Jewish-Capitalism-Media' conspiracy theories current at the time and another pamphlet, *Australia Must Be Heard,* called on the pope to intervene in World War I. Gocher stood for election several times at state and federal level but was never elected. In 1901 he finished 49th of 50 candidates in the senate elections.

In 1900 Gocher inherited money and set up the *Manly and North Sydney News*. He was not, as many have claimed, editor of the famous *Manly Daily*, which was not established until 1906. The *Australian Dictionary of Biography* entry on Gocher, written by Bruce Mitchell in 1983, states that:

> In 1900 he moved his family to Manly and established a short-lived newspaper, the *Manly and North Sydney News*. Through this paper he staged the scene at Manly for which he is remembered. He determined to expose the irrelevance of the local government regulations which forbade sea-bathing in daylight hours. The issue was one of public decency as there were no changing sheds and swimming costumes were rare. Clad in a neck-to-knee costume, Gocher in October 1902 swam at midday after announcing his intentions in his paper. Twice ignored by the authorities, he duly criticized their lack of zeal; on a third occasion he was escorted from the water and interviewed by the police who brought no charges. In November 1903 the reluctant Manly council resolved to allow all-day bathing, rapidly growing in popularity, provided that a neck-to-knee costume was worn. Gocher claimed a triumph and in 1907 friends presented him with a gold watch and a purse of fifty sovereigns.

Some elements of Mitchell's *Australian Dictionary of Biography* entry are true, others are not. As a supporter of the Manly Progress Association, Gocher had apparently campaigned for changing sheds at the beach, but there is no evidence of the headlines or stories of the supposed 'protests' in police records, and no copies of the relevant *Manly and North Sydney News* exist.

In an article, written in 1910, Gocher claimed that he questioned the police about the arrest of several yachtsmen for having a swim and learned that 'bathing in the open ocean was forbidden after 7 a.m.'. (It was actually 6 a.m.) Gocher wrote:

> My ire was aroused at the absurdity and injustice, so I rose up on my hind legs and informed the police that they would have to arrest me on the following Sunday as well, for I meant to test the matter.

According to Gocher, neither the police nor anyone else turned up on the beach to witness his swim the next Sunday, so:

> The next issue of my paper was flavoured with cayenne pepper for the police for not doing their duty. I announced my intention of going in for a bathe at precisely the same time and at the same place . . . Certainly more people rolled up to watch events still, no police.

However:

> On the occasion of my third dip matters commenced to be merrier. The law swooped on me and I was trotted along to the limbo. Frank Donovan bailed me out.

On 11 November 1951 the Sydney *Sunday Herald*, in response to a letter from Gocher's daughter, Mrs Mahoney, about her dad's supposedly forgotten place in surfing history, ran a nostalgia piece in which a retired police officer, Peter Eppel, claimed the incident happened between 1885 and 1892:

> It was probably some time in 1885, just after he joined the police. It was certainly before 1892—the year he resigned . . . He was patrolling The Corso at Manly when his sergeant gripped his arm and pointed. 'What is that man doing in the surf?' he demanded. 'Bring him in at once. The damn fool—the sharks will get him.'
> It was about 8 o'clock in the morning. In the sparkling water a figure was splashing. Constable Eppel obeyed orders. He walked down to the water's edge and called the man to the beach. It was Mr. Gocher. He was wearing a pair of old grey trousers cut off at the knees, and from the waist up he was naked. Constable Eppel and his sergeant ordered him to dress and come along with them. In a little while he was facing a magistrate. The actual wording of the charge against him eludes Mr. Eppel to-day. But it was something to the effect that he had been found in the ocean, whither he had gone to the danger of his life and limb.
> The magistrate was obviously aghast. Yet he was a tolerant man, and after cautioning Mr. Gocher on the folly of his act allowed him

to go. A day or two later Mr. Gocher was back. Constable Eppel and his sergeant had espied him in the surf again at the very same spot. This was open defiance and the magistrate showed his displeasure by imposing a fine of 10/. But when the same offender was observed again in the surf only a few days later, Constable Eppel considered that other treatment was necessary and this time brought him to the city.

The magistrate's eyebrows rose as he listened to this strange recital. Clearly, he decided, the man's mentality should be examined. He announced: 'You will be remanded to the Reception House for seven days.' So Mr. Gocher was taken away, and a week later stood again in the place of law. Two doctors who had studied him during his remand gave evidence that, in spite of his persistence in going into the surf, his brain was clear, he was in full possession of his senses, and was undoubtedly sane.

The following edition of the *Sunday Herald* reported, on 18 November:

Last week 'The Sunday Herald' told the story of ex-Constable Peter John Eppel who remembered—he said—exactly what befell Mr. Gocher because he was one of the policemen who arrested him three times for bathing in the surf at Manly.

That story really started something. The ink was hardly dry on it before telephones began ringing in our office. Then letters arrived. Everybody wanted to tell us how wrong Mr. Eppel was.

Other versions of the incident that rolled in, to be collected and published in the *Sunday Herald* the following week, included Gocher's own 1910 account from a press clipping kept by the Manly town clerk.

Another retired policeman, Mr J.L. Jones, claimed that he was present and that local police had been instructed to allow bathers to swim until 8 a.m.:

A deputation of bathers from Manly had been to see the Chief Secretary before this, and the police were told to leave them in until 8 o'clock. It was against the law, but those were our instructions. They went on bathing until 8 o'clock for a few months.

On the day in question, according to ex-Constable Jones:

> Mr. Gocher went in wearing a three quarter-length frock coat, striped trousers and a hard hat, and he had an umbrella under his left arm. I can see it all quite clearly . . .
>
> There were three of us there—Senior Constable A.J. Taylor, Constable John Kiley and myself. We had reported Mr. Gocher's intention to headquarters and we had been advised to take no notice.
>
> He waded in up to his armpits, made two strokes, and then came out and walked up to us expecting to be arrested. There were 200 or 300 people watching. They opened up to make way for him.
>
> We took no notice. He was never arrested.

William Gocher's daughter, Mrs Mahoney, countered:

> Mr. Eppel and Mr. Jones are both wrong. It was in 1902, and dad was in his neck to knee swimming costume. No man would go in for a swim with a hard hat on and a frock coat and with an umbrella . . . And he certainly was arrested, although he was never fined. I can vow to that.

What we have here is a perfect example of how fake news, unreliable memories and furphies can, with the passing of time, create the myths that are believed and repeated until they are part of a false history—in this case the history of how swimming in the surf became part of our lifestyle.

What is the truth?

Well, the truth is that none of the jumbled tale of Mr Gocher and the police on Manly Beach is really relevant to how local government attitudes to bathing in daylight hours were challenged and changed.

For a start, swimming at ocean beaches had been occurring since the 1880s. The real problem was the one of decency, caused by some men either skinny-dipping or wearing quite skimpy swimsuits. This prevented the small number of female bathers, who would have enjoyed swimming in the surf, from doing so. Female swimmers felt they should keep away from where men might be indecently dressed and ladies were, therefore, restricted to the 'ladies only' ocean baths, which were situated on many beaches.

Historian Pauline Curby, whose meticulous research gets us closer to the truth than any number of newspaper articles, states:

In the early twentieth century, swimming in daylight hours was quite common in Sydney and, provided that modest bathing costumes were worn, caused little concern. But this was easier said than done and there were regular complaints that beachgoers' bathing attire did not provide sufficient coverage. With no real swimming costume manufacturing industry at the time, the bulky costumes that were available were expensive. Many working people therefore cobbled together swimming gear that did not always stay in place, especially in the surf.

The real catalyst for change came not at Manly, but on the other side of the harbour, at Bondi, and it was an officer of the law who precipitated the change, rather than the bathers, although they certainly had a role to play.

It is due to Pauline Curby's research that Gocher's shenanigans on Manly Beach (no matter which version you choose to believe) can be shown to have had a minimal effect on how attitudes and council by-laws concerning daylight bathing were changed. As she points out, the real heroes of the change to 'common sense' were Inspector General of Police Edmund Fosbery and fifteen anonymous bathers on Bondi Beach:

Swimming and surfing in daylight hours became legal in Sydney as the result of an incident on what would later become Australia's best known beach, Bondi. As at Coogee and Manly, 'ocean bathing' had been popular there since the 1880s, so when on 13 November 1902 two policemen unexpectedly appeared on the beach with notebooks in hand, regular early morning surfers were defiant.

This police visitation was the result of a complaint to Waverley Council that 'unless they are properly and becomingly clad', bathers at Bondi were in breach of the *Police Offences Act (No. 5) of 1901*. When they saw the officers, most of the bathers held back, but about fifteen—only two were in 'proper bathing costumes'—plunged into the water. The police officers immediately began taking the names of those clad in small trunks. With a well-known local clergyman and several equally respectable men among the miscreants, a furore erupted.

As a result of the commotion, the police were reined in. Inspector General of Police Edmund Fosbery wrote to Waverley Council, putting his policy on public record:

> So long as the bathers wear suitable bathing costumes and public decency is not outraged, I am unable to see that a practice permitted for so many years should be stopped . . . Unless, therefore, I receive instructions from the Government to the contrary I do not see my way to take action beyond instructing the police that decency is to be observed.

Despite the *Police Offences Act*, no one was going to be prosecuted at Sydney's beaches as long as Fosbery was in charge.

Ten days after this declaration, Randwick Municipality proposed allowing daylight bathing, the first to do so in New South Wales. In early December the executive council gave its approval for this by-law. Thereafter, males and females were allowed to bathe in the sea in the municipality 'at all times and at all hours of the day', provided they were clothed 'from the neck and shoulders to the knees with a suitable bathing dress or costume'.

Other local councils followed suit. Apparently Manly Council delayed for some time because councillors felt that the operators of the local baths, who leased the area from the council, would be adversely affected. As the lease on the baths expired in 1903, they felt that a change would be unfair before that time. When the lease expired they followed other councils in making the change in the by-laws.

Inspector General of Police Edmund Fosbery will never get the recognition he deserves as the man who changed surf-bathing history with the common-sense solution he proposed in 1902. On the other hand, there was a proposal to build a statue of William Gocher at Manly and, in 1952, a block of housing commission flats was named after him. The statue never eventuated but, in 1980, a plaque was placed at South Steyne Beach to mark the spot where he is said to have swum in defiance of council by-laws.

The *Sunday Herald* pointed out, in 1951, that the *Police Offences Act (No. 5) of 1901, Section 77,* was still technically valid at that time and millions of Sydneysiders were happily breaking the law on Sydney's beaches with impunity. What the *Herald* never mentioned, however, was that the credit should go to a sensible old copper named Edmund Fosbery—not William Gocher.

MELBOURNE CUP MYTHOLOGY

Since the Melbourne Cup was first run in 1861, the Australian public have clamoured to believe the most ridiculous and romantic tales of coincidence, supernatural premonition and divine intervention. Each year brings new examples of heroism and perseverance as horses, jockeys and trainers battle, overcoming seemingly insurmountable odds, to achieve victory.

This all began with the furphy of Archer's long walk to Melbourne to win the first Cup. Some gullible souls even believe he did this walk twice to win the first two Cups. This 'walk' never happened the first time around, and to suggest that Australia's most successful trainer of the era, Etienne de Mestre, would have sent his valuable Cup winner from the previous year on a second arduous marathon walk is laughable. Yet many believe it, despite accounts from the time that Archer, like all other normal human beings and horses, made his way to Melbourne by ship.

Newspaper accounts of the day show that Archer left Sydney on 18 September 1861 on the steamer *City of Sydney*, together with two stablemates, Exeter and Inheritor, and arrived at Port Melbourne three days later.

Also on board were Etienne de Mestre and jockey Johnny 'Cutts', who was, in fact, John 'Cutts' Dillon, one of the most respected jockeys in New South Wales. Despite stories to the contrary, Cutts was not from the Nowra district and never lived there, although his brother-in-law Walter Bradbury worked for de Mestre and lived at Terara, about 3 kilometres northeast of Nowra.

This pretty much puts a hole in the theory, or 'legend', that Johnny Cutts was born and raised in the area around Nowra, supposedly one of many Aboriginal stockmen who replaced the stockmen of European descent when they left to join the goldrushes.

There is even a more ridiculous 'legend' that Archer's strapper, Dave Power, not only walked him to Melbourne, but rode him under Cutts' name in the Cup . . . and was of Aboriginal descent.

Perhaps Power walked Archer to the nearest port of embarkation from his home on the south coast of New South Wales, or perhaps he walked him from the Port Melbourne docks to the hotel stables at South Yarra, where he was trained for the first Cup, but he certainly never walked him to Melbourne from his home near Nowra, nor did he ride him in the Cup.

Archer went by steamboat from Sydney to Melbourne three times to compete in Victorian races, in 1861, 1862 and 1863.

De Mestre's horses usually boarded the steamer at Adam's Wharf near his property at Terara, on the Shoalhaven River. However, floods in 1860 altered the course of the river channels and made navigation dangerous. So, from 1860 to 1863, horses needed to be walked to the wharf at Greenwell Point, 13 kilometres to the east. Perhaps this was the origin of the 'walking to Melbourne' legend.

The longest distance Archer ever walked was the 250 kilometres from the end of the railway line at Campbelltown to his owners' paddock near Braidwood when he retired from racing in 1864.

Etienne de Mestre, cunning as he was, may have enjoyed spreading the ridiculous rumour about the walk as part of his plan to empty the pockets of Melbourne's bookmakers. It is more obvious, however, that he achieved his goal by keeping the Sydney horse away from prying eyes and training him in what was then known as St Kilda Park, opposite the Botanical Hotel, where he was stabled in South Yarra.

Archer had won his last seven starts in Sydney, but those wins were spread out over a year and the form of the various colonial horses was not easy to compare. It was the Cup that would eventually bring Australian champions together from around the continent and give us a real 'Australian racing scene'.

De Mestre single-handedly backed his victorious horse in from 8 to 1 to 6 to 1, with the result that the bookmakers of Melbourne were left reeling and more grist was added to the mill of interstate rivalry, or intercolonial rivalry, as it then was.

Neither the handicapper nor the bookmakers of Melbourne missed Archer the following year. He was given 10 st 2 lb (64.5 kg) to carry and was favourite at 2 to 1. Of course, he added another chapter to Cup history by winning yet again.

In the true spirit of colonial rivalry, Archer was given the massive weight of 11 st 4 lb (72 kg) by the handicapper in 1863. De Mestre had paid the first acceptance fee of 5 sovereigns and was incensed when weights were announced. However, he eventually relented and Archer and another runner from his stable, Haidee, left by steamboat for Melbourne on 16 June.

De Mestre's agents reminded him on 1 July that he needed to send final payment and acceptance that day, so a telegram was sent to the Melbourne office of George Kirk & Co., asking them to accept on his behalf. De Mestre sent the telegram himself, as the due date was a normal working day in New South Wales, and records show it was received at the Melbourne Telegraph Office at 1 p.m.

However, Wednesday 1 July was a public holiday in Melbourne, and the telegram was not delivered until 7.30 p.m.

Acceptances closed at 8 p.m., and when George Kirk handed the telegram to the stewards at the Victorian Turf Club the next morning, those honourable sporting men, having found a loophole to stop Archer once and for all, decided it was too late.

This decision caused a furore at the time; even Victorian owners lobbied the club to accept the entry, but to no avail. Mind you, it was highly unlikely that Archer, carrying 11 st 4 lb, could have won anyway, and the Victorian owners doubtless realised this. If he had run, it would have been the biggest weight carried in the history of the Melbourne Cup.

All the interstate entrants pulled out in protest and only seven local horses ran in what is considered the worst and weakest Cup in history. It was won, in front of 7000 people, by Banker, carrying 5 st 4 lb (34 kg).

It is both fitting and ironic that the public holiday that enabled this unsportsmanlike decision to be made was Separation Day, the day that Victoria celebrated its official separation from New South Wales in 1851.

Archer was taken by train to Ballarat in August 1863 and ran poorly in a sweepstakes race. He was suffering from fever and an injured fetlock and returned to Sydney to recover and be trained for the Metropolitan Handicap of 1864. He broke down once more on the eve of the race, however, and never raced again.

Although Archer is shown in the record books as being owned by de Mestre, and he raced in the trainer's famous all-black colours, he was actually leased by de Mestre and was always owned by an old school friend of de Mestre's, J.T. Roberts, in partnership with his brother-in-law and two nephews.

Archer was retired to stand at stud at his owners' property, Exeter Farm, near Braidwood, where he was foaled, for a fee of 10 guineas, but his progeny failed to win a stakes race, bearing out, perhaps, de Mestre's opinion that Archer was not among the best horses he had ever trained.

Archer died, aged sixteen, in 1872. An ornament made from his tail hair, coiled into a horseshoe shape, set in silver and mounted on red satin, can be seen at the Australian Racing Museum in Melbourne.

So, right from its very beginnings, the Cup was shrouded in myths, tall stories and romance.

If looked at devoid of its myths and fairytales, the first Melbourne Cup was a rough-and-tumble affair. One horse bolted off the course during the race, three of the seventeen runners fell and two died. Two jockeys were seriously injured and suffered broken bones.

Archer defeated the favourite, and local champion, Mormon, by 6 lengths in the slowest time in Cup history, 3 minutes 52 seconds, in front of the smallest crowd ever, 4000 people.

Archer had previously defeated Mormon over 2½ miles in the Australia Plate at Randwick. So the form was there to see and de Mestre's betting coup was a real triumph over local pride. An injury to Archer, real or feigned, leading up to the race may have helped the price get out to an appetising 8 to 1 before de Mestre pounced and reduced the odds to 6 to 1.

De Mestre also took home £710 and a handmade gold watch for the win. There was no second prize, so the locals were left empty-handed.

The second year the odds were not as juicy. Archer won by 8 lengths, a feat not equalled until Rain Lover won by the same margin in 1968. His trainer took home £810 and another watch. Mormon again ran second and collected £20.

Etienne de Mestre was a colourful character who became part of Cup legend by training five winners, a record that lasted for 99 years, until Bart Cummings broke it in 1977. The famous trainer was one of ten children of another fascinating character in our history, Prosper de Mestre.

The son of a French officer fleeing the Revolution, Prosper was born at sea on a British ship after his father's death. He was raised and educated in America after his mother remarried, and he lived and traded in China, India and Mauritius before arriving in Sydney, where his right to trade as a 'foreigner' was challenged and he subsequently became the first person ever to be naturalised as an 'Australian', or at least a British subject in Australia!

Etienne himself had eleven children and developed the land his father was granted at Terara, near Nowra, into a successful racehorse training and breeding establishment. Archer's stable is still there. In fact, it's a bed and breakfast establishment today and, if you are prepared to believe Cup and local folklore, you can spend a weekend sleeping where Archer was supposedly stabled for most of his racing life.

Maybe you believe he walked to Melbourne, too.

Other Melbourne Cup folklore includes the tale of the twelve-year-old 'Aboriginal' boy named Peter riding Briseis, the first female horse to win, in 1876. The story goes that Peter was born on the St Albans Stud property near Geelong to an Aboriginal mother; perhaps he was the son of St Albans' owner, Jim Wilson senior, or his son, also Jim. Another version has the boy being left as a baby on the doorstep of one of St Albans' grooms, Michael Bowden, to be raised by him and his wife.

As he had no 'real' surname, so the story goes, he was given the name of the property and became Peter St Albans, youngest jockey and first Aboriginal rider to win the Cup!

Unfortunately, this wonderful story, like Archer's walk to Melbourne with his Aboriginal 'strapper/jockey', has more holes in it than Swiss cheese.

Two elements of the story are true. He was known as Peter, and he was very young; in fact, he was only twelve and, oddly enough, this explains the whole wonderful concoction.

Peter had ridden Briseis, as a two-year-old, to three victories at Randwick earlier in the year, including an incredible win in the Doncaster Handicap where he rode her at 5 st 7 lb (35 kg). However, the Victoria Racing Club (VRC) rules did not allow jockeys to ride in the Melbourne Cup until they were aged thirteen, and Peter was a few days shy of his thirteenth birthday on Cup Day 1876.

The regular jockey for St Albans' horses was the legendary Tom Hales, who could not make the Cup weight at 6 st 4 lb (40 kg). As Briseis won most of her big races as a two- and three-year-old, she was given a very light weight to carry, which meant that a good lightweight jockey was required.

Few grown men could ride at those weights, but Peter was an excellent rider who knew the horse as a stable boy at St Albans and had ridden her to victory in three races in Sydney. So, cunning old Jim Wilson came up with the 'cock-and-bull' story of Peter's origins to allow him to ride Briseis in the Cup. He argued to the VRC that both the boy's birthdate and parents were unknown, but he was probably older than thirteen.

'Peter St Albans' was actually born Michael Peter Bowden in Geelong on 15 November 1864, and there is a birth certificate to prove it. He was the son of Michael Bowden, who worked at St Albans, and his wife. Although christened 'Michael', he was known as 'Peter' from an early age. There is a painting at the State Library of Victoria by Frederick Woodhouse showing Peter as a youth, looking very white and European, standing alongside Briseis as her strapper, with Tom Hales in the saddle.

Michael 'Peter St Albans' Bowden was a successful jockey for several years around Geelong and also rode successfully interstate until a bad fall at age nineteen saw him switch to training. He died in 1900 at the age of 35. The Geelong Thoroughbred Club awards the Peter St Albans Trophy each year to the jockey who rides the most winners at the Geelong track.

OUR DRINKING REPUTATION

Although Australia has a very alcoholic history, many of the things that people believe about our drinking habits are not necessarily true.

It is true that we are probably the only nation in the world who can boast a prime minister (Bob Hawke) who held a record for beer drinking (1.4 litres in eleven seconds), if such a thing is something to boast about.

As far as I know, we are also the only nation in the world to have had alcohol as our official currency although, at that stage of course, we were not a nation; it was merely the colony of New South Wales that used rum as currency.

Perhaps some of us tend to exaggerate the historic influence of alcohol on Australia. After all, the attitude to drinking and the tendency to drink to excess was something we inherited with our British background. There is no real evidence to suggest that the levels of drinking and results of the evils of alcohol were any different in the British colonies in Australia from what they were in Britain at the time of colonisation. The only way to reach the colonies in the Antipodes was by sailing ship, and alcohol was part and parcel of both the Royal Navy and the merchant navy.

The German botanist Johann Forster, who replaced Joseph Banks on Cook's second voyage of discovery, described the crew as 'solicitous to get very drunk, though they are commonly solicitous about nothing else'. The acceptance of drunkenness, and the tolerance of overindulgence in alcohol as a lifestyle, was part and parcel of both naval life and working-class life in Britain in the 18th century, and it was transferred to the colonies of Australasia, along with everything else British.

The mutiny by the 99th Regiment in Sydney in 1846 was ostensibly caused by the abolition of the daily grog allowance—on the order of Colonel Despard. It was really a 'strike' that lasted approximately four weeks and ended when the 'rebels' learned that 400 troops from Hobart were on board the ship *Tasmania* standing off Sydney Heads. The mutiny was, in fact, a protest against Despard's over-officious style of leadership and his attempts to separate the troops from the townspeople. Evidently he was of the opinion that the troops might have to be used against the unruly part-convict population, and he was dead against them being seen to be a part of the general community. He was concerned that the 'foreign service' grog ration encouraged the troops to be far too like the people they were there to control.

Despard, who famously led a disastrous campaign in the Maori Wars, also gave an order that prohibited citizens from walking on any part of the grass-covered area in front of the barracks when listening to the band play. This had been the town's chief entertainment for many years.

The 99th were so annoyed when Despard stopped their grog ration that they 'forgot their obligations to their Queen and country', by refusing to obey the lawful commands of their Officers, or to perform any further duty', and went on strike.

The barque *Tasmania* was chartered and 400 men and officers of the 11th Regiment in Hobart embarked for Sydney to disarm the mutineers of the 99th Regiment.

An offshore gale kept the vessel from entering the harbour for seven days but eventually the 11th Regiment arrived in Sydney on 8 January 1846 and marched four-deep, with fixed bayonets, along George Street with the band playing 'Paddy Will You Now' until they entered the Barrack Square to a hearty welcome and cheers from the 99th Regiment and their families, together with as many citizens as could fit into the barrack grounds.

Thus ended the mutiny of the 99th Regiment. The grog ration was restored and Sydney's citizens were again allowed to walk on the grass in front of Barrack Square, and listen to the band play on Thursday afternoons.

One thing to note here is that the 99th were a *British* regiment!

One of the most common myths about Australians is that we are great beer drinkers. This is simply not true anymore. Before the advent of refrigeration, rum and other spirits were the popular drinks, along with some styles of beer that are drunk at room temperature, like ale and porter.

After it became possible to refrigerate beer, we became prone to drinking relatively large amounts of cold lager, due to the climate being rather hotter here than in Europe, which is quite understandable.

There was a period when we were quite famous for overindulgence in lager. The soldiers' riots that occurred on Valentine's Day 1916 in Liverpool and Sydney were the result of trainee soldiers being denied access to alcohol at the overcrowded army training camps in the Liverpool district.

This 'mutiny' was one of the reasons New South Wales adopted the infamous 'six o'clock' closing, which led to binge-drinking of cold lager and many social problems. Some other states had similar legislation, and similar social problems such as illegal liquor sales, the development of criminal networks and police corruption.

Today Australia rates a lowly 17th in the list of nations judged on the consumption of beer per head of population. Our figure is 75 litres per head per year, which puts us in the same ballpark as the USA (73 litres) and the UK (70 litres), and way behind European nations like the Czech Republic (189 litres), Austria (108 litres), Romania (100 litres) and Germany (99 litres). In Africa, Namibia (96 litres) beats us hands down, and in Central America we lag a full 3 litres behind Panama (78 litres).

I regret to inform those who take pride in our beer-drinking reputation that we rank higher, 14th place, in the list of wine-drinking nations!

THE 'RUM REBELLION'

The so-called 'Rum Rebellion' of 1808 was not called by that name until after 1855 when an English Quaker historian, William Howitt, wrote a history of Australia and exaggerated the 'alcoholic' aspect of the rebellion in order to stress the evils of drink. Howitt invented the term 'Rum Rebellion' and it stuck, which meant other important aspects of the power struggle have been forgotten. Before Howitt intervened, the event was known generally as 'The Great Rebellion'.

Howitt was an interesting character. Born in Derbyshire in 1792, he was educated in Quaker schools and became an author and radical free-thinker. He worked as a farmer and travelled the English countryside studying nature. He taught himself languages, botany and chemistry and worked as an apothecary. After his marriage in 1821 he and his wife began publishing his varied writings and he served as an alderman in Nottingham before moving his family to Germany for several years.

In 1852, aged 60, he sailed for Victoria with his two sons and spent two years on the goldfields. They found very little gold but the two years spent travelling the colonies provided material for Howitt's writing. After returning home he produced, among his many writings: *A Boy's Adventures in the Wilds of Australia* (1854), *Land, Labour, and Gold; or, Two Years in Victoria* (1855), *Tallangetta, the Squatter's Home* (1857), and *The History of Discovery in Australia, Tasmania, and New Zealand* (1865).

In England the family continued their writing, publishing and philanthropy until 1870 when they moved to Rome, where Howitt died in 1879.

There was, of course, some truth in the idea that the rebellion was partly connected to rum.

The rum monopoly began in 1793. Just after Governor Arthur Phillip had returned to Britain and left Major Francis Grose temporarily in charge of the fledgling colony, an American ship with the ironic name of the *Hope* sailed into Sydney with a cargo that included 7500 gallons of rum. The captain, one Benjamin Page, refused to sell his cargo except in one lot, including the rum.

The colony had almost starved three years earlier and all supplies were scarce. In light of this and partly to prevent the captain from holding the colony to ransom, the officers of the New South Wales Corps banded together with Major Grose's blessing to purchase the entire cargo. This gave them a monopoly on rum, which they exploited whenever a new ship arrived in the colony.

Until 1814 rum was an accepted currency in New South Wales. Soldiers were paid in rum, as were convicts who worked on officers' land. According to historian George Mackaness, the population of Sydney in 1806 'was divided into two classes, those who sold rum and those who drank it'.

Simplifying history is, however, always a dangerous practice. In a *Sydney Morning Herald* article dated 26 January 2006, historian, journalist and publisher Michael Duffy made an attempt to give a more balanced view, claiming Bligh's removal was not about him preventing army officers profiteering through rum: '... almost no one at the time of the rebellion thought it was about rum ... Howitt took Bligh's side and invented the phrase "Rum Rebellion", and it has stuck ever since.'

Duffy points out that the colony's per capita intake of alcohol was no more, and possibly a little less, than Britain's at the time. He also makes the point that by the time Bligh became governor, in 1806, 'ex-convict entrepreneurs such as Simeon Lord and immigrant businessmen like Robert Campbell' were making inroads into the officers' monopoly of trade.

Duffy could have added another ex-convict to that list.

James Squire, transported for stealing chickens, was the first successful brewer in Australia. After receiving his ticket of leave in 1791, he obtained a licence to sell liquor, in partnership with Simeon Lord. In 1792 they set up the Malting Shovel Tavern on the river at Kissing Point, near Ryde. It was at the halfway point on the river between the two settlements of Sydney and Parramatta—and it proved a great success.

Squire added twelve other land grants to his own 30 acres (12 hectares) at Ryde and eventually had an estate of more than 800 acres (324 hectares) along the Parramatta River. He cleverly complained to the colonial secretary about neighbouring land grants not being taken up and consequently purchased several of them for a shilling each.

Oddly enough, the brewing of beer was seen as a good thing for a colony that was corrupted by the trade in rum. Beer was considered a sobering influence and Governor King tried hard to get the inhabitants of New South Wales to drink beer rather than rum. Squire was much praised for his efforts in growing hops and grain and producing and selling a decent brew. Beer was actually considered to be a healthy and efficacious beverage!

This belief was partly due to the fact that 'small beer', very mildly alcoholic beer (less than 1%), was universally consumed in parts of Europe, especially northern Europe and the 'low countries', throughout medieval times and into the 17th and 18th centuries. Small beer was brewed in most households for consumption by workers, children and servants because water sources were polluted and the brewing process meant small beer was a safer way to quench the thirst. It was common for men doing heavy manual labour in hot weather to consume 6 litres or more a day of 'small beer'.

Squire was an industrious and successful farmer; he was also a gypsy (or Romani), one of only two on the First Fleet. Gypsies were denied civil rights in Britain, but they had good knowledge of hop cultivation as they provided the itinerant workforce for hop planting and picking. One hop vine Squire cultivated in 1806 covered 5 acres (2 hectares) by 1812 and produced 700 kilograms of hops. As a brewer he was similarly successful. By 1820 his brewery was producing 40 hogsheads (about 10,000 litres) of beer a week.

When he managed to cultivate a hop vine in 1806, from plants he had been given a few years before, he took the first small crop to Governor King, who was so overjoyed at Squire's achievement that he 'directed that a cow to be given to Mr Squire from the Government herd'.

When he died in 1822, his funeral was the largest ever seen in the colony up to that time. His grandson, James Squire Farnell, was premier of New South Wales from 1877 to 1878. But I digress.

Back in 1806, Bligh, who took over from King as governor, had been given the unenviable task of wresting control of the twenty-year-old convict colony away from the officers of the New South Wales Corps, especially John Macarthur and Major George Johnston, who had, along with others like Surgeon-General Thomas Jamison, managed to effectively run the colony to suit themselves, receiving huge land grants and monopolising trade in food and goods, including rum, which was the colony's de facto currency. Previous governors Hunter and King had failed to break the power of the New South Wales Corps and had retired defeated.

The problem was, in part, due to the fact that the governors before Macquarie (Phillip, Hunter, King and Bligh) were *navy* men—while those in control in the colony were *army* officers, or ex-officers, who had established themselves as the colony's leading free citizens.

Governor William Bligh was a hero in the eyes of the admiralty, having helped win the naval battle of Camperdown off the Dutch coast during the French Revolutionary War. He also defied the mutineers on the *Bounty* and then navigated the ship's launch, in which he and eighteen loyal crew members were set adrift, across 7000 kilometres of open sea via the island of Tofua, where they were attacked and one man was killed. They then sailed past Fiji and across the Coral Sea to the coast of northeast Australia, through the Great Barrier Reef and on to Dutch Timor. The launch was designed to hold ten men; the voyage lasted 45 days and the remaining seventeen men and Bligh made it to Timor.

Bligh was seen as a hard man who could take control of the colony and sort out the problems caused by opportunism and monopolies, but he was short-tempered and undiplomatic. He was given direct instructions in London to take control of the rum trade out of the hands of the officers and he did ban the use of spirits as payment for other goods and stopped John Macarthur importing stills to make rum, but that was only a small part of the power struggle that led to the 'rebellion'.

Bligh stopped land grants, removed military men from the court system and favoured the poorer free settlers who needed help after the Hawkesbury River floods of 1806. Poorer settlers and ex-convicts were being forced to pay high prices for meat and other goods, which were monopolised by the officers of the New South Wales Corps and other large land-holders.

In order to maintain a more usual style of authority, Bligh's successor Major-General Lachlan Macquarie (who was, obviously, not a naval officer) arrived with his own regiment in 1810 and the New South Wales Corps was renamed the 102nd Regiment of Foot and sent back home. At last the colony had an army man in charge. A canny Scot, Macquarie cleverly established a currency by purchasing a cargo of 10,000 Spanish dollars in 1814 and having the centre cut out of every coin. This had the double purpose of providing two coins of different denominations and rendering the coins useless outside the colony, so the currency remained in New South Wales. This strange coin, known as the 'holey dollar' (the bit in the middle, of less value, was known as the 'dump'), replaced rum as the colony's currency.

Macquarie was to write another chapter in the alcoholic history of New South Wales. In order to further control the rum trade, he gave the monopoly to import the spirit to a group of businessmen. In exchange they built Sydney Hospital, in Macquarie Street. So, Sydney's first major public institution was built in exchange for the monopoly on importing rum, and was known for years as the 'Rum Hospital'.

The so-called 'Rum Rebellion' was about many things. Like all events in the past it can only be truly understood by studying the political and social context in which it occurred—and the events leading up to it. Sadly, time and space prevent me from doing that here. But we can take a quick look at just one factor.

Bligh's arrival marked the end of the policy of making generous land grants. His immediate predecessor, Philip Gidley King, had granted about 62,000 acres (25,000 hectares) to businessmen, government officials and officers of the New South Wales Corps. Macarthur, for example, had been gifted 5000 acres of prime grazing land at Camden. During Bligh's relatively short reign a mere 4000 acres were granted, and half of those were to Bligh and his family.

Macarthur and Bligh had been sniping at each other since Bligh's arrival. Macarthur had made life unbearable for previous governors Hunter and King. Basically it was a case of navy men being appointed to govern a colony that army men were running to suit themselves, riding roughshod over any official attempt to thwart their often-corrupt practices.

The actual events that precipitated the 'mutiny' were all ridiculously trivial. After a convict apparently stowed away and fled the colony on one of Macarthur's vessels, Bligh ordered forfeiture of the normal bond paid by ship owners to guarantee convicts did not escape on their ships.

Then Macarthur had paid to import a still, one of two that eventually arrived in the colony and, by Bligh's orders, it had to be sent to the government store. Macarthur had ordered the second still, but had agreed to comply and to hand it over as soon as it arrived.

On arrival it was delivered direct to Macarthur and Bligh demanded it be handed over. Macarthur agreed to do so, but said he wished to keep and use the boiler component and would hand the alcohol-making component over soon. Bligh then sent soldiers to seize the still.

Macarthur was summoned to appear before Judge Atkins, and when he failed to do so Bligh had him arrested. He was bailed and refused to be tried by a court that included Atkins, who was his debtor and sworn enemy. The other six magistrates, all members of the New South Wales Corps, sided with Macarthur. Bligh accused them of mutiny.

On 24 January 1808 things came to a head. Bligh ordered Macarthur's arrest, the corps refused to carry out the order . . . and so it progressed. Finally the officers of the corps and some 'prominent citizens' signed a petition declaring Bligh 'unfit to exercise the supreme authority another moment in this colony' and the naval hero was placed under house arrest by the colonial army officers.

The only resistance to the army invading Government House was offered by Bligh's daughter, who attacked the soldiers with her parasol.

Johnston, who had by now been promoted to lieutenant-colonel, took over the colony, and he appointed the surveyor-general, Charles Grimes, as judge-advocate. Macarthur and the six officers were tried and found 'not guilty'. Macarthur then became colonial secretary.

Colonel William Paterson returned from Tasmania to attempt to keep some semblance of order and Lieutenant-Colonel Joseph Foveaux was sent back to the colony and appointed acting governor. The result was that, finally, an army man, Major-General Lachlan Macquarie, was appointed as the next governor and he reversed all land grants made by Johnston and Macarthur and reinstated all the officials they had sacked.

Johnston was court-martialled and found guilty. Cashiered from the army, he returned to the colony as a private citizen. Macarthur was banned from the colony until 1817 and Bligh was promoted to rear-admiral.

The irony is that Johnston was the one man who could have prevented the mutiny, as he was often able to negotiate a mutually agreeable way forward between the short-tempered Bligh and the devious Macarthur. When Bligh summoned him to sort out the mess on 25 January, he failed to show up as he was 'indisposed' and injured. He had 'dined with officers of the corps' the evening before, over-indulged and crashed his gig on the way home.

So it was an early 'drink-driving' accident that prevented Johnston from turning up to work the next day—and possibly preventing what would later be called the 'Rum Rebellion'.

HOW AUSTRALIAN IS FOSTER'S?

In the 1970s and 1980s you may well have heard the phrase 'as Aussie as Foster's lager' in Britain and the USA especially, where Foster's was marketed as the beer Aussies made and loved to drink. The slogan for Foster's was 'It's Australian for *beer*'.

Well, it may have been marketed as 'Australian for *beer*', but what *is* the answer to the question 'How Aussie is Foster's?'

If you take the nationality of the founders of Foster's famous beer into account, it's not Aussie at all—it's American!

The Foster brothers, William and Ralph, arrived in Melbourne in 1887 and they were not primarily interested in beer or brewing. They were pioneers in the refrigeration industry and they arrived with the latest in refrigeration equipment. They brewed beer in order to demonstrate the wonders of refrigeration.

They set up their brewery and, in 1888, successfully brewed the very first local 'lager-style' beer in Australia, a beer that needed to be kept cold to be enjoyed properly.

Having done what they had planned to do, Ralph and William promptly sold their entire enterprise to some locals in 1889 and Ralph went to Italy and then back to the USA. William moved to Sydney, where he lived out his life quietly; his descendants live there still.

In 1908 there was a massive amalgamation of breweries in Melbourne. Carlton, McCracken's City, Castlemaine, Shamrock and Foster's breweries all combined to form Carlton United, and the Foster's brewery in Rokeby Street was closed and the Foster's name was almost lost. Carlton United only continued to brew a beer branded as 'Foster's' because there was some demand for the label in Queensland and Western Australia.

In 1971 Foster's was introduced to England through Barry Humphries' highly successful cartoon strip in the magazine *Private Eye*. The strip was used as the basis for two very successful movies, *The Adventures of Barry McKenzie* and *Barry McKenzie Holds His Own*.

The hero of the cartoon strip and movies was rarely seen without a can of Foster's in his hand and Foster's took off in Britain, where cold, lager-style beer was just taking over the beer market from the more traditional styles of porter and ale.

Foster's then launched into the USA in 1972, where it was marketed along with sport. Foster's sponsored the 1972 America's Cup challenge and tennis championships, and was the official Olympic beer for Australia at the 1984 Los Angeles Olympics.

For more than a decade from 1985, the Melbourne Cup was known as the Foster's Melbourne Cup, and John Newcombe claimed in advertisements that he drank five cans after each tennis match. Then Paul Hogan was brought into the advertising campaign.

Hoge's first Foster's commercial script read:

> G'Day. They've asked me over from Oz to introduce youse all to Foster's Draught, here it is. Cripes! I'd better start with the basics. It's a light, golden liquid, except for the white bit on top, the head, and it's brewed from malt, yeast and hops. Technical term is Lager. That's L-A-G-E-R. But everyone calls it Foster's. Ahhhh, ripper! Tastes like an angel cryin' on yer tongue. Foster's.

Of course, the famous 'Aussie Foster's Lager' marketed to Poms and Yanks was also brewed to local tastes locally—not here in Australia. Foster's is brewed in eight countries, including China, Spain and Sweden! It is sold in 135 countries.

Us Aussies living in Britain, and the USA, in the 1980s spent a lot of our time telling the locals we didn't drink Foster's at home. After all, it was an American invention!

While we're on the subject of iconic Australian brews, Castlemaine beer is not strictly Aussie either.

Castlemaine Brewery had been founded by the two Irish Fitzgerald brothers. They migrated from Galway in 1859 and began their brewing business at Castlemaine in Victoria. In 1875 they established a brewery in South Melbourne and, in 1877, they had also set up in Brisbane where, from 1878, they brewed the famous Castlemaine ale that became associated with Queensland—although it was named after a town in Victoria!

The beer became Castlemaine XXXX in 1916 and ever since that time the joke has been that it's called XXXX because Queenslanders can't spell 'beer'.

If you wondering what 4X was called before 1916 . . . cease wondering. From 1878 to 1916 it was called 'Castlemaine XXX Sparkling Ale' . . . 3X!

PART TWO

AUSTRALIA IS NOT THE GREAT SOUTH LAND

'What's the good of Mercator's North Poles and Equators,
Tropics, Zones and Meridian lines?'
The Bellman would cry: and the crew would reply,
'They are only conventional signs!'

'The Hunting of the Snark', Lewis Carroll, 1876

BIRTH OF A LEGEND

I have to risk upsetting fans of much-loved 1980s rock-synth band Icehouse by announcing that Iva Davies' inspirational song 'Great Southern Land' is based on a false premise. Our country, the continent now known as Australia, is not, and really was never thought to be, the much-fabled and sought-after Great South Land.

To understand fully why we are *not* the Great South Land, and how the title (along with the name 'Australia') was eventually attached to our continent, we need to follow a thread of connected events that begins when scholars realised that the world was a globe, in about 350 BC, and continues until James Cook proved, once and for all, in 1775, that the mythical Great South Land did not exist.

The Great South Land was a large landmass believed to exist in the South Atlantic or South Pacific Ocean, perhaps in both, at a similar latitude south to that of Eurasia's latitude north—i.e. between 40 degrees and the pole. The idea that there *had* to be a Great South Land developed this way . . .

Scholars had known that the world was round since the time of the ancient Greeks. Pythagoras, after studying the moon, proposed the idea around 500 BC and, some 50 years later, Anaxagoras studied eclipses and came to the same conclusion. Around 350 BC Aristotle declared, quite confidently, that the Earth was a sphere.

Late in the 2nd century AD the Graeco-Roman scholar Ptolemy, living in Egypt, produced reasonably accurate descriptions and maps of the geography of the northern hemisphere, excluding North America, by using a grid to plot latitude and longitude. His work was mostly forgotten until the 14th century, when it was copied and translated by monks in Constantinople and introduced to European academics by the Byzantine scholar Emmanuel Chrysoloras and the Italian Jacobus Angelus. Using Ptolemy's ideas, European map-makers and geographers, like Johannes Honter in Romania, began making 'predictive' maps of the world.

Honter's 1545 map shows a large continent called 'Australia' extending from the South Pole northward to around latitude 45 degrees south. Basically, it looks like a huge Antarctica stretching up to about where New Zealand's South Island is. This was, of course, quite wrong, but the idea had developed that there had to be a huge landmass at the bottom of the world to balance the huge landmass at the top. Crazy as it may seem, this idea persisted among scholars and geographers right up until James Cook's time.

As these latitudes in the northern hemisphere were conducive to habitation that had led to farming, civilisation, trade and wealth, it was believed that similar conditions in the southern hemisphere would have produced the same sorts of results and these southern civilisations would therefore have products to trade, like the spices of Asia, or treasures for the taking, like the slaves of Africa and the silver, gold and emeralds of Central America.

The idea of balanced hemispheres, and curiosity about the unknown southern half of the planet, was apparent in the popularity of the term 'antipodes' (Latin 'opposite the feet') in the 17th and 18th centuries. Europeans were fascinated by the idea that they lived on a globe and there was a world diametrically opposite to their feet on the other side.

Fantastic adventure stories, published as accounts of actual voyages, were popular in Europe in the 17th and 18th centuries and many were written. In 1676 Frenchman Gabriel de Goigny published *La Terre Australe Connue* (*The South Land Revealed*), an account of a journey to 'Australia', where the inhabitants were eight-foot-tall vegetarians who lived in an idyllic democracy. English books like *The Life and Adventures of Peter Wilkins* (Robert Paltock, 1751) and *The Life and Astonishing Adventures of John Daniel* (Ralph Morris, 1751), and satirical books like

Jonathan Swift's *Gulliver's Travels* (1726) were set in 'The Antipodes'. Belief in the Great South Land was reinforced by these books.

While the term 'antipodes' tended to be used in literature, '*australis*' (Latin 'south') was more common on maps. Names used for the Great South Land were '*Terra Australis*' or '*Terra Australe*' (land of the south), '*Australia*' (south continent) and the slightly more sceptical '*Terra Incognita*' (unknown land). Indeed, the Great South Land, as it was perceived by those who believed in it, was not only unknown, it was non-existent. By giving this undiscovered, fabled land meaningful Latin names, geographers and map-makers placed it in the realm of probability. Most geographers assumed it was there . . . somewhere.

Once ship-building technology and navigation science had developed to a point that made it possible to explore the oceans outside of Europe, the exploration of the southern hemisphere was only a matter of time. It turned out to be quite a long time: four centuries.

THE AGE OF DISCOVERY

Prince Henry and the Knights of Christ

The ancient world was relatively small in global terms. Indeed, 'Mediterranean' means 'in the middle of the world'. Until medieval times, the Mediterranean and North Seas were the only oceans Europeans could explore with the maritime knowledge and nautical technology available. Other oceans were beyond the realms of European knowledge.

A vast improvement in maritime technology took place during the lifetime of Prince Henry (Infante Dom Henrique) of Portugal (1394–1460). He is the man credited with beginning the 'Age of Discovery'. He set up a maritime and navigational training school at Sagres Point, at the tip of the peninsula where Europe ends and the vast Atlantic Ocean stretches to the horizon. The place was known as '*el fim do mundo*'—'the end of the world'.

Henry was the third son of King John (Joao) 1st of Portugal and Philippa of Lancaster, a member of the English royal family, whose marriage to John in 1386 created the Treaty of Windsor, a long-standing alliance between England and Portugal that led to the special relationship the two nations have maintained ever since.

Prince Henry is known in English as 'Henry the Navigator', although this term is not used in Portuguese and Henry never sailed on any of the voyages of exploration. He had access to vast amounts of money, which he used to finance expeditions to attack Moorish cities and fund the organisation of his nautical training institution and build fleets of ships. Where did that money come from?

Well, back in 1305, the French king, Philip IV, owed a fortune to the Knights Templar, who were the bankers of Christendom and the protectors of the faith in the Mediterranean. Philip managed to get his lifelong friend Raymond Bertrand de Got, Archbishop of Bordeaux, elected pope (although he was not even a cardinal). He became Pope Clement V. Under the influence of Philip IV, Clement V supported an evil scheme to have the Templars declared heretics. On Friday 13 October 1307, in a surprise move throughout France, the Templars were arrested and imprisoned, their monies and treasures and properties were seized by the state and many knights were tortured and burned at the stake as heretics. This wiped out Philip's debt and gave him access to a fortune. Clement V moved the papal court to Avignon, in the Kingdom of Arles to the south of France, in 1309.

Although the Order of the Knights Templar had been annihilated throughout France and in many other parts of Europe, King Dinis I of Portugal had not joined in the persecution and, after the next Pope, John XXII, retrospectively absolved the Templars of heresy and ordered that what was left of their assets be held by the church, Dinis revived the order at the Templars' Tomar stronghold in central Portugal, under the name 'The Order of the Knights of Christ'. Pope John XXII issued a papal bull, *Ad ea ex quibus*, on 14 March 1319, which recognised the new order and gave it the right to inherit Templar assets and properties.

For most of his adult life, Prince Henry of Portugal, born a century later, was the grandmaster of the Military Order of the Knights of Christ, and the vast wealth of the order financed the Age of Discovery. During Henry's lifetime the Portuguese developed and refined the caravel, a seaworthy manoeuvrable ship that was able to tack and sail against the wind, and a larger, partly square-rigged, sea-going vessel called the 'carrak'. These vessels were originally 50 to 100 tons—going to sea in one would have been quite terrifying.

Henry's captains found Madeira (1418), The Azores (1427) and the Cape Verde Islands (1456), which all became Portuguese colonies. In 1473, thirteen years after Henry died, Lopes Gonçalves became the first European to sail across the equator and in 1488, fifteen years later, another Portuguese captain, Bartholomew Dias, rounded the bottom of Africa and sailed into the Indian Ocean.

In May 1498, a fleet of Portuguese ships, led by Vasco da Gama, reached India. The Portuguese opened trade routes and formed alliances with various rulers along the east coast of Africa and in India and the Spice Islands, and thus fulfilled Prince Henry's dream of breaking the monopoly on the Asian spice trade, until then held by Islamic nations. Da Gama was appointed Portuguese viceroy to India in 1524. Both Dias and da Gama were knights of the Order of Christ. The success of the Portuguese Empire was to be built on the African slave trade and spice, and the remnants of the treasury of the once mighty Knights Templar.

The Pope Divides the Planet

Portugal, and the Spanish kingdoms of Castile and Aragon, dominated world exploration and waged war on each other intermittently until Aragon and Castile were united by a royal marriage. The Treaty of Alcáçovas in 1479 divided overseas discoveries into two agreed zones: Spanish and Portuguese. In 1494, Pope Alexander VI sanctioned the Treaty of Tordesillas, which divided the 'new world' territories between Portugal and Spain by papal decree. An imaginary line was drawn 370 degrees west of the Cape Verde Islands. Spain could claim new lands to the west of the line and Portugal everything to the east.

By a quirk of fate, the dividing line drawn down the Atlantic intersected the landmass of South America and ran through what is now Brazil and thus Portugal claimed it! The problem was that no one was sure what happened when the line was extended around the other side of the globe, so another papal decree tried to sort that out in the Treaty of Zaragoza (1529) and Portugal got the Moluccas (Spice Islands).

Christopher Columbus, a Genoese Italian sailing for Spain, found the Caribbean Islands and Americas in 1492. In South America, Hernán Cortés conquered the Aztecs (1520) and Francisco Pizarro conquered the Incas (1533). Portugal kept Brazil, the rest of Central and South America was Spanish.

Ferdinand Magellan, a Portuguese employed by Spain, entered the Pacific Ocean from the east and found the Philippines in 1521 and Spain began to colonise the islands in 1565.

In 1567, Alvaro de Mendana, crossed the Pacific from Peru, discovered the Solomon Islands, lost most of his men to scurvy and was horrified to discover the inhabitants were cannibals. Twenty-five years later, he led a second expedition of four ships carrying 380 men, women and children to settle the islands, but couldn't find them again! They attempted to settle on the largest of the Santa Cruz Islands, about 400 kilometres southeast of the Solomons, where Mendana and others died of fever. Guided by a young navigator named de Queirós, two of the ships made it to the Philippines where, three months later, Mendana's widow married the governor's son. Of the 380 who left Peru, 290 died of starvation, fever and scurvy.

De Queirós made another attempt to find the elusive Solomon Islands in 1605, and, in May 1606, reached Vanuatu, which he assumed to be a northern extension of the Great South Land and named *Australia del Espíritu Santo* (South Land of the Holy Spirit). He later altered it to *Austrialia del Espíritu Santo* (Austrian Land of the Holy Spirit) in honour of Spanish King Philip III, a member of the Royal House of Austria.

After conflict with local tribes the explorers left the island in two ships and became separated in a storm. On de Queirós' ship the crew mutinied, locked him in his cabin, and sailed to Mexico. On the other ship, Luis Váez de Torres decided to go his own way and, while charting the southern coast of New Guinea, saw 'very large islands' at 'the 11th degree of south latitude'. What he saw was the coast of Australia where, six months earlier, Dutchman Willem Janszoon (also known as Jansz) had sailed, making maps of what he thought was the coast of New Guinea.

Torres wrote an account of his discovery, which remained a secret for 155 years. During the Seven Years War the British East India Company captured the city of Manila in 1762 and held it till the end of the war. An ambitious young employee of the company, Alexander Dalrymple, found the account in the Manila library and translated it. Mr Dalrymple has a major part to play in our story, but not yet.

The Age of Discovery coincided with the period of astonishing brutality called the Spanish Inquisition. All the Holy Lands, won in the Crusades, were lost to Christianity by 1291 and Spain's neighbours, to the east and south, were Moslem. Islamic rulers controlled the Middle East and the lands that stretched to India. Religious fervour and fear of losing power led to a desperate desire to control both the known and unknown areas of the world. As a result, 32,000 individuals who wanted to think differently about religion were officially tortured and executed by the church.

Spreading this dreadful version of Christianity was not only one motivation for the Age of Discovery, it was also a very good excuse to use when the real motivations were things far more basic and less Christian—conquest, slavery and greed.

The Spanish and Portuguese empires were built on religious fanaticism and conquest, slavery, spices, gold, silver, emeralds and tobacco. It has been said that the Spanish took the gold and silver of the Americas and turned them into stone, building huge cathedrals, castles and fortresses across southern Spain.

So, the Age of Discovery was not about finding the Great South Land, but European ships were now sailing the waters of the Indian and Pacific oceans.

In 1580, the matter of Portuguese/Spanish 'ownership' of 'new lands' became further complicated by the fact that, as a result of a royal marriage, Portugal and Spain became one unified kingdom (the Iberian Union). Under the Hapsburg rulers Philip II, III and IV, this situation lasted until 1640.

By the time this happened, however, it had become apparent that there was another problem with papal decrees and the treaties of Tordesillas and Zaragoza—some nations simply ignored them.

CORPORATE RAIDERS

The Protestants Take to the Sea

The two nations that ignored the papal decrees most vehemently were England and the Netherlands. Both of these nations broke from the Catholic Church and the control of the pope in the 16th century.

Henry VIII established the Church of England, with himself as its head, when parliament passed the *Act of Supremacy* in 1534. When the Spanish invasion of England failed in 1588, during the reign of Henry's daughter Elizabeth I, England was free to establish itself as a major seafaring nation. Francis Drake circumnavigated the globe from 1577 to 1580, and was the second captain to do so. He attacked and plundered Spanish colonies and ships along the west coast of South America and explored the west coast of California (which he claimed for Elizabeth I). Thomas Cavendish emulated Drake's feats in 1586–88. Both were knighted for their efforts as part of the war against Spain.

The Dutch situation was different. The Netherlands had been ruled by Burgundy, and became part of the Hapsburg Empire by royal marriage and thus under Spanish sovereignty until 1581 when the northern region, which had adopted Protestant Calvinism, declared independence, in what was known as the 'Dutch Revolt'. This occurred as part of what is known as the 'Eighty Years War', or 'Dutch War of Independence' (1568–1648). In effect the northern Netherlands acted as the Dutch Republic from 1588.

The Dutch, at war with their Spanish rulers but now operating as an independent nation, did not take long to start exploring and challenging

Portugal for access to the Spice Islands. The first Dutch fleet to the East Indies, four ships financed by seven different merchant companies, sailed in 1595. Then, in 1598, Olivier van Noort left Rotterdam with four ships to harass the Spanish in the Philippines and attempt to open trade with China. Entering the Pacific through the Straits of Magellan, he lost two ships but sank the galleon *San Antonio* near Manila and made it home with one ship and 45 of his original 248 men.

In 1601 a fleet of thirteen Dutch vessels, belonging to different merchant companies and sailing under two different admirals, made its way to Bantam on the island of Java, and part of the fleet (five Dutch vessels commanded by Admiral Walter Harmensz) fought a pitched sea battle with a Portuguese and Spanish fleet made up of eight galleons and many smaller ships. The Dutch won a decisive victory and captured three ships. The smallest of Harmensz's five vessels, a messenger ship called the *Duyfken*, would later play a major role in Australia's history.

The Dutch States General, the ruling body that represented the seven Netherland provinces, realised that fleets of ships belonging to various merchant companies and ship owners, with more than one admiral or decision-maker, were prone to many problems. A more unified and disciplined approach was required. Across the North Sea in England, Queen Elizabeth I was thinking the exact same thing!

As early as 1579, Sir Francis Drake's voyage around the world plundering Spanish ships and colonies had added substantially to the royal treasury and returned a massive 5000 per cent profit to investors. After the defeat of the Spanish armada in 1588, Queen Elizabeth gave her blessing to several expeditions into Spanish- and Portuguese-controlled waters. In 1592 an expedition organised by the Earl of Cumberland, led by Sir Walter Raleigh and made up of ships owned by various adventurers, merchants and captains, captured several enemy vessels, including a carrak, the *Madre de Deus* (*Mother of God*), in a sea battle near the island of Flores in the Azores.

The *Madre de Deus* was three times larger than any British vessel ever built at the time and caused a sensation when she was brought back to Dartmouth. In her holds were chests filled with jewels, pearls, gold, silver coins, ambergris, ebony, cochineal, cloth and tapestries. She was also carrying huge quantities of spices, including nutmeg, pepper, cinnamon, frankincense and cloves. Also on board the vessel was a book that contained information about trade with India, China and Japan.

The capture of the *Madre de Deus* changed the course of British history and provided a dilemma for Elizabeth I. Here, in one vessel, was treasure equal to half of the annual royal revenue of her kingdom. On the other hand, there was no prescribed way of dividing the spoils and arguments developed between the various ship owners and captains. Much of the precious cargo was stolen or misappropriated by those who had been involved in the expedition. Elizabeth realised that there had to be better methods for the Crown to benefit from some form of control over the revenue from such expeditions. It was time to find a new way to access the riches of the Indies.

The old European ideas of spreading Catholicism, colonising and plundering were about to be replaced by a 'new greed'—commercial trading monopolies—and 200 years of war between European powers.

The VOC and British East India Company

Out there on a lawless ocean, there were enemy ships as well as pirates. Spain and Portugal were now united under one king, had established colonies in Africa, America and Asia, and were at war with both England and the Netherlands. Individual merchants, or small groups of merchants, who sent ships on speculative trading missions to distant parts of the world risked losing everything on one voyage.

In 1600 Elizabeth I gave a monopoly by royal charter to explore, trade and attack enemy ships and territories in the East Indies to the 'Governor and Company of Merchants of London Trading into the East-Indies', which became the English East India Company, later the British East India Company, often simply called 'The Company'. At the peak of its powers in the 18th century, the company controlled more than half of all the trade in the entire world and ruled over India and other parts of what would become the British Empire, with its own army and fleet of ships. Any merchants trading in breach of the charter without a licence from the company were liable to indefinite imprisonment at the 'royal pleasure' and all their ships and cargoes would be forfeited in equal parts to the Crown and the English East India Company. The charter, originally for fifteen years, was renewed by all reigning British monarchs until 1858, when the British government took over the company's Indian possessions, its administrative powers, its property, its army and its empire, and the company was dissolved.

Although the English East India Company was established two years before the Dutch version, it would be the Dutch East India Company (Vereenigde Oostindische Compagnie or VOC) that was the first of the two organisations to make a major impact on the history of Australia.

Established on 20 March 1602, the VOC has been accurately described by the American author Peter Gelderloos as:

A chartered company, the first with publicly traded stocks, and— within a few decades of its foundation—the richest company in the world, the VOC was not merely a business interest. It constituted . . . a state in itself. By 1669, it commanded over two hundred ships, a quarter of them warships, and ten thousand soldiers. The Dutch state had granted the VOC law-making, war-making, and judicial author- ity. It founded colonies that proved to be fully functioning, if not fully independent, states that lasted for centuries.

Both the VOC and British East India Company espoused the concept of *mare liberum* (freedom of the seas) in direct defiance of the *mare clausum* (the right to 'close' the ocean to others) that was claimed by the Spanish and Portuguese and originated in the papal decrees of 1498 and 1529. *Mare liberum* provided ideological justification for the VOC, equipped with superior vessels and armaments, to end the Portuguese control of the spice trade. After decades of war, a peace settlement in 1663 left the VOC in possession of the Cape Colony in Africa and most of the Spice Islands. The Portuguese were left with Brazil, colonies in Africa and only small footholds in Asia—Goa in India, East Timor and Macau.

The English East India Company used the conflict as an opportunity to send vessels and establish contacts in India and the Spice Islands, while the other two powers were at war and distracted. By 1700, the English East India Company and the VOC had gained control of far eastern trade, from India to Japan.

WHO WANTS NEW HOLLAND?

The Winds of Change

With the Netherlands now a dominant power in the Spice Islands, the VOC's main problem was the length of the voyage to the islands around Africa and across the northern Indian Ocean. This problem was solved in 1611 when VOC Captain Hendrik Brouwer ventured further south of the Cape Peninsula, instead of following the coast and rounding the bottom of Africa, and discovered the strong westerly winds called the 'Roaring Forties'. These powerful air currents are caused by air being displaced from the equator into latitudes 40 to 50 degrees south. This, combined with the effect of the Earth's rotation and the lack of any significant landmass to block the flow, causes the strong prevailing westerlies.

By following these winds across the Southern Ocean and then turning north, the time for the journey was cut in half. The problem then, however, was to accurately calculate longitude and decide when to turn north. Before the invention of accurate chronometers, calculating longitude was done by 'dead reckoning', which was inaccurate and little better than guesswork. In spite of this problem, in 1616 the VOC made it compulsory for all its captains to use the new route. One result of this directive was increased profits for the VOC, as sailing time was reduced and more voyages could be made. On the other hand, several valuable ships and cargoes were lost when VOC vessels ran aground or sank after hitting reefs, or the shore, along the coast of Western Australia.

Another incidental consequence of captains being instructed to use the 'Brouwer' or southern route was, of course, the discovery and mapping of much of the continent that became Australia. In 1616 Dirk Hartog, captain of the VOC vessel *Eendracht* (*Concord*), lost contact with the fleet in a storm and, on 25 October 1616, anchored near an island just off the west coast of Australia at Shark Bay. Hartog explored the island for three days and left a pewter plate nailed to a tree as evidence of his discovery. He named the coast 'Eendrachtsland'.

The name *Eendracht* was a common one for Dutch ships, referring to the successful alliance of the seven provinces that made up the Dutch Republic. Just over a year before Hartog's landing, another vessel of that name, captained by Willem Schouten, had made the first ever passage under Cape Horn and sighted a land to the southeast, which he named 'Staten Landt' (in honour of the parliament of the seven provinces of the Netherlands, the *Staaten Generaal*). Schouten wondered whether the land was part of the Great South Land's south-western extremity. Twenty-seven years later, in 1642, Abel Tasman found New Zealand and considered the possibility that it was a western extension of Staten Landt, so he gave it the same name. One year later Hendrik Brouwer proved Staten Landt under South America was an island, so Dutch map-makers changed Tasman's 'Staten Landt' to *Nova Zeelandia* (New Zeeland) after the Dutch province of Zeeland.

A number of large VOC ships with valuable trade cargoes and passengers were wrecked along the coast of Western Australia in the following century, most notably the *Batavia* in 1629, the *Vergulde Draeck* (*Gilt Dragon*) in 1656, the *Ridderschap van Holland* (*Knighthood of Holland*) in 1694 and the *Zuytdorp* (*South Village*) in 1712.

In 1696 Willem de Vlamingh commanded an extensive search with three ships, looking for survivors of the *Ridderschap van Holland*, a vessel that had carried 324 passengers. He explored and charted hundreds of miles of coastline, including Rottnest Island, the Swan River and Shark Bay, found Hartog's plate and replaced it with one of his own.*

In May 1626 *'t Gulden Zeepgaert* (*The Golden Seahorse*) departed Amsterdam with Pieter van Nuyts, a member of the VOC's India Council, on board. Instead of turning north, the ship continued east and mapped 1500 kilometres of the Australian southern coast to near modern-day Ceduna. Francois Thijssen, the captain of the ship, named the region *Landt van Pieter Nuyts* (Pieter Nuyts' Land) as Nuyts was the highest-ranking VOC official on the ship. We still have Nuyts Reef, Cape Nuyts and the Nuyts Archipelago, and Western Australian Christmas bush is named *Nuytsia floribunda*.

On the north coast the *Duyfken*, which had taken part in the sea battle at Bantam in December 1601, was now a VOC vessel captained by Willem Janszoon. *Duyfken* was a three-masted manoeuvrable vessel of about 100 tons that was used as a scouting and messenger vessel. She had a shallow draught and could carry cargoes of up to 60 tons. Often named *Duyf* or *Duyfken*, these vessels carried small cargoes between ports and were used to scout coastlines and survey new territories. The names meaning 'Dove' and 'Little Dove' were a reference to the dove sent by Noah to scout for land and check for signs that the world was safe after the flood.

In 1603, the *Duyfken* became the first European vessel to explore the coast of Australia, although Captain Janszoon thought he was exploring and mapping part of New Guinea when he made the first maps of the west coast of Cape York.

After Francois Thijssen mapped a large portion of the south coast, it seemed that this landmass was not part of the fabled Great South Land. In 1642 VOC captain Abel Tasman was sent by the company with two ships, *Heemskerck* and *Zeehaen,* to search the Southern Ocean below 40 degrees south.

In August 1642, Tasman left Mauritius, headed south and turned east. He discovered Tasmania, which he named 'Van Diemen's Land' in honour of the governor-general of the Dutch East Indies, charted the southern half of the island and sailed east, where he found and charted the west coast of New Zealand before sailing back to Batavia via Tonga and Fiji. He had circumnavigated the Australian continent without once seeing the mainland. The following year Tasman, following explorations twenty years earlier by VOC captains Jan Carstenszoon and Willem Joosten van Colsteerdt, charted the north and west coasts of the continent, from Cape York to just north of Shark Bay.

Dutch cartographer Joan Blaeu produced a map labelling the whole landmass officially *Nova Hollandia* (New Holland) in 1663. From that time, all accurate maps of the world showed about three-quarters of the coast of New Holland, with open sea to the east and south. It was obvious that it was *not* the Great South Land.

Why didn't the Dutch ever claim or settle 'New Holland'? Well, the answer can be found in the report by Jan Carstenszoon after his 1623 exploration of Cape York and the Gulf of Carpentaria, where his crew fought a pitched battle with some two hundred local tribesmen. The people, who he described as 'poor and miserable', had 'no knowledge of precious metals or spices'.

These Dutch captains, like those of the British East India Company, belonged to a commercial enterprise; they were interested in trade. They had no interest in establishing settlements that could not make profits.

After William Dampier called in at Timor in 1699, the VOC became wary of British interest and sent expeditions to both New Holland and New Guinea in 1705 to make sure there was nothing there that made the territories worth claiming or settling. The Maarten Van Delft expedition spent three months on the Tiwi Islands and north coast of New Holland (near present-day Darwin) studying the locals and trading. Van Delft, who died on the return voyage, concluded they were 'primitive and treacherous' people. Similarly, the New Guinea expedition, led by Jacob Weyland, found nothing worthy of interest to the VOC. These were the final attempts by the VOC to find any reason to settle or claim New Holland or New Guinea.

The British Are Coming

The first English East India Company captain to use the 'Brouwer' route was Humphrey Fitzherbert, who helped establish an English enclave at Table Bay at the Cape of Good Hope. The second English East India Company ship to attempt the route was the ill-fated *Tryal*, the first British ship to sight the coast of New Holland, captained by John Brooke, in 1622.

Carrying a valuable cargo of silver for trading purposes and precious gifts for the king of Siam (present-day Thailand), the vessel travelled too far east and ran onto a reef near Barrow Island and sank. Brooke had misread Dutch charts and later blamed Fitzherbert for giving him inaccurate information. With his son and nine others he took what he could of the treasures on board, scrambled into the ship's skiff, abandoned the rest of the crew and sailed to Batavia. To cover his ineptitude and cowardice, he lied about the circumstances of the wreck and location of the reef, making it appear the ship was lost further west.

Meanwhile, the ship's factor (head merchant), Thomas Bright, managed to get 44 men and the ship's longboat ashore on one of the Monte Bello Islands. A week later they set sail and reached Batavia three days after Brooke. Ninety men drowned in the shipwreck.

Bright wrote a report blaming Brooke for the wreck and loss of life and investigations were carried out, but Brooke was cleared of blame. Three hundred years later, in 1934, the true position of the 'Tryal Rocks' was calculated by historian Ida Lee and the wreck was found in 1969, proving Brooke was guilty as charged.

However, as a result of the wreck, English East India Company ships were banned from using the faster 'Brouwer' route for several decades and there was no significant British contact with the coast of New Holland until the arrival of William Dampier, an adventurer, botanist, anthropologist and hydrographer who managed to circumnavigate the world three times in his lifetime.

In 1688, as a member of the crew of the pirate ship *Cygnet*, Dampier spent three months exploring the land around the Fitzroy River in Western Australia while the ship was being repaired. His book, *A New Voyage Round the World*, published in 1697, was a best-seller and so impressed the British admiralty that, in an unprecedented move, they gave him captaincy of a naval vessel, the 26-gun warship HMS *Roebuck*, and sent him, in January 1699, to find the east coast of New Holland and explore the continent.

As it was mid-winter, however, entry into the Pacific via Tierra del Fuego was impossible, so the *Roebuck* went via the Cape of Good Hope and Indian Ocean to Shark Bay and followed the coast north and east. Dampier charted the coast and also made the first detailed scholarly records and drawings of Australian flora and fauna and seashells. After visiting the Dutch port at Timor for supplies, he charted the north coast of New Guinea, New Ireland and New Britain. He sailed within 700 kilometres of the east coast of Australia but, with the *Roebuck* leaking badly with worm-eaten timbers, Dampier abandoned the voyage and attempted to return to England via Cape Horn.

He made it as far as Ascension Island in the South Atlantic where, in February 1701, with the *Roebuck* about to sink, he ran her aground in an attempt to save his collection of specimens, charts and papers. Five weeks later an East Indiaman arrived and all were rescued. The specimens and drawings are in the Fielding-Druce Herbarium at Oxford University. Dampier's account of the expedition, *A Voyage to New Holland*, was published in 1703.

In 2001 a team from the Western Australian Maritime Museum located the wreck of HMS *Roebuck* in Clarence Bay at Ascension Island.

None of this exploration, however interesting it may be in the history of Australia, had anything to do with attempting to find the Great South Land. It would take another 70 years and a 'world war' before the race to find the Great South Land began in earnest.

Meanwhile, between 1740 and 1743, Commodore George Anson circumnavigated the globe during the 'War of Jenkins' Ear', 1739–48. This war, over trading rights in the Caribbean, started when Welsh merchant captain Robert Jenkins was accused of smuggling and had his ear removed by a Spanish coast guard commander.

Anson set out, with six warships and two store ships, on a poorly planned mission to the Pacific. After only two months at sea, dysentery and typhus spread among the crews and later scurvy appeared as they battled to reach the Pacific under Cape Horn in gales and ice. Two ships became separated from the fleet and turned back. One ship was wrecked on the coast of Chile and two were lost at sea. Anson sacked the Spanish port of Paita, 1100 kilometres north of Lima, captured several Spanish ships and headed across the Pacific. Most of the men died of scurvy but one ship, HMS *Centurion*, made it to Macau, where it was refitted. Anson intercepted, attacked and captured the Acapulco galleon *Nuestra Señora de Covadonga* (*Our Lady of Covadonga*) as it neared the Philippines, carrying 35 tons of silver coins and ingots.

Anson sailed home a hero with 188 of the original 1854 men who had set out almost four years earlier. One hundred and sixty-six of the more than 600 men from the two ships that turned back and the one wrecked on the coast of Chile also made it home. He had lost five ships and 1500 men, but his share of the prize money made him one of the wealthiest men in Britain. Promoted to admiral and elected to parliament, his 1748 account, *A Voyage Round the World in the*

Years 1740–1744, included charts, captured from Spanish vessels, that contained quite a lot of misinformation about the Pacific, including 'phantom islands' and bits of coastlines, which later caused Alexander Dalrymple and others to make false assumptions about the Great South Land.

Anson, who became First Lord of the Admiralty in 1751, suggested a British settlement on the Falkland Islands, as they were conveniently located to be used as a base for exploring the Pacific. His plan was not implemented for fear it could cause yet another war with the Spanish.

Britain's next major war would, however, change the world forever and lead to a race to claim the Falklands and explore the Pacific.

ET LES FRANÇAIS?

Gonneville Land and New France

France, as a Catholic nation that had taken no part in the treaties of Tordesillas and Zaragoza, had no religious 'legal' right to explore unknown seas or claim territories. It was left to individual French ship owners to advocate the idea of 'freedom of the seas' and explore them with the tacit approval of expansionist French monarchs Louis XII (1498–1515) and François I (1515–47).

In 1503 a ship owner from Honfleur, Binot Paulmier de Gonneville, defied the Portuguese *mare clausum* and, with the help of two Portuguese pilots, set sail for the Spice Islands in his ship *L'Espoir* (*Hope*). South of the Cape of Good Hope they were driven in a great storm for six weeks to a land where the natives lived in peace and farmed crops. Gonneville and his crew stayed there for six months before returning home with a native boy, the son of a local ruler. The boy later married into the Paulmier family and, 160 years later, his great-grandson Jean Paulmier de Courtonne, Canon of the Church of Saint-Pierre at Lisieux, wrote an account of the voyage and, in 1667, published a small book, *Mémoires touchant l'établissement d'une mission chrestienne dans le Troisième Monde* (*Memoirs Concerning the Establishment of a Christian Mission in the Third World*), which called upon France to find, Christianise and colonise *La Terre Australe*, the land of his ancestors.

Historians generally agree that Paulmier de Gonneville landed in the southern part of Brazil. As a result of this story, however, the French name for the mythical Great South Land became 'Gonneville

Land' and was often also referred to as *le Troisième Monde* (the Third World). The French belief in this land led to writers, like Gabriel de Goigny, using it as the setting for utopian fantasy adventure stories, in the form of accounts of 'real' voyages.

Because of the papal restrictions and Portuguese control, the French were slow to establish colonies in the East Indies; they were, however, busy elsewhere. Between 1534 and 1542 Jacques Cartier made three voyages from Saint-Malo, explored the coast of Canada and the St Lawrence River and claimed the land for France. It became the first province of New France and, in 1608, Samuel de Champlain started a settlement at Québec, which was the beginning of a huge French empire in North America. We tend to forget that, before the Seven Years War, 'New France' covered an area more than four times larger than the territory controlled by the British in North America.

After the French East India Company was finally formed in 1664 and a trading post was established in India in 1668, one of their captains, Bouvet de Lozier, searching for 'Gonneville Land' in 1739, found, in a sea of ice and fog at latitude 54 degrees south, Bouvet Island, the only speck of land in the vast South Atlantic. He reported that trade appeared unlikely—as there was no sign of habitation.

Bougainville, the Seven Years War and the Falklands Fiasco

Louis-Antoine, Le Comte de Bougainville, was a French nobleman, diplomat, mathematician, army colonel and navy admiral and a dedicated enemy of Britain although, while he was attached to the French embassy in London in 1755, he became a member of the Royal Society at the age of 27 after the publication of his *Treatise on Integral Calculus*. A year later he was commanding French troops against the British in Canada.

The Seven Years War actually lasted nine years, from 1754 to 1763, and began in, of all places, Ohio as a border dispute between French and British colonists. This war changed the world drastically and had a major impact on Australian history. It intensified the race to find the Great South Land, which didn't exist, and the east coast of New Holland, which did!

Britain's allies included the 'German' kingdoms of Prussia, Hesse, Hanover, Brunswick and Schaumburg, as well as Portugal and the

Native American nations of the Iroquois and Cherokee. On the French side were Austria, Russia, Spain, Sweden, Saxony, the Moghul Empire and the Native American Wabanaki, Algonquin, Mohawk, Ojibwe, Ottawa and Shawnee nations.

The war was fought in Europe, North America, Central America, South America, the Caribbean, Africa, India, the Spice Islands, the Philippines and on the waters of the Mediterranean, North Sea, and the Atlantic, Pacific and Indian oceans. After nine years of fighting and negotiating the French lost 'New France', and almost all of their other overseas territories, to Britain. This was a devastating blow to French colonial aspirations and, in the aftermath, their search for new territories to claim and colonise became almost frantic, as did British attempts to counter the French aspirations.

Bougainville took part, as a commanding officer, in the pivotal Battle of Québec, which ended in a humiliating defeat for the French and the surrender of Québec to the British. A 30-year-old midshipman named James Cook was instrumental in the charting and navigating that enabled the British fleet to carry troops along the St Lawrence River to capture the city. Bougainville helped negotiate the surrender of both Québec and Montréal, as well as the terms of the Treaty of Paris in 1763, and then quickly set about planning to re-establish France as a world power by exploring and acquiring new territories. After the Seven Years War, lying, spying and subterfuge about discoveries and maps, which had always been standard practice, reached new levels of paranoia between the French and British.

Even before the peace treaty was signed, Bougainville began hatching a plan with French foreign minister, the Duc de Choiseul, to secretly establish a French colony on the uninhabited *Îles Malouines* (Falkland Islands) and use it as a base to explore the Pacific. This involved taking volunteers, mostly refugees from the North American maritime province of Acadia, who had refused to sign British loyalty oaths, to settle the islands and claim them for France by act of 'first settlement'. Bougainville personally funded the whole operation.

This plan was the same one proposed by George Anson in 1748. As European nations had no idea what islands or continents existed in the Pacific, the Falklands were the only known strategic base for exploration.

Bougainville, a colonel in the French Army, was quickly made a captain in the French Navy in June 1763 and left in September from Saint-Malo with two ships and 29 settlers. He established the Port St Louis colony in February and officially claimed the islands in April, making his cousin, Michel-François de Nerville, governor. Louis XV formally ratified possession on 12 September 1764 and Bougainville took another 50 settlers to Port St Louis in October and then visited Tierra del Fuego to collect timber, as the Falklands were virtually treeless, before returning to France in August 1765.

When the British admiralty got wind of what the French were up to, in March 1764 a secret expedition was hastily organised by the secretary to the lords of the admiralty, Sir Philip Stephens, the most powerful person in the organisation. The Lords of the Admiralty left decision-making to Stephens and often didn't know what he and his staff were planning. (It was usually new ways to thwart French colonial ambitions.)

Britain had previously claimed the Falkland Islands by act of discovery, in 1592, by Captain John Davis and Sir Richard Hawkins in 1593. Englishman John Strong and his crew were the first people known to land on and explore the islands in 1690.

As soon as Stephens at the admiralty had news of the French enterprise, the British frigates HMS *Dolphin* and *Tamar* were hastily prepared and sailed, on 3 July, to reassert the British claims to the Falkland Islands and California, and search for the Great South Land under the command of 'Foul-Weather Jack', Commander John Byron.**

The expedition was disguised as a 'voyage to India' and not even the crews knew the true purpose until the ships left Rio de Janeiro for the Falklands. In mid-January 1765, Byron found a good harbour on Saunders Island, which he named Port Egmont, and in a ceremony on 22 January he re-established the British claim to the islands.

Unknown to Byron, 120 kilometres to the east, on East Falkland Island, the French colony at Port St Louis was almost a year old.

Byron had been ordered to survey the islands, but, due to 'foul weather', he quit before finding the French and sailed to Port Famine in the Straits of Magellan to rendezvous with the store ship HMS *Florida*, which arrived back in London in June with Byron's maps and a report that a 'strange ship' had followed him to Port Famine, flying French colours. It was Bougainville, on his wood-collecting expedition!

In September 1765 the admiralty despatched Captain John McBride with three ships, a pre-fabricated wooden blockhouse and 25 marines to make a permanent settlement at Port Egmont, survey the islands and map them. Over a year later, in December 1766, McBride finally found the French at Port St Louis. He politely asked them to leave— and they politely refused.

Meanwhile, back in Paris in August 1765, Bougainville had discovered that, owing to complaints from Spain and the formal family agreement, *Pacte de Famille*, between the Bourbon kings of France and Spain (who were cousins), the islands were to be formally handed over to Spain. Bougainville was paid a massive compensation of 600,000 livres (about £25,000) and the settlement was handed to Spain and renamed *Puerto de Nuestra Señora de la Soledad* (Port of Our Lady of Solitude).***

On 6 December 1766, Bougainville left France on his secret expedition to become the first Frenchman to circumnavigate the globe and explore the Pacific. The voyage was disguised as a visit to the Falklands, to formally hand over the colony to the Spanish and evacuate settlers wanting to leave. Once this was done the Falkland Islands/*Islas Malvinas* became an Anglo–Spanish problem and Bougainville went to search for new French territories—and the east coast of New Holland.

SOUTH PACIFIC SECRETS

Tahiti and Beyond

After Commander John Byron 'reclaimed' the Falklands and was reprovisioned by the *Florida*, he negotiated the Straits of Magellan, entered the Pacific in late April 1765 and sailed home via the Mariana Islands and Batavia. He just missed Tahiti but found several islands to the northeast and named them after King George. Although his 'secret orders' were to look for the Great South Land and reinforce the British claim to America's northwest coast made by Francis Drake in 1579, he failed to do either, claiming his ships were in poor condition. He reported huge flocks of birds heading south, which suggested the possible existence of the Great South Land.

After the fastest circumnavigation to that date, Byron arrived home on 7 May 1766, and Sir Philip Stephens made sure all officers' journals were seized by the admiralty and all crew members were made to swear a vow of secrecy in front of a judge. Apparently, however, there was a French agent in the admiralty and Byron's log and maps were copied and sent to Paris.

The race to explore the Pacific was now on in earnest.

The admiralty, fearing that the French were possibly one step ahead, had the *Dolphin* refitted and sent back to the Pacific less than four months later, on 22 August, under the command of Captain Samuel Wallis. The second vessel on the voyage, HMS *Swallow*, was under the command of Philip Carteret, who had sailed with Byron, as had at least seven of the crew members on the two ships.

After suffering dreadful weather in the Straits of Magellan for four months, Wallis lost contact with the *Swallow* and entered the Pacific on 11 April 1767. He attempted to follow orders and sail west to where Abel Tasman had charted the west coast of New Zealand, but weather and sickness among the crew made it impossible.

With the ship undermanned Wallis turned north then west and found Tahiti. By then he was seriously ill and bed-ridden with bilious attacks, and Second Lieutenant Tobias Furneaux was in command of the day-to-day running of the ship.

Several days before making landfall at Tahiti, some of the crew thought they saw land to the south. As this was in the same area that Byron had reported seeing large flocks of birds flying south, this fuelled more speculation about a southern continent.

The first attempt to make a landing on Tahiti met with such hostility from the locals that the ship's cannons were fired and the *Dolphin* retreated, sailed around the island and found a safe haven on the north side, at Matavai Bay, on 23 June 1767. Tobias Furneaux exchanged 'emblems of peace' with a local chieftain and conducted a possession ceremony, naming the island 'King George III Island'. During the five-week stay at Matavai Bay the crew, including Wallis, were restored to health and the *Dolphin* made the same passage home as previously, arriving on 6 May 1768 with news of the discovery of Tahiti, just eighty days before the *Endeavour* was due to sail to the Pacific to observe the transit of Venus.

Meanwhile, back in October 1766, Bougainville had received formal permission from Louis XV for his proposed expedition to search the Pacific and circumnavigate the globe, partly as compensation for the Falklands Islands/*Îles Malouines*/*Islas Malvinas* fiasco. His two vessels entered the Pacific in late January 1768. His written instructions from King Louis XV did not mention the Great South Land. He was instructed to search for, and claim if possible, 'the lands lying between the Indies and the western shores of America . . . called Diemen Land, New Holland, Carpentaria, Land of the Holy Spirit, New Guinea etc.'.

It is uncertain whether or not Bougainville was in possession of the information stolen from the British admiralty, but he followed a similar path to that taken by John Byron. Unlike Byron, however,

Bougainville found Tahiti and anchored in a lagoon on the east coast, about 20 coastal kilometres from where Wallis had anchored ten months previously. Bougainville assumed he was the first European to find the island and claimed it for France. Due to the difficult anchorage (they lost six anchors in nine days) Bougainville set sail after only ten days at Tahiti, taking with him the local chief's brother, Ahutoru, who volunteered to accompany the foreigners to their homeland.

Bougainville found the Samoan islands, then headed to Vanuatu and quickly proved that de Queirós' *Austrialia del Espíritu Santo* was just another chain of islands, which he claimed for France. He then crossed the Coral Sea with the specific intention, as stated in his journal, 'to verify our conjectures by getting sight of the eastern coast of New Holland'.

On 4 June 1768, eight days out of Vanuatu, the *Boudeuse* and *L'Etoile* were confronted by a line of huge waves breaking on a submerged reef that Bougainville named Diana Reef. The next day fruit and wood were seen in the sea and Bougainville noted, 'I have no doubt that there is land SSE of us.' On 6 June the ships encountered a line of shoals and reefs stretching to the horizon north and south: it was obviously a massive coastal reef. Bougainville was sure that 'this land is nothing else than the eastern coast of New Holland'.

The first version of the map of the voyage, produced by *Saillant et Nyon* in Paris in 1771, shows an arc of Australian coastline to the south of the line of the voyage that looks vaguely like the coast from Point Melville to Cairns, and dotted reefs to the west and south west. A second edition of the map contradicts this and shows instead a small piece of coastline to the north of the most easterly position of the voyage, at which point Bougainville turned northward. Both versions of the chart are obviously mere guesswork, but Bougainville was certain he had found the east coast of New Holland and, although he never saw the coast, he was right.

Evidently some crew members claimed to see land from the mast tops, but that is highly unlikely. The original charts were made by the expedition's cartographer, Charles Routier de Romainville; Bougainville never made a chart in his life. We don't know how many engravers and copiers made approximations before they were published.

Fearing scurvy, which had already taken some of his crew, and faced by a seemingly impenetrable barrier, with only a few weeks fresh water left and enough food for three months, Bougainville's choice was now to turn south, into the unknown, or north, where he knew there was land. Louis XV had ordered Bougainville to search for 'Diemen Land' as well as New Guinea. As he stood the ships safely away from the seemingly endless reefs, Bougainville said he heard *la voix de Dieu* (the voice of God) in the roar of the breakers and it said, 'Go north.'

Bougainville did so, and was the first European to find the largest and most northerly of the Solomon Islands, which still bears his name. After exploring the same islands that Dampier had studied 70 years earlier, the expedition returned home via Batavia.

In retrospect, Bougainville made two mistakes. Firstly, he turned north instead of south at the critical moment and, secondly, he failed to make any French claim on the east coast. He did, however, establish that there was ocean between the east coast of New Holland and *Austrialia del Espíritu Santo* (Vanuatu). The previous French maps, showing New Holland bulging eastward from Cape York to incorporate the islands of Vanuatu, could now be corrected, and the French now knew where the east coast of New Holland was and the British didn't, but they would within a year.

Mr Dalrymple's Theory

Both the admiralty and British East India Company were interested in the possibility of the existence of the Great South Land: the admiralty for strategic and logistic reasons, and shareholders of the British East India Company for commercial reasons. If the continent existed, it was important to find it before the French.

The main advocate of the possibility of the existence of the Great South Land was Alexander Dalrymple, a man who spent most of his working life with the British East India Company. Dalrymple was born into a noble Scottish family in 1737, on the family estate, Newhailes, near Edinburgh. He was the seventh of sixteen children born by Lady Christian Hamilton, a daughter of the Earl of Haddington, to her husband, Lieutenant-Colonel Sir James Dalrymple.

After his father died, his mother's family connections secured Alexander a job with the East India Company in Madras at just fifteen years of age. The ambitious young man enthusiastically explored the seas and islands between Borneo and the Philippines and visited Canton. He negotiated a trade deal with the Moslem Sultanate of Sulu, which governed parts of Borneo and Mindanao, south of the Philippines, to set up a trading station on the island of Balambangan.

As part of the Seven Years War, a British fleet captured the city of Manila and surrounding areas in the Philippines in 1762. The city was governed by the British East India Company for two years before being returned to Spain, as part of the Treaty of Paris, at the end of the war. During those two years, documents relating to the exploration of the Pacific found in the Manila library were given to Dalrymple to translate, among them the long-hidden account of Luis Váez de Torres' voyage, which told of a passage south of New Guinea from the Pacific Ocean to the Spice Islands.

In 1765 Dalrymple was back in London, where the East India Company rejected his plans for the Balambangan trading station. He was, however, elected a fellow of the Royal Society for his work mapping the Malay Archipelago and researching exploration in the Pacific. His book, *An Account of the Discoveries Made in The South Pacifick Ocean, Previous to 1764*, was published in late 1768, but a shorter, earlier printing was made to support his ambition to lead the British expedition to the Pacific, to plot the transit of Venus across the face of the sun in 1769 and explore the Southern Ocean.

In 1764 Dalrymple proposed a theory about the Great South Land. His map shows the west coast of New Zealand, as charted by Abel Tasman, and an empty southern Pacific Ocean stretching to a point about 1550 kilometres east of the coast of Chile. At that point, at 40 degrees south latitude, Dalrymple shows a small stretch of eastern coastline charted by Juan Fernández. At latitude 50 degrees south, on the same longitude, there's a small stretch of eastern coastline supposedly charted by the Dutch.

Fernández was a Spanish explorer who discovered the islands that bear his name, 670 kilometres off the coast of Santiago. The east coast fragment on Dalrymple's 1764 map lies 1300 kilometres southwest of those islands and was supposedly charted when Fernández was looking for the Great South Land. An account exists in the Spanish naval archive of an unofficial Fernández voyage to a land rather like New Zealand.

Dalrymple's map also shows, further northwest around latitude 30 degrees, just south of Easter Island (found by Dutchman Jacob Roggeveen in 1722), a line labelled 'signs of land'. Dalrymple's theory was that the Great South Land stretched from New Zealand across the Pacific to where part of its east coast terminated at one, two or all three of the aforementioned locations on his map.

Supported by the Royal Society, Dalrymple was appointed, in December 1767, to lead the *Endeavour* expedition. Four months later, however, he was informed that only a Royal Navy officer could command an admiralty vessel. He was offered the compromise of leading the scientific party but not commanding the ship. He bluntly refused and never forgave what he saw as the insult of being replaced by James Cook.

Dalrymple accused Cook of plotting behind his back, but the man who wielded the real power at the admiralty, Sir Philip Stephens, was not going to let a servant of the East India Company take charge of an expedition that had a secret admiralty agenda. He needed a man who could keep secrets, a tough, capable officer who could discover what Byron and Wallis had not.

In spite of having lost command of the expedition, Dalrymple made his maps available to Joseph Banks and expounded his theories to the wealthy young botanist, who had paid a small fortune (£10,000) to be allowed to join the expedition, along with an entourage of four artists, a fellow botanist, four servants and three hunting dogs.

THE PROOF IS
IN THE SAILING

The Odd Couple

Joseph Banks, who was just 25 years old when the expedition departed in August 1768, shared the *Endeavour*'s great cabin with James Cook, who turned 40 as the *Endeavour* sailed down the Atlantic in November. During the voyage of almost three years, the two men had only a few minor disagreements and became lifelong friends.

Cook had studied every account and map available—de Queirós, Fernández, Tasman, Roggeveen, Schouten, Anson, Byron and Wallis. He studied the science of currents, winds and waves and developed his own theory about a large habitable continent in the South Pacific—he didn't believe it existed.

Banks added more than 100 volumes to the library in the great cabin, including Dalrymple's maps and writings, other navigational material and an entire library of botanical works. He was convinced by Dalrymple's theories and believed that they would discover a great continent in the South Pacific.

The *Endeavour* passed under Cape Horn and entered the Pacific on 25 January 1769. To the great dismay of his crew, James Cook spent the next ten days exploring the stormy seas as far south as 60 degrees latitude, making sure there was nothing there and almost touching the Antarctic Circle, before proceeding back and crossing to the north of where he had entered the Pacific.

Cook then set a course more westerly than either Byron or Wallis and sailed northwest at an angle of some 45 degrees across the Pacific.

It soon became obvious, even to Banks, that the *Endeavour* was now sailing in the wide open ocean across the area where Dalrymple believed the Great South Land existed.

By this time the scientists, officers and artists on board, and indeed many of the crew, had divided into two camps. On one side were the 'Continent-mongers', led by Joseph Banks. On the other side were Cook and the 'No-continenters'. The debate was generally good-natured but bets were made and there was money at stake.

After observing the transit of Venus at Tahiti, Cook once again sailed south of latitude 40 degrees, well under the latitude of New Zealand on Tasman's map, and found only open sea. He then zig-zagged north-west and southwest and found the northwest coast of the North Island of New Zealand on 7 October 1769.

The 'Continent-mongers' were ecstatic, believing that this was indeed a northern extremity of the Great South Land, which would stretch southwest across that area of the Pacific that the *Endeavour* had not explored. Cook, however, spent the next six months exploring, charting and circumnavigating New Zealand, to prove that it was indeed two large islands and *not* the Great South Land. Sailing south of South Cape, at the bottom of Stewart Island, Cook was sure that 'This was the Southermost land . . . a large hollow swell from the South-West ever since we had the last gale of wind from that Quarter . . . makes one think there is no land in that direction.' Banks admitted defeat, commenting that, 'Although we hoped to make discoveries more interesting to trade at least than any we had yet made, we were obligd [sic] intirely to give up our first grand object, the Southern Continent.'

Cook's next objective, according to his secret orders, was to find the east coast of New Holland, which he did, and charted it. The *Endeavour* arrived home in July 1771 and Cook left again in HMS *Resolution* in July 1772.

In the meantime the French, who realised full well that New Holland was not the Great South Land, were still looking for 'Gonneville Land', alias *Terra Australis* or *le Troisième Monde*. Jean-Françoise-Marie de Surville crossed the South Pacific from New Zealand to Peru in 1770, Marc-Joseph Marion du Fresne found the Prince Edward Islands and Crozet Islands in the Southern Indian Ocean in 1771. Yves-Joseph de Kerguelen-Trémarec sailed from

Mauritius with two vessels, found Kerguelen Island in 1772 and assumed it was the tip of 'Gonneville Land'. ****

In July 1772, James Cook departed on his second circumnavigation of the world with the *Resolution* and *Adventure*. He sailed close to the Antarctic Circle, across the Atlantic, Indian and Pacific oceans and proved that the French discoveries were just barren islands. Although he never saw Antarctica, he was the first captain to cross the Antarctic Circle, which he did on three occasions to latitudes lower than the Antarctic continent, until the frozen ocean prevented him going any further.

When Cook stated in the journal of his second voyage 'I have sailed further than any man and found nothing', he was not expressing disappointment. He was simply stating the fact that he had proved there was no Great South Land.

The Man Who Named Australia

It was more than 30 years after Cook proved beyond any doubt that the fabled Great South Land did not exist that the idea of New Holland being referred to as the 'Great South Land', '*Terra Australis*' or 'Australia' developed, and it was due to Matthew Flinders.

There were two reasons for Flinders' suggestion. Firstly, it was now certain that New Holland was the only habitable landmass of continental size entirely in the southern hemisphere. Secondly, Flinders had a somewhat delicate political dilemma with naming the landmass he had circumnavigated in 1801–02, because part of it was called 'New Holland' and another part 'New South Wales':

> It is necessary, however, to geographical precision, that so soon as New Holland and New South Wales were known to form one land, there should be a general name applicable to the whole ...
> I have ... ventured upon the re-adoption of the original TERRA AUSTRALIS;
> There is no probability, that any other detached body of land, of nearly equal extent, will ever be found in a more southern latitude; the name Terra Australis will, therefore, remain descriptive of the geographical importance of this country ... Had I permitted myself any innovation upon the original term, it would have been to convert

it into AUSTRALIA; as being more agreeable to the ear, and an
assimilation to the names of the other great portions of the earth.

The Real *Terra Australis*

Flinders was wrong about one thing. There was another large detached
body of land in the Southern Hemisphere, a real *Terra Australis*. It
wasn't quite as big as Honter had proposed in the 16th century and
called *Australia*, but it was bigger than the one Flinders called 'Australia'. It wasn't the fabled inhabitable Great South Land people had
imagined, but it was there. As Flinders had already misappropriated
its name for the continent comprising New Holland and New South
Wales, cartographers had to find another name for it.

They called it Antarctica.

In February 1819, British merchant William Smith sailed his ship, *The
Williams*, well south of Cape Horn in order to catch the wind to sail
northwest, and sighted some unknown islands. He reported this to Royal
Navy officials on arrival at Valparaíso in Chile, and they chartered his ship
and sent Lieutenant Edward Bransfield with Smith back to the islands.
Bransfield landed on King George Island and took formal possession for
Britain. The islands became known as the South Shetlands.

On 30 January 1820, under Cape Horn, Bransfield sighted the
northernmost tip of Antarctica at latitude 63°50'S and longitude
60°30'W. He followed the coast east and also found and claimed
Elephant Island and Clarence Island for Britain.

It just so happened that the Russian Bellingshausen expedition
(1819–21), also exploring below the Antarctic Circle, had sighted
the coast of the continent just two days earlier, to the east and much
further south, at 69°21'28"S, longitude 2°14'50"W, and marked it on
their chart as an 'ice shelf'.

Fabian Gottlieb Benjamin von Bellingshausen, who, with Commander Mikhail Lazarev, circumnavigated Antarctica twice with two
ships, the *Vostok* and *Mirny*, had visited Sir Joseph Banks before setting
out. Banks, as president of the Royal Society, had helped the expedition
with maps, charts and advice and the expedition used Sydney as a base.
Bellingshausen never claimed to have discovered Antarctica, but a later
study of his journal by British historian A.G. Jones, in 1982, proved that
he was first to do so.

So a gentlemanly soldier, explorer and scientist, born in the small Baltic state of Estonia and sailing for the Czar of Russia, a nation that lies partly within the Arctic Circle, finally discovered the southern-most continent on the planet, Antarctica, the true *Terra Australis*—it was *incognita* no longer.

*Footnote 1—The 'de Vlamingh Plate'
In 1696 Willem de Vlamingh commanded an expedition to Australia's west coast in three ships, *Geelvinck* (*Yellowfinch*), *Nijptang* (*Nippers*) and *Weseltje* (*Little Weasel*), to look for survivors of the *Ridderschap van Holland* (*Knighthood of Holland*) that had gone missing two years earlier with 325 on board. He found Hartog's plate and replaced it with one that had been prepared in Batavia. Hartog's plate was sent to the VOC's headquarters in Holland. It is in the Rijksmuseum in Amsterdam.

In 1801, Captain Jacques Hamelin of the corvette *Naturaliste* on the Baudin expedition landed in Shark Bay. His second-in-com-mand, Louis de Freycinet, went to Dirk Hartog Island and found de Vlamingh's plate. Hamelin made a careful copy of the inscription and ordered it be returned to where it was found.

In 1818, de Freycinet on his own circumnavigation returned to Shark Bay on the *Uranie* and recovered de Vlamingh's plate to take to France for safekeeping. Although the *Uranie* was wrecked at the Falkland Islands on its return voyage, both de Freycinet and the de Vlamingh plate survived the wreck. De Freycinet deposited the plate in the Académie Française on his return—and it was lost.

A century later, in 1940, it was discovered on a store room bottom shelf among some old engraving plates. After the liberation of Paris Australia requested its return as a goodwill gesture. In May 1947 the French ambassador presented it to Prime Minister Ben Chifley. It is in the Shipwrecks Galleries of the Maritime Museum in Fremantle.

**Footnote 2—'Foul-Weather Jack'
The 18th century British press bestowed this nickname on Vice-Admiral John Byron, who always seemed to encounter, or be conservatively wary of sailing in, bad weather. As a midshipman on HMS *Wager* on the Anson expedition he survived shipwreck, mutiny,

exposure in the harsh Patagonian winter and six years of imprisonment and hardship before being one of only ten men of a crew of 300
to return to England. He commanded a squadron in the Seven Years
War and defeated a French flotilla in the Battle of Restigouche. He was
later governor of Newfoundland. He was the grandfather of the poet
and adventurer Lord George Gordon Byron and also Lord George
Anson Byron, explorer and admiral.

***Footnote 3—The Falklands/*Malvinas*

Puerto de Nuestra Señora de la Soledad was abandoned in 1812 and,
although the population over the 44 years of its existence only averaged
around 60, mostly convicts, *Puerto Soledad* managed to have 21 different governors!

Spain's (and Argentina's) subsequent claim to the Falkland Islands
is based on the fact that France, who claimed them by right of settlement, officially handed them to Spain. The Spanish name for the
islands, *Islas Malvinas*, is a translation of the French *Îles Malouines*
(The Islands of Malo), which derives from the French port of Saint-
Malo, named after a 5th century Welsh missionary, one of the seven
founding saints of Brittany.

In June 1770 five armed ships and 1400 soldiers arrived from
Argentina and the British were forced to leave the Falklands under a
flag of truce. This incident was almost the tipping point for another
major war. Britain demanded that the settlement be handed back and,
after a flurry of diplomatic measures, the Spanish King Charles III
declared 'things shall be restored in the Malouines, at the Port called
Egmont, precisely to the state in which they were before the tenth of
June, 1770'. The king added that this could not 'affect the question of
the prior right of sovereignty of the Malouine Islands otherwise called
Falkland Islands'. The French foreign minister, the Duc de Choiseul,
who had been using the situation to attempt to drag Spain into a war
against Britain, was sacked and banished from Court and from Paris.

The British returned to Port Egmont in September 1771 and abandoned it in April 1774, leaving only a flag flying and an inscription on
the blockhouse stating Britain's claim to the islands. In the interim,
islands had been found and claimed in the Pacific, which rendered the
'base camp' on the Falklands much less important. Twenty years after

Puerto Soledad was abandoned Captain James Onslow of HMS *Clio* reasserted Britain's claim and the islands were colonised by Britain in the 1840s.

****Footnote 4—French attempts to find The Great South Land 1769–73
Jean-François-Marie de Surville: sailing for the French East India Company in 1769, he left India, visited the Solomons and New Zealand, ran into cultural problems with the locals, and sailed to Peru, with a Maori chieftain on board. Surville drowned attempting to get ashore in a small boat on the coast of Peru. Most of the crew, and the Maori chief, died of scurvy but the ship made the port of Callao and finally 66 of the original 173 crew reached the French island of Mauritius. Surville and James Cook passed within two days of each other just north of New Zealand.

Marc-Joseph Marion du Fresne: a French East India Company captain. In 1770, after the company was dissolved, he volunteered to partly fund a voyage of two ships to return the Tahitian Ahutoru, brought to France by Bougainville, to his homeland and then search for 'Gonneville Land'. Ahutoru, however, died of smallpox within days of the ships departing Mauritius. Du Fresne found the Prince Edward and Crozet Islands in the South Indian Ocean in 1771 and made first European contact with Tasmanian Aborigines. In June 1772, he was attacked and killed at the Bay of Islands in New Zealand, along with 24 of his crew, by the previously friendly Maori. In reprisals 250 Maori were killed. His second in command, Julien-Marie Crozet, took both vessels safely back to Mauritius via the Philippines. Crozet left a message in a bottle claiming New Zealand for France.

Yves-Joseph de Kerguelen-Trémarec was sent in 1772 by Louis XV to find 'Gonneville Land'. At Mauritius he traded the ship he'd been given for the task, a 56-gun East Indiaman, for two armed storeships named *Fortune* and *Gros Ventre* (*Big Belly*).

In the second week of February 1772 he found what is now known as Kerguelen Island, which he mistook for the continent of 'Gonneville Land'. One boat from each vessel was sent, in very rough conditions, to explore the island's southern bay and make charts. When a huge storm rolled in Kerguelen-Trémarec, assuming there was a huge continent extending to the east and south of his ship and afraid of being wrecked on a lee shore, put out to sea and, when the *Gros Ventre* didn't appear after two days, he sailed back to Mauritius.

The captain of the *Gros Ventre*, Louis Francois Marie Aleno de Saint Aloüarn, picked up the two boat crews, annexed the land for France and then sailed east, to the previously agreed rendezvous point at Cape Leeuwin, New Holland. When Kerguelen-Trémarec failed to arrive, Saint Aloüarn followed the coast northward to Dirk Hartog Island where, on 30 March 1772, one of his officers, Jean Mengaud de la Hage, raised the French ensign, buried a bottle containing a document and two coins valued at 6 francs, and claimed the land for France. They sailed back to Mauritius via Timor and Batavia.

As the Dutch had a prior claim due to 'discovery', the French needed to follow up their claim to New Holland by 'right of settlement', which they never quite managed to do. Both Saint Aloüarn and de la Hage died, probably of fever or scurvy, in September 1772, a few days after reaching Mauritius.

Kerguelen-Trémarec, who had only observed what he claimed was 'Gonneville Land' from his ship and never set foot on it, gave glowing reports to Louis XV and claimed to have discovered a continent. He was consequently sent on a second voyage and departed just before the *Gros Ventre* arrived home with the truth about the barren island. As a result, on his return Kerguelen-Trémarec was court-martialled and imprisoned. Freed during the French Revolution, he was given a ship by the revolutionary government to explore the southern oceans but the ship was captured by a British privateer just after leaving France. He died in 1797. The *Îles Kerguelen* are also known in French as *les Îles de la Désolation*.

PART THREE

DEMYTHIFYING CAPTAIN COOK

'What I tell you three times is true.'

'The Hunting of the Snark', Lewis Carroll, 1876

SIMPLIFYING CAPTAIN COOK

When I was a kid in primary school, I heard what was probably the standard 'potted' version of the story of Captain Cook's *Endeavour* voyage and the 'discovery' of Australia. It went something like this . . .

Captain Cook was a brave officer in the British Navy and a wonderful navigator. He decided to go exploring in the Pacific Ocean after he had taken some scientists to Tahiti so that they could observe an astronomical event that could be seen well from that position.

He had chosen the *Endeavour* as being the best kind of ship to explore coastlines, because he had worked as a sailor on similar cargo ships and colliers and wanted a ship with shallow draught that could sail in coastal water and be easily pulled ashore and repaired.

He was looking for the Great South Land and discovered it when Lieutenant Hicks sighted the east coast of Australia.

Cook was the first European explorer to sail along our east coast, which he called New South Wales. He didn't land until he reached a bay he called Botany Bay, where he gave his wife's nephew, Isaac Smith, the honour of stepping ashore first. (There was a flat stone at Kurnell marked as the landing place, and a sign told the story of Isaac stepping ashore.)

He sailed past Sydney Harbour and named it Port Jackson, but never saw it or explored it. Governor Arthur Phillip was the first European to see Sydney Harbour, eighteen years later.

Cook made his way north then negotiated the Great Barrier Reef and, when the *Endeavour* struck a coral reef near what would become

Cooktown, it was pulled ashore and repaired. He claimed the land for Britain at Possession Island and sailed home via Batavia and Cape Town. The captain discovered how to prevent scurvy by making his crew eat vegetables and drink fruit juice.

The cottage in which James Cook grew up, at Great Ayton in Yorkshire, was moved stone by stone in 1934 and is now in Fitzroy Gardens, in Melbourne.

Any of that sound familiar?

Simplifying history for school textbooks and general public consumption always means that much of the story is not told, particularly the political agendas and social issues of the time that led to the events. Kids are often curious about details that teachers mostly don't know and have no time to research. Adults are simply not interested in too much detail; they are not historians and they want the simple version. Often they like the version they were told at school and believe the myths and, consequently, perpetuate them.

The problem with the 'simple' version of the *Endeavour* voyage, however, is that most of it is simply not true.

Here are ten commonly believed myths about James Cook and HMB *Endeavour*—debunked and explained.

TEN JAMES COOK FURPHIES

Number one: Captain Cook sailed in the *Endeavour*

L et's begin by getting one thing straight. 'Captain' Cook did not exist until 1775, so to say that Captain Cook did anything at all on the *Endeavour* voyage (1768–71) is technically incorrect.

Lieutenant James Cook, having been given his commission in 1768, was the highest ranking officer on board and therefore 'in command' (i.e. ship's captain) of the *Endeavour*. Promoted in 1771 to the official rank of commander, a rank higher than lieutenant but below captain, he was 'in command' of the *Resolution* on his second voyage of discovery (1772–75). Having been promoted, on his return, to captain, he was later appointed in 1775 to the position of 'officer in charge' at the Greenwich Hospital (retired sailors' home) and given the higher rank of 'post captain'.

In the preface to the 1893 publication *Captain Cook's Journal During His First Voyage Round the World*, compiled from three different copies of Cook's journal, editor William Wharton notes:

> It must be understood, that although this book is styled CAPTAIN COOK'S JOURNAL, he was on this voyage only a Lieutenant in Command, and therefore only Captain by courtesy.

In June 1755, James Cook resigned his position as 'mate' on Walker Brothers' collier *Friendship* and voluntarily joined the navy as an able seaman when he signed on at the 'rondy' in Wapping, London. The 'rondy' was the nickname given to any pub chosen as the 'rendezvous' by the impress officer or 'regulating captain'. These men were naval officers who used a pub near the docks as a base for recruiting. As part of the recruiting system, the impress service used retired naval men, or those on leave, as 'press gangs' to force men into the navy.

Impressment was commonly enforced during the 18th century by acts of parliament passed in 1703, 1705, 1740 and 1779. Royal Navy vessels could also stop British merchant ships at sea, or arriving in port, and take crew members forcibly into service. James Cook reports this happening, on his orders, several times on ships on which he served.

There was a war brewing in 1755 and the navy was recruiting. Many men also joined of their own free will, and one of them was James Cook. We don't know why he resigned from Walker Brothers Shipping Company of Whitby and signed on, but we do know that leaving Walker Brothers was an amicable agreement and James Cook and John Walker remained lifelong friends. Walker later wrote that Cook had always wanted to join the navy. After signing on at Wapping, Cook was sent to Portsmouth to join HMS *Eagle*.

When Captain Hugh Palliser took command of the *Eagle*, in October 1755, Cook was acting as 'master's mate'. The Seven Years War began a year later and, after HMS *Eagle* captured the French East Indiaman *Duc d'Aquitaine* after a furious battle in the Bay of Biscay, Cook passed the required examination in London and became a 'ship's master'. This meant he was responsible for navigation and the day-to-day running of the vessel and was required to keep a logbook for the admiralty.

After the war, as a 'senior warrant officer', he was 'master in command' of a navigation and charting vessel, the schooner *Grenville*, but he wasn't an officer by rank and did not have a commission. In order to take command of the *Endeavour* on an admiralty expedition, regulations said he had to be a commissioned officer. So Cook was made a lieutenant on 25 May 1768. The practice of appointing lieutenants to command vessels, especially smaller ones, was common. The term given to this was 'lieutenant commanding', which later evolved into the rank of 'lieutenant commander'.

So, while there is no doubt that James Cook was a brave and an *extremely* talented navigator and chart-maker, he was not a commissioned officer when he was chosen to captain the *Endeavour*. He came from a humble background and had joined the navy quite late, at 26 years of age, as a midshipman. The skills he had gained during his nine years as a merchant mariner (including several years as 'mate') with Walker Brothers, along with his remarkable charting and navigational abilities, had enabled him to rise as high as any man could in the Royal Navy without having a commission.

It was only on his third and final voyage (1776–80), also on the *Resolution*, after he came out of 'semi-retirement', that he would have been referred to as 'Captain James Cook'. On the *Endeavour* voyage he was in command of the vessel, but he didn't hold the rank of captain.

Footnote

To make things even more confusing, until 1794 the commissioned rank of commander was referred to as 'master and commander'. This became simply 'commander' after 1794 to save confusion, as there was also a 'warrant officer' (i.e. non-commissioned officer with a warrant to give orders) on every Royal Navy ship of a certain size who was known as the 'ship's master'. This non-commissioned warrant officer gave the crew specific orders for running the vessel. James Cook had been the 'sailing master' and 'ship's master' of several vessels before receiving his commission as a lieutenant and becoming the *Endeavour*'s 'lieutenant in command'. The 'master' on the *Endeavour*, incidentally, was a very capable young man named Robert Molineux, who died at Cape Town on the journey home.

Number two: Cook went exploring in the Pacific Ocean in his ship, *Endeavour*

The implication was always that the *Endeavour* was Cook's ship and he made the decisions about what it did and where it went. However, anyone who knows anything about how the Royal Navy worked in 1768, or how James Cook became involved in the *Endeavour* voyage, would understand that he decided very little about the *Endeavour* expedition.

The admiralty had been involved in the 'Transit of Venus' project for two years before the *Endeavour* sailed and James Cook's command of the vessel was confirmed on 25 May 1768, exactly *three months* before she sailed. In April, James Cook was busily preparing his own Royal Navy vessel, the *Grenville*, to depart for Newfoundland so he could continue the navigation and charting duties he had been undertaking for the past five years—every summer since 1763.

James Cook was not the first choice to lead the expedition. He was an eleventh-hour replacement for the man who had promoted and helped to plan the expedition since 1766, the man who was officially appointed as the leader of the project in December 1767, Alexander Dalrymple.

The only input Cook had into preparing the *Endeavour* would have been some decisions about provisioning. He also bought navigational and astronomical instruments to take on board, for which he was reimbursed the sum of £25. As lieutenant in command, he would have decided how the ship sailed to the places he was ordered to take it, but he had very specific orders from the admiralty about where he was to sail, including at what latitude. He also had secret sealed orders telling him where to go and what to do after the ship left Tahiti. It is also certain that he had other secret unwritten orders from his superiors at the admiralty.

When Cook was relieved of his position as master of the *Grenville* on 9 April, the *Endeavour* had already been purchased and redesigned. She was in drydock at Deptford being prepared for sea and having new decks and cabins built and a new outer hull installed. James Cook was 'appointed' to the vessel—he didn't choose her or decide where she was to go or what she was to do.

Number three: Cook took some scientists of the Royal Society to Tahiti so they could observe an astronomical event

I remember thinking, as a kid, that half the members of the Royal Society must have been on the *Endeavour*. In fact, there were only two, and they were there because one of them, an extremely wealthy 25-year-old gentleman named Joseph Banks, had actually partly funded the voyage.

Banks was elected to membership of the Royal Society in 1766, when he was just 22. The other fellow of the Royal Society on board was Banks's Swedish private secretary and personal assistant, Dr Daniel

Solander. He had been elected to the society in 1763, when he was 30 years old, for his work in cataloguing the natural history collection at the British Museum. Banks and Solander were botanists, not astronomers.

The two men who were paid by the Royal Society to undertake the observation of the transit of Venus across the face of the sun at Tahiti were not members of the Royal Society. One was an astronomer named Charles Green, who had previously been assistant to the Astronomer Royal and had naval experience as a purser on an admiralty vessel. Green was paid £200 for his involvement in the expedition. The second 'observer' was James Cook himself. He was paid £100 by the Royal Society, over and above his naval pay, to perform and record the observation. Both men were also paid an expenses and living allowance by the society. Green's wife was provided with a living allowance of £50 for each year the *Endeavour* was away.

Back in August 1766, while James Cook was engaged in his annual task of charting the coast of Newfoundland as master of the *Grenville*, he had taken time to carefully observe an eclipse of the sun and record his calculations. In November of that year, when he returned to London, he prepared a paper that he sent to the Royal Society. The paper was read to a meeting of the fellows of the society by Dr John Bevis, who called Cook 'a good mathematician and very expert in his business'. The paper was then published in the society's journal.

So Cook had established his credibility as an astronomer and mathematician almost two years before the *Endeavour* expedition departed, and eighteen months before he was chosen to lead the expedition. Like the man he replaced, Alexander Dalrymple (who *was* a member of the Royal Society), Cook could captain a ship and make and record scientific and astronomical observations.

Sadly, Charles Green died on the voyage home, along with the artist Sydney Parkinson and 28 other members of the expedition, after the *Endeavour* left the disease-ridden port of Batavia (modern-day Jakarta), where fever and dysentery were rife.

James Cook was eventually elected a fellow of the Royal Society in March 1776, after his second voyage.

Number four: Cook chose the *Endeavour*

Simply not true.

The search for a suitable vessel occurred early in March 1768 and Adam Hayes, master shipwright at Deptford Naval Dockyards, inspected two colliers, *Valentine* and the slightly larger *Earl of Pembroke*. The latter was purchased on 27 March and entered in the navy list renamed HMB *Endeavour*. This happened before Cook was taken from the *Grenville* on 9 April to be considered for commanding the expedition. James Cook had no part in choosing the vessel, although he would have approved the choice. His comments about the suitability of such ships for exploration were written a few years later, in the introduction to his account of his second voyage and after the *Endeavour* had proved a very suitable vessel. He expressed the belief that vessels for exploration should be of shallow draught and:

> ... must also be of a construction that will bear to take the ground; and of a size which, in case of necessity, may be safely and conveniently laid on shore, to repair any accidental damage or defects. These properties are not to be found in ships of war of forty guns, nor in frigates, nor in East India Company's ships, nor in large three-decked West India ships, nor indeed in any other but north-country-built ships, or such as are built for the coal-trade, which are peculiarly adapted to this purpose.

It is possible that Alexander Dalrymple, the man who was originally chosen to lead the expedition but who was replaced by James Cook, was involved in choosing the vessel; he certainly claimed he was.

The search for a suitable vessel was quite possibly done by the surveyor of the navy, Sir Thomas Slade, perhaps accompanied by Alexander Dalrymple. The two vessels inspected were, however, both on the Thames at the time, so the search was not exactly extensive. Nevertheless, it was Adam Hayes who notified the Navy Board that a suitable vessel had been chosen.

Another common error made by writers, and even historians, is to designate the *Endeavour* as HMS. She was, in fact, designated 'HMB', or 'HM Bark' (His Majesty's Bark). There were two reasons for this.

The Royal Navy used the term 'bark' for vessels that did not fit any of the usual naval categories. Secondly, the Royal Navy already had a sloop named HMS *Endeavour* in service.

Footnote
The designation 'HM Bark' did not imply that a vessel was a 'barquentine'. A barquentine was a three-masted vessel rigged in a particular way—with the two main masts square-rigged and the smaller mizzen mast 'lateen rigged' (like a yacht). The *Endeavour* wasn't a barquentine; she was a redesigned collier.

Number five: Cook found the Great South Land and called it New South Wales

New Holland was not thought to be the Great South Land. James Cook never thought New South Wales was the Great South Land, he knew full well that it was the east coast of New Holland. Cook didn't *find* the fabled Great South Land—in fact, he was the man who proved, conclusively, that it didn't exist.

Cook, and every other navigator who could read a map, knew where New Holland was. Most of it had appeared on maps from 1663 onwards, and it was too far north to be the Great South Land (believed to exist between latitude 40 degrees south and the pole). From 1644, when Abel Tasman sailed under Tasmania and then found the west coast of New Zealand, it was apparent that New Holland was not the Great South Land.

James Cook was given three separate tasks to perform and two of them were in his 'secret orders'. Firstly, he was to set up an observatory on Tahiti and observe and record the transit of Venus across the face of the sun. Secondly, he was to explore the Southern Ocean and attempt to ascertain if the Great South Land existed. Thirdly, if there was time, he was to attempt to find the east coast of New Holland.

Although there were some on the *Endeavour* who were looking for the fabled Great South Land, or at least hoping to find it, James Cook was not one of them. In fact, he believed that it did not exist. He spent two of his three voyages of exploration proving that it did not exist.

The *Endeavour* expedition was not the first the admiralty had sent with secret orders to explore the Southern Ocean: it was the third.

The captains of the HMS *Dolphin* on its two circumnavigations, John Byron (1764–66) and Samuel Wallis (1766–68), both had secret orders to look for the Great South Land but, for various reasons, both failed to do what they were told to do.

When those in charge at the admiralty were presented with another opportunity to find out, once and for all, if the Great South Land existed and was habitable, they took it. The first two 'secret' expeditions had been disguised as 'voyages to India', and this one could be disguised as a scientific expedition to make astronomical calculations for the Royal Society.

For 32 years the real 'power behind the throne' at the admiralty was the secretary to the Lords Commissioners, Sir Philip Stephens. He wanted to know if the Great South Land existed and, if it did, to get to it, and claim it, before the French.

Alexander Dalrymple, who was a member of the Royal Society and had very close and strong connections to the British East India Company, was not an admiralty man and, therefore, could not be trusted to put the admiralty's secret agenda before all else, so he was removed from the project and replaced by someone who could be trusted to do that.

Stephens made sure that the man leading the expedition was a loyal, reliable and trusted servant of the admiralty. He wanted a fearless and talented navigator who would do as he was told, a man who owed all his loyalty only to the admiralty and had no political connections or powerful friends other than admiralty men. Stephens wanted a man who could keep secrets, falsify charts and tell lies, if necessary, to ensure naval supremacy for the admiralty and world domination for Britain. That man was James Cook.

The *Endeavour* passed under Cape Horn and entered the Pacific on 25 January 1769, four months before the transit of Venus was due. Cook spent 78 days looking for the Great South Land, firstly as far south as 60 degrees latitude and then northwest across the area where many believed the Great South Land was situated. When he reached the latitude of Tahiti, he turned due west and anchored in Matavai Bay on 13 April.

Three months later, having completed the observation of the transit of Venus, Cook explored the Society Islands for a month and then, on 17 August, headed south, zig-zagging across the ocean until he sighted New Zealand's North Island 52 days later, on 7 October 1769. He then circumnavigated New Zealand, and proved it was not part of a southern continent.

Number six: Lieutenant Hicks sighted the east coast of Australia at a point Cook named Point Hicks

There can be no doubt that Lieutenant Hicks, second in command on the *Endeavour*, who sadly died of tuberculosis on the voyage home, was the first man on board to sight mainland Australia. At about 6 a.m. on 17 April 1770, he spied a speck on the edge of the skyline, some high point of land visible above the horizon, but it *wasn't* the east coast.

What is interesting is the direction Lieutenant Hicks was looking when he saw the distant land and cried, 'Land-Ho!'

He was, in fact, looking to the *northeast*. The *Endeavour* had actually sailed into the open eastern end of Bass Strait from the southeast, heading northwesterly. When the coastline became visible, Cook described it as 'extending from North-East to West'. In other words, the land was sighted on the starboard (right) side of the ship, as they sailed westward. Hicks wasn't looking to the west hoping to see the east coast appear, he was looking to the north and back to the east—so what he saw was the south coast of mainland Australia.

Cook continued sailing west into a strong headwind for two more hours before turning back to the east at 8 a.m. and then rounding the southeastern corner of what is now Victoria, and heading north. It seems he had checked a few of his suspicions, theories he had formed by studying Tasman's map: the currents in the southern Pacific (none of which seemed to be the type caused by large continents further south), and the size and power of the waves coming towards the *Endeavour* from the west as she sailed into them. After two hours he had made up his mind.

He didn't name the point of land Hicks actually saw, away to the northeast, after the lieutenant. He gave the name 'Point Hicks' to what he said was the most southerly point of land they saw, away to the southwest. He plotted Point Hicks to be:

The Southernmost point of land we had in sight, which bore from us
West 1/4 South, I judged to lay in the Latitude of 38 degrees 0 minutes
South and in the Longitude of 211 degrees 7 minutes West from
the Meridian of Greenwich. I have named it Point Hicks, because
Lieutenant Hicks was the first who discover'd this Land.

Now, Cook was a meticulous navigator who took pride in being able
to fix exact positions in order to accurately verify his charts and maps.
Doing so had been his daily work for more than a decade, the special
skill that made him so respected at the admiralty.

It is important to stress that Cook does not say he gave the name
'Point Hicks' to the point of land Hicks saw—he states that he gave the
name to the southernmost point of land on the horizon.

Given all that, it is rather odd that anyone plotting the exact position
of Cook's 'Point Hicks' on the planet (you can do it yourself relatively
easily, using Google Maps) will quickly discover that the 'landmark'
does not exist. It is, in fact, a spot in the ocean 15 or more kilometres
off the south coast of Australia, below Cape Conran.

What on earth is going on here? Well, on Earth, nothing, because to
the south and west, where Cook's journal implies there is land, there is
nothing but hundreds of kilometres of ocean.

If this shakes your faith in Cook's reputation for accuracy, don't
despair. If you're puzzled by this glaring 'error' made by the greatest
navigator of his age, you're in good company. All the historians,
cartographers and experts who read or edited Cook's journal, and
were obliged to check the facts, were puzzled too.

Did Cook miscalculate? Did he transcribe the position wrongly in
his journal when he came to write it up a few days later? Or did he,
perhaps, tell a great big 'porky pie' in order to hide the fact that he
strongly suspected there was a strait between Van Diemen's Land and
New Holland?

Welcome to the devious and dark world of keeping secrets,
falsifying charts and telling lies for the admiralty. Margaret
Cameron-Ash's excellent book on the subject (to which I am greatly
indebted for this part of the story) is called, quite simply, *Lying for
the Admiralty.*

What was this all about?

Bear with me for a moment or two while I explain how important it was that any 'newly discovered lands' were separated from other lands by sea, or not.

The way in which European nations were able to 'claim' supposedly 'undiscovered' lands had changed over the centuries. Way back in 1498 the pope had decided that only Spain and Portugal had the right to claim newly discovered lands and a line was drawn down the Atlantic Ocean to separate the world into two halves. Spain, according to the pope, could claim land west of the line and Portugal land to the east. This became the Treaty of Tordesillas.

Papal decree, however, was becoming rather a tenuous claim by 1770. 'First discovery' (whether the land 'discovered' was inhabited or not) was seen as one valid way of claiming new lands, and 'first settlement' was also considered a valid, slightly stronger, claim. Conquest during war, where one European nation ousted another from lands distant to Europe, was very common from 1500 to 1800. Subsequent 'ownership' was then decided by the treaties signed to end the war.

If Van Diemen's Land (Tasmania) and New Holland were separate landmasses, any nation attempting to claim them had *two* claims to establish rather than one. So it was in Britain's best interests that other European powers (i.e. the French) were led to believe that Van Diemen's Land and New Holland were part of the one landmass.

James Cook had to decide whether to sail north or south. He could not do both and, although he was convinced that there was a strait between the two landmasses, he had to hide the fact from the world as best he could. That meant keeping his opinion to himself and deceiving even those on board the *Endeavour*.

It was the French that the British admiralty were concerned about. After the end of the Seven Years War in 1763, the race to explore and claim lands in the Pacific really only had two starters, France and Britain. The Dutch and the Spanish still had to be treated carefully and diplomatically respected but they were no longer a real threat to British expansionism in the Pacific.

The truth was that the ancient Spanish claim to the Pacific, by papal decree, was virtually extinct and the Dutch, who had explored and named much of New Holland, had never actually claimed it, although it was considered to be in their 'sphere of influence'. They would later go to war with Britain over disputed territory in the commercially valuable East Indies, but they were not likely to waste time or effort fighting over spice-less territories they had not considered worth claiming or settling for 250 years.

There was a well-justified British paranoia about information falling into the hands of any other European powers. The admiralty collected all journals at the end of every voyage and crews were sworn to secrecy. When the *Endeavour* reached Batavia, all journals on board were 'confiscated' and locked in the safe in the great cabin. This was quite normal when admiralty ships entered foreign ports, as sailors were not well paid and it was common for foreign spies to offer very lucrative incentives for any information that had been gathered on voyages of discovery.

What Cook did, in hiding hydrographic and geographic information, was not unusual or uncommon, it was what the admiralty expected of its commanding officers. It was perfectly 'normal' behaviour among the navigators and explorers who sailed for all the nations of Europe.

Cook was very aware of how claims to territory worked.

In the Treaty of Paris, at the end of the Seven Years War, France lost all its territories in North America but retained fishing rights off Newfoundland and was given back the small islands of St Pierre, Miquelon and Petite Miquelon, which it had lost to Britain in the Treaty of Utrecht of 1715. These islands, 22 kilometres off the coast of Newfoundland, were handed back to France on the condition that it did not fortify them and used them only as bases for fishing. The British prime minister, William Pitt, the secretary of state, Lord Egmont, and Philip Stephens at the admiralty all foresaw future problems and were vehemently opposed to this concession but, for the sake of getting the treaty signed, it was agreed to.

In April 1763, James Cook was appointed by the admiralty as 'Surveyor to Newfoundland' for the express purpose of making a detailed survey of the islands and charting them before they were handed back to France. The admiralty was keen to have detailed charts of the coasts, bays and possible harbours of what was to become foreign territory before it handed the islands over to the old enemy. Cook's commanding officer during the war, Rear-Admiral Lord Colville, recommended the man whose charts and navigation had been instrumental in the British victory at Québec as the man for the task.

Cook left for Newfoundland on 15 May 1763. The date for the handover had passed when he arrived and, while the French garrison and settlers were kept waiting at sea for three weeks, he surveyed the coastline of St Pierre. After the French landed on St Pierre, Cook completed the survey of Miquelon and Petite Miquelon by the end of July, when the islands were finally handed over officially.

The French were soon disputing British claims about the limits of the treaty and threatening to resume hostilities in Newfoundland. Cook's old friend from the *Eagle*, Hugh Palliser, commanding a small fleet of warships, confronted a French fleet that was 'protecting' the French fishing rights. It was James Cook's map of Newfoundland and its islands, showing accurately the established historic claims to fishing grounds and the areas agreed in the treaty, that prevented another outbreak of war and substantiated the British version of the treaty.

In 1764 Palliser was appointed governor of Newfoundland. As suspected, the French kept breaking the terms of the Treaty of Paris, using the three small islands as a base to take timber and furs from unprotected areas on Newfoundland, setting up small settlements in uninhabited coastal areas along Newfoundland's shoreline, and further disputing landmarks and charts to cover their transgressions. Palliser needed his old 'master's mate' from HMS *Eagle* to sort it out by accurately surveying the entire coast of Newfoundland. For the next four summers James Cook, as master of the schooner *Grenville*, with a crew of eighteen men, did exactly that.

This diplomatic and administrative nightmare, caused by the French having possession of a few islands close to British territory, was something that occupied James Cook's working life for six years, and he never forgot it.

So, when he was faced with the dilemma of confirming or denying that Van Diemen's Land was separated from New Holland, it seems that he chose to disguise what he knew, or suspected, with a deliberate error on a chart and a vague entry in his log:

To the Southward of this point we could see no land, and yet it was clear in that Quarter, and by our Longitude compared with that of

Tasman's, the body of Van Diemen's land ought to have bore due South from us, and from the soon falling of the Sea after the wind abated I had reason to think it did; but as we did not see it, and finding the Coast to trend North-East and South-West, or rather more to the Westward, makes me Doubtfull whether they are one land or no.

Later historians who came to read, edit and comment on the various versions of Cook's journals as they came to light in the 19th century were either astounded by the apparent 'mistake' made by the great navigator, or tried to find excuses for the 'oversight'.

Hydrographer to the admiralty, Captain William Wharton (later Rear-Admiral Sir William Wharton), editing the journals of Cook and Banks that were available to him in 1893, blames the weather and is also puzzled about 'Point Hicks':

Had not the gale on the day before forced Cook to run to the northward, he would have made the north end of the Furneaux Group, and probably have discovered Bass Strait, which would have cleared up the doubt, which he evidently felt, as to whether Tasmania was an island or not. The fact was not positively known until Dr. Bass sailed through the Strait in a whale-boat in 1797. Point Hicks was merely a rise in the coast-line, where it dipped below the horizon to the westward, and the name of Point Hicks Hill is now borne by an elevation that seems to agree with the position.

In 1912, Professor Ernest Scott was less forgiving. Writing in the *Victorian Historical Magazine*, volume 2, number 4, he stated: 'There can be no doubt that Cook believed at this time that Australia and Tasmania were divided by a strait.'

Evidence adding to the probability that Cook was hiding something comes in the form of his manuscript chart of the east coast of New South Wales. It begins exactly where the false Point Hicks was calculated, oddly showing none of the ocean below through which the *Endeavour* had sailed to reach Point Hicks. As Cook's original map of the east coast shows ocean above Cape York, as well as the south coast of New Guinea, the fact that he shows nothing south of Point Hicks makes his map look oddly unbalanced. In Dr John Hawkesworth's 1773 account of the voyage, the engraver has lopped off the top of Cook's map (no doubt under instructions from the admiralty), so the imbalance is not so obvious.

There is a precedent for this skulduggery, an even more glaring example of chart-altering by James Cook. It is his attempt to hide the fact that New Zealand's third largest island, Stewart Island, is, in fact, an island. It is about the same distance from the South Island of New Zealand as the French islands of St Pierre and Miquelon are from the coast of Newfoundland.

Just about everybody on the *Endeavour* realised that Stewart Island was indeed an island. Even non-naval men, like artist Sydney Parkinson and others, were confident enough to call it that in their journals. The first chart, drawn by ship's master Robert Molineux, shows it to be an island. It seems that Cook, on reflection, amended the chart. He had claimed the two larger islands for Britain and was running out of time to search for the east coast of New Holland. It was easier to hide the fact that Stewart Island was an island than to spend time landing and claiming it, so his chart leaves the coastline unfinished and seven lines of his journal for 11 March 1770, that appear to describe a strait, are partially erased and written over, claiming there is probably an isthmus connecting it to the mainland:

> ... now we thought that the land to the Southward, or that we have been sailing round these 2 days past, was an Island, because there appeared an Open Channell between the North part of that land and the South part of the other in which we thought we saw the Small Island we were in with the 6th Instant; but when I came to lay this land down upon paper from the several bearings I had taken, it appeared that there was but little reason to suppose it an Island. On the contrary, I hardly have a doubt but what it joins to, and makes a part of, the Mainland.

Whoever made the copy of the map that was given to the engraver to prepare for the printed version, in Hawkesworth's account of the voyage sanctioned by the admiralty, has added a very distinct, substantial, but highly improbable isthmus.

In spite of other journals written on the *Endeavour* claiming otherwise, the deception worked for 40 years. American sealer Owen Smith charted the strait in 1804. He gave his chart to Governor King in

Sydney in 1805, but the discovery was not made known until 1809 when a shipwreck there was reported in the *Sydney Gazette*. The name was then changed from Smith Strait to Foveaux Strait, in honour of the New South Wales colony's lieutenant-governor at that time.

New Zealand historian John Beaglehole, the first editor to have access to Cook's own personal journal of the *Endeavour* voyage, published in 1955, tried to understand what Cook was thinking when he made the obvious falsification: 'It is difficult to follow Cook's reasoning here without knowing all that was in his mind. On paper he is unconvincing.'

In November 1802 Philip Gidley King, governor of New South Wales and the man who later did not bother to tell the world that Stewart Island was indeed an island, commented in a letter to the minister for war and colonies, Lord Hobart, that the French 'may have some intention of laying claim to van Demons [sic] land, now it is known to be insulated from New Holland . . . request instructions for my conduct in case the latter conjecture should be verified'.

We can guess what the reply was by the fact that, in September 1803, two ships sent by Governor King arrived at Risdon Cove on the Derwent River to establish a British colony in Van Diemen's Land.

The French writer Victor-Donatien de Musset-Pathay, writing in 1810, accused Britain of a 'real evil' when he claimed that the British printed and made public 'false accounts, and charts full of errors . . . When these charts were compared with those preserved in London, the fraud was discovered in all its blackness.'

He is right, of course. In spite of Captain John Hunter suggesting in his journal published in 1793 that there was 'a very deep gulf, or a straight, which may separate Van Diemen's Land from New Holland', the British 'hid' what became known as Bass Strait until 1798. There are, however, similar British claims against the French and, had *les Français* been here first (or the Dutch or the Spanish or the Portuguese), who can say how truthful their published charts might have been?

Number seven: Cook was the first European explorer to find our east coast, which he called New South Wales
While it's quite true that Cook named the east coast of Australia 'New South Wales' due to the similarity of the southern coastal cliffs to those

of Carmarthenshire, he was certainly not the first European to find the east coast of the continent.

Louis de Bougainville found the east coast of Australia in June 1768, almost two years before Cook arrived, but never set foot on shore, and there is circumstantial evidence that others, Portuguese and Spanish, were there long before that. Artefacts, such as Spanish coins, sword hilts, cannons and ballast stones carved with ships' names, have been found or reported found along the east coast of Australia.

While artefacts themselves can appear and disappear, a more reliable source of evidence, that other Europeans had explored the east coast long before Cook, can be found in old maps. In some cases, however, it takes a stretch of the imagination and a few possibilities and probabilities for these to be taken as evidence of exploration.

Explorer and maritime expert Ben Cropp believes there is evidence of a temporary Spanish settlement in the 1640s at Bamaga, near the tip of Cape York, possibly connected with the extraction of alluvial gold. There is certainly a map, dated 1703, that shows the east coast of Australia quite accurately down as far as about present-day Towns-ville. The map was found in the collection of a German cartographer, the Jesuit priest Heinrich Scherer, but whether it was made by him or someone else we don't know.

The most contentious claim to be made about earlier discovery, based on the evidence of maps, is the one that has Portuguese explorer Cristóvão de Mendonça charting almost the entire east and south coast of Australia between 1521 and 1524.

By 1520 the Portuguese were established as the only European power in what is today Malaysia and Indonesia, having annexed Malacca in 1511 and set up strongholds in Ambon and other places in the region. According to historian João de Barros, Mendonça set out on an expedition with three caravels from Malacca and proceeded to explore and chart the coast of Australia, which was then known as 'Jave la Grande' (Big Java); it had been mentioned by Marco Polo, in 1300 AD, as the 'largest island in the world'.

Mendonça, some believe, sailed as far as modern-day Warrnam-bool, charting the coast as he went but missing certain sections when the small fleet travelled out at sea. He made the standard 'strip maps' of the day, charting each section of the coast separately in a linear fashion. Near Warrnambool, one of the caravels was either wrecked, careened for repairs and abandoned, ran aground accidentally, or was abandoned at sea and washed ashore. It could be the 'mahogany ship'.

The 'mahogany ship' was found in 1836 on the beach between Warrnambool and Port Fairy, on the south coast of Victoria, and was well documented until 1876, when it became lost in the sandhills. There are almost a hundred references to the wreck, including detailed descriptions, in letters and writings throughout the 19th century. It was a common landmark well known to locals who used the site as a picnic spot. Whether it is, as many believe, the wreck of one of the Portuguese vessels from the expedition led by Cristóvão de Mendonça down the east coast of Australia in 1522–23, or something else, is still hotly debated and we will never know for certain unless what remains of the wreck can be found again.

Mendonça decided not to continue the exploration without the third vessel and returned to Malacca, where he later became the commander of the Portuguese fleet. Later still, he became governor of Hormuz, which was then a Portuguese possession, in the Persian Gulf.

The 1529 Treaty of Zaragoza drew a meridian east of the Moluccas, to finally delineate the two halves of the Earth and divide them between Spain and Portugal, and Spain then relinquished its claim to the Moluccas. As it turned out, eastern Australia was in Spain's half, so Mendonça's expedition had been in an area where Portugal had no legitimate claim and Mendonça should not have been there—a good reason to tell no one about it.

Mendonça's strip maps were kept hidden from other foreign powers for two other reasons. Firstly, it was in Portugal's best interest not to encourage other nations into the area. Secondly, it was not common practice to share maps.

The original strip maps were probably lost when the Lisbon earthquake of 1755 destroyed the Portuguese Archive of the Indies, but copies had been made and some found their way to Dieppe in France, the centre of map-making in Europe at the time.

Having been ignored when the Spanish-born Pope Alexander VI drew the imaginary line from pole to pole through the mid-Atlantic that led to the Treaty of Tordesillas, the French were still manifestly interested in maritime exploration. Dieppe, where ship owner Jean

Ango operated a fleet of 70 vessels, became a major centre of map-making, exploration and commercial fishing. French cartographers at Dieppe used copies of Mendonça's strip maps to construct Jave la Grande, which they placed on maps and in atlases, notably the 1547 Vallard Atlas.

One of the earliest depictions of Jave la Grande was on a map given to Henry VIII of England by French cartographer Jean Rotz. In Dieppe, Rotz had prepared a book, called *Boke of Idrography* (*Book of Hydrography*). Denied patronage by the French court, however, he found his way to England, where he became cartographer to Henry VIII in 1542.

Similar depictions of Jave la Grande were made by Pierre Desceliers on his world map in 1546, and again in 1550 and 1553. The east coast of Jave la Grande can be seen as a rough representation of the coast of Queensland and New South Wales, but further south the coast turns the wrong way: southeast, instead of southwest.

However, if the map is broken up into sections, as it would have been when the charts were first made, it is remarkable that it can be made to closely resemble the Australian coast between Cape York and Warrnambool. There are also at least 60 instances where the map bears a close relationship to particular landmarks. If corrections are made to allow for 'certain factors', the whole coastline fits into the shape of our east and south coast, and many landmarks line up perfectly.

What are the 'certain factors'?

Well, some of the strip charts need to be 'juggled'. If Jave la Grande is Australia, pieces of the coastline are out of order: it appears the Dieppe map-makers either made errors, or didn't know the correct sequence of the linear charts.

Secondly, some charts need to be rotated to fit. For example, there is an uncannily accurate Dieppe map of the Furneaux Islands group that appears to indicate that Mendonça visited the Bass Strait islands either coming or going. The orientation is wrong, but strip charts made in the 16th century did not use later standard map-making devices, such as an indication of north. Moreton, Stradbroke and Fraser islands are reasonably accurately shown and the Brisbane River estuary appears to be depicted as *Bonno Porto* (Good Port).

Thirdly, when you are working with pieces of a coastline and attempting to make a globe fit onto a flat page or two, errors can easily occur. One wrong fold and everything is out, and the discrepancy is repeated as maps are copied. If one particular fold is reversed, the map of Jave la Grande suddenly appears to be a very close representation of Australia's east and south coast down as far as Warrnambool.

As for the location of Jave la Grande, in relation to Australia, it appears that the original Portuguese maps, now lost, placed the continent slightly to the west of where Australia actually is . . . which strangely (said with tongue firmly in cheek) placed it in the *Portuguese* half of the globe.

The names on the Dieppe maps show evidence of French, Spanish, Portuguese and Galician words and phrases. Mendonça was from Galicia, in northwest Portugal.

Another depiction of Jave la Grande is a large, profusely illustrated map, now in the British Museum, that was made as a gift for the young French dauphin (crown prince) around 1547, probably by Pierre Desceliers.

How this map came to Britain in the first place is unknown, but as the heraldic arms depicted on the map have been changed from those of the young prince to those he took when he became King Henry II of France, it appears that the map remained in France during his reign at least. (Henry II married Catherine de Medici, had ten children and died in 1559.)

The 'Dauphin Map' is also known as the 'Harleian Map', as it came into the possession of either Robert or Edward Harley sometime before 1741.

Robert Harley and his son Edward were the first and second 'Earls of Oxford and Earl Mortimer', a title created especially for politician Robert in 1711. Both men were book and map collectors and, twelve years after Edward's death, his enormous library was bequeathed to the nation by his widow and became part of the newly created British Museum in 1753.

Apparently, however, the Dauphin Map was kept by one of the family servants; it was only given to the British Museum in 1790, by none other than Sir Joseph Banks. If the map was in Banks' possession when he sailed as a 25-year-old on the *Endeavour*, then it, or a copy of it, would most certainly have been among the hundred or more books and volumes of charts that he took on board the *Endeavour* with him.

Our old friend Alexander Dalrymple mentions that he was lent the Dauphin Map by Dr Daniel Solander sometime before 1786. Solander was also, of course, Joseph Banks' private secretary and resided with him in London. Although Solander possibly delivered it to Dalrymple, it was Banks who owned the Dauphin Map and finally gave it to the museum in 1790, after Dalrymple had used it to make copies and engravings. Dalrymple pointed out that the map corresponded to Cook's charts in several ways, or vice versa.

Some place names are similar. Cook changed 'Stingray Bay' to 'Botany Bay'; the Dieppe maps call it *Côté des Herbages* (Herbage Shore). There is also the rather obvious *Costa Dangeroza* (Dangerous Coast), where Cook hit the reef. Port Jackson is marked as a small, unexplored indent on the Dieppe map and also on Cook's charts. It appears Mendonça's ships didn't enter it, nor did the *Endeavour* (though Cook may have seen it while ashore). Botany Bay *is* marked and charted on both maps, and Cook made landfall there.

Dalrymple certainly believed the maps were genuine charts of the same coastline Cook explored, and openly hints that Cook had knowledge of them. Of course, Dalrymple, as one of those who supported the idea of the voyage of exploration and was originally chosen to lead it, had an axe to grind. Having examined the Dauphin Map and copied it for engraving and publication, Dalrymple made observations about similarities in names on Cook's charts and concluded sarcastically: 'We may say with Solomon, "There is nothing new under the Sun".'

Taking the 'map conspiracy' rather too far, some exponents of the theory have noted that, when Cook needed to repair the *Endeavour* after grounding her on the Great Barrier Reef, he headed on a diagonal course northward to shore, rather than using a direct one, and made a suspicious entry in his journal, noting that the bay where the ship was careened was 'much smaller than I had been told'. It seems perfectly reasonable to me to assume that the *reef* prevented a direct course to shore, and Cook's journal tells us the ship's smaller boats had gone ahead to scout for a suitable bay!

It is interesting, however, that Matthew Flinders, 30 years after the *Endeavour* voyage, talks of the Dieppe maps as being earlier maps of the continent and appears to assume the possibility of a Portuguese discovery.

Number eight: Cook didn't land until he reached Botany Bay, where he gave his wife's nephew, Isaac Smith, the honour of stepping ashore first

When I was a kid at school, I was told a 'Boys' Own' version of Cook's first landing on Australian soil. I was told the same story by my mum when we visited the place at Kurnell where it all happened, or didn't happen.

It was a well-known and much told (and much loved) story that involved Isaac Smith, who was the son of Cook's wife's cousin Charles Smith. This made Isaac Elizabeth Cook's first cousin once removed, but it was always 'nephew' in the story.

In the version told to kids in my childhood, Isaac was a 'cabin boy' (he was actually a midshipman) on the *Endeavour* and was in the first boat ashore at Botany Bay. According to the legend Cook said, 'Jump out, Isaac,' (in my mum's version it was 'You go first, Isaac') and thus the young cabin boy became the first European to set foot on the east coast of Australia. I remember one illustrated version of the tale that had Isaac looking like a boy of twelve; he was, in fact, almost eighteen when the *Endeavour* was in Botany Bay.

Needless to say, the story does not appear in any of the journals written by those on board the *Endeavour* and Cook certainly never mentions it, because it never happened.

Isaac Smith joined the navy at thirteen and sailed, with Cook as his patron and mentor, in the *Grenville*, then the *Endeavour* and again in the *Resolution* on Cook's second voyage of discovery. He was the first man to make charts of the southern parts of South America, was commander of the 36-gun frigate HMS *Perseverance* at the Battle of Tellicherry against the French in 1791 and retired, due to having contracted hepatitis, as rear-admiral in 1807. Isaac was obviously like a younger brother to Cook's widow, Elizabeth, and, as she outlived all her children, she and Isaac shared a house when he retired. Isaac died in 1831 at the age of 78 and Elizabeth Cook died four years later in 1835, aged 93.

Evidently the story of Isaac being the first European to set foot on eastern Australia was first told publicly years after Elizabeth's death by her second cousin Canon Frederick Bennett, a respectable clergyman, who said the story was a 'family legend'.

Wikipedia still perpetuates this myth in Isaac Smith's biographical entry: 'On 28 April 1770 he became the first European to set foot on eastern Australian soil, Cook telling him "Jump out, Isaac" as the ship's boat touched the shore at Botany Bay.'

The truth is, as usual, quite another story, and Wikipedia also has the date wrong.

Botany Bay *was* the first landing, although Cook tried to land at Jervis Bay, where adverse winds prevented him from doing so, and again near Bulli, where the surf was too strong. His journal for Saturday 28 April 1770 describes the attempted landing near Bulli, seeing canoes and people ashore and the dangerous surf that forced him back to the ship, after which the *Endeavour* continued north.

Due to the fact that, until 1805, ships' logs entries ran from noon to noon (when solar sightings were taken by quadrant or sextant for latitude and longitude), the following information, included in the entry for Saturday 28 April, is actually referring to the morning of 29 April:

> At daylight in the morning we discover'd a Bay, which appeared to be tollerably well shelter'd from all winds, into which I resolved to go with the Ship, and with this View sent the Master in the Pinnace to sound the Entrance.

The account continues on the afternoon of the same day:

> Sunday, 29th. In the P.M. wind Southerly and Clear weather, with which we stood into the bay and Anchored under the South shore about 2 miles within the Entrance in 5 fathoms.

As far as setting foot on shore goes, Cook doesn't mention it except to say, 'we landed'. His journal account deals with attempting to befriend the locals and failing to do so. He's too busy observing the Aborigines and worrying about their weapons to give a detailed account of how they landed and who went ashore first:

> I went in the Boats in hopes of speaking with them, accompanied by Mr. Banks, Dr. Solander, and Tupia. As we approached the Shore they

all made off, except 2 Men, who seem'd resolved to oppose our landing. As soon as I saw this I order'd the boats to lay upon their Oars, in order to speak to them; but this was to little purpose, for neither us nor Tupia could understand one word they said. We then threw them some nails, beads, etc., a shore, which they took up, and seem'd not ill pleased with, in so much that I thought that they beckon'd to us to come ashore; but in this we were mistaken, for as soon as we put the boat in they again came to oppose us, upon which I fir'd a musquet between the 2, which had no other Effect than to make them retire back, where bundles of their darts lay, and one of them took up a stone and threw at us, which caused my firing a Second Musquet, load with small Shott; and altho' some of the shott struck the man, yet it had no other effect than making him lay hold on a Target (Shield). Immediately after this we landed, which we had no sooner done than they throw'd 2 darts at us; this obliged me to fire a third shott, soon after which they both made off.

So, as far as that magic moment we were told about as kids, the young cabin boy becoming the first Britisher to set foot on Australian soil (well, eastern Australia anyway), there is no evidence that Isaac was even in the boats that went ashore; usually the marines accompanied the landing party rather than crew members. All Cook was thinking about was firing his musket at the locals!

Given that he was busy taking pot shots at seemingly aggressive natives on the shore, it would seem that telling a member of your wife's family 'You go first' might not be the sort of thing you would want the in-laws to know!

Joseph Banks' account of the occasion is even more prosaic than James Cook's. He describes the momentous event like this: 'In the mean time we had landed on the rock.'

Number nine: Cook discovered how to prevent scurvy by making his crew eat vegetables and drink fruit juice

Scurvy is a condition caused by lack of vitamins in the C and B groups. It causes the cell structure of the body to start to break down and flesh and bones soften and putrefy. Symptoms are: skin turning black, ulcers, difficulty breathing, teeth falling out and gum tissue extruding from the mouth and putrefying, causing disgusting breath odour.

As scurvy did not appear until long voyages in the southern oceans began in the 15th century, it was little understood and often mistaken for leprosy, syphilis, dysentery or madness caused by the sun. Many sailors believed that the disease was caused by lack of contact with soil and carried sods of earth with them on voyages.

Being a crew member on a voyage of discovery any time between the 15th and 18th centuries was not conducive to a long life. Vasco da Gama lost two-thirds of his crew and Ferdinand Magellan lost 80 per cent of his men. Only 354 of George Anson's original 1854 men returned from his expedition against the Spanish in 1744 and only one ship, of the original eight, completed the circumnavigation.

Although battles, shipwrecks and drowning contributed to these losses, the vast majority were caused by scurvy.

Sir Richard Hawkins, a contemporary of Francis Drake, called scurvy 'the plague of the Sea, and the Spoyle of Mariners'. Captains were justifiably terrified of scurvy and often tried to claim it didn't appear on their vessels and blamed sailors' deaths on other causes.

By the 18th century it was common knowledge that, once victims of the disease reached land, they could recover quickly by eating grasses like wild celery, wood sorrel, nasturtiums, cabbage tree and other plants commonly growing along the shorelines of the American continent and southern islands. These were known generically as 'scurvy grass'. Fruit and palm wine were also considered good remedies.

In 1747 the Scottish Royal Naval surgeon James Lind conducted experiments on board a vessel when scurvy appeared. He gave six different supplements, all of which had been touted as cures, to six small groups of men afflicted by scurvy. The only cures that worked were fresh citrus and, to a lesser extent, apple cider. In 1753, after his retirement, Lind published *A Treatise of the Scurvy*, noting that there was experimental proof that fresh citrus had a rapid beneficial effect. He also argued that good ventilation and the cleaning and airing of bedding were beneficial to health on navy ships.

All three admiralty circumnavigations, led by John Byron, Samuel Wallis and James Cook, were directed to practise strict cleanliness measures and were supplied with 'cures' for scurvy and warm jackets for the crews to make ventilation tolerable. Wallis and Philip Carteret, on the second voyage, carried copious quantities of sauerkraut, vinegar, mustard, mixed dried vegetables (which could be made into soup), and malt (crushed dried grain used in beer making, which could be made into a liquid called 'wort').

So, Cook didn't discover or invent any cures for scurvy. What he did do was insist that his crew took the various preventatives and practised strict regimes for cleanliness on board. Men were punished for any failures to obey these orders. According to the journals, there were only five reported cases of scurvy during the *Endeavour* voyage and all were quickly cured. One victim was Joseph Banks, who carried a special medical kit of his own with various expensive remedies, and he soon recovered.

It has been suggested, by certain conspiracy theorists, that Cook avoided the mention of death by scurvy, as did many ships' captains. Some have suggested that Forby Sutherland, who died when the ship reached Botany Bay, and Lieutenant Hicks, who died just weeks before the *Endeavour* returned home, could have died of scurvy.

In his journal (May 1771) Cook attributes Hicks' death to consumption (tuberculosis):

> Sunday, 26th. A Steady Trade and Cloudy Weather. About 1 o'Clock P.M. departed this Life Lieutenant Hicks, and in the Evening his body was committed to the Sea with the usual ceremonys. He died of a Consumption which he was not free from when we sail'd from England, so that it may be truly said that he hath been dying ever since, tho' he held out tolerable well until we got to Batavia.

Cook gives no cause of death for Sutherland, who was the ship's poulterer (in charge of cleaning and preparing birds kept on board or shot for food)—he merely notes that he 'departed this life' and was buried ashore. Others have attributed Sutherland's demise to 'consumption' and there's really no evidence to show that this was not the case.

In a paper delivered to the Royal Society after his second voyage, Cook praised wort (malt) as 'without doubt one of the best antiscorbutic sea-medicines yet found' and said he was convinced that it did 'prevent the scurvy from making any great progress for a considerable time'.

Later medical opinion, however, tended to agree with what James Lind had already discovered—that fresh vegetables and citrus juice were the only real cures as they contained the necessary amounts of vitamin C. It has also been pointed out that 'rob', the condensed form of citrus juice carried by admiralty ships, including the *Endeavour* and the *Resolution*, and issued to prevent scurvy, had been boiled in the process—so that all the vitamin C was lost.

Number ten: The cottage in which Cook grew up, at Great Ayton in Yorkshire, was moved stone by stone in 1934 and is now in Fitzroy Gardens, in Melbourne

Cook's father, also James, was a Scot from Ednam in Roxburghshire who moved to Yorkshire to work as a day labourer some years after the Jacobite Rising failed in 1715, possibly in around 1720. In 1725 at Stainton Parish Church he married Grace Pace from Thornaby on Tees, County Durham.

Day labouring was semi-itinerant work but James secured a permanent position working for a farmer named George Mewburn, and the couple were living in a simple two-room, mud-and-thatch labourer's cottage just 3 kilometres from where they were married, at Marton-in-Cleveland, when their second child, named James after his father, was born on 27 October 1728. Little James was baptised at the local church, St Cuthbert's, on 3 November 1728.

In 1736 James senior was given the position of foreman at Airey-holme Farm, on Thomas Skottowe's estate at Great Ayton, and the family lived in a simple cottage on the estate until James left home at sixteen.

The cottage that now stands in Fitzroy Gardens in Melbourne was built either by or for James Cook senior in Great Ayton village in 1755 (ten years after his son James left home) on a plot of land given to him by Thomas Skottowe, the lord of the manor, as a reward for services rendered as a farm foreman for almost twenty years.

When his parents moved into the cottage, James was 26 years old and had just signed on as a midshipman in the Royal Navy in London. For the next seven years he was busy fighting in the Seven Years War, mostly in North America. When the war ended in 1763, he had been married to Elizabeth Batts for a year and was living in London although, until the three voyages of discovery, he spent seven or eight months of every year charting the coast of Newfoundland.

The Fitzroy Gardens cottage was purchased by Victorian industrialist and philanthropist Sir Russell Grimwade in 1933 for £800, and given, in 1934, as a gift to the state of Victoria to mark the centenary of European settlement. The woman who owned the cottage had stipulated, as a condition of the sale, that it must remain in Britain. When the highest British offer was £300, however, she changed the stipulation to 'remain in the British Empire', and happily accepted Sir Russell's 800 quid. The cottage was dismantled and shipped in 300 crates to be reassembled, complete with ivy cuttings taken before the removal, in Fitzroy Gardens.

How often James Cook stayed in the cottage is unknown. It is believed he visited Great Ayton at least once during the Seven Years War, probably in 1757. HMS *Eagle*, on which he served for the first two years of his naval career, patrolled the Irish Sea and the Bay of Biscay as part of the British blockade of French ports, but HMS *Solebay*, on which Cook served for several months after his promotion to master, patrolled the North Sea from the Scottish coast to the Shetlands. Cook probably visited Great Ayton on his way north to join the *Solebay* at Leith Harbour in Edinburgh, and possibly on his way south in September 1757 to join the *Pembroke* at Portsmouth.

From 1758, however, Cook spent the next four years on HMS *Pembroke* and later HMS *Northumberland*, as part of the war in Canada. The war was almost over when he returned, to marry Elizabeth in December 1762.

He certainly visited Great Ayton for his sister Margaret's wedding in 1764, and could have stayed at the cottage. When his mother Grace died, aged 62, on 18 February 1765, it is possible her son attended her funeral at All Saints Church, Great Ayton (where she is buried with five of her eight children), as he didn't sail for Newfoundland that year until April. If he did attend the funeral, he could have stayed at the cottage on that occasion as well.

It is also possible that, as Thomas Skottowe had taken a great interest in young James and been a patron to him from an early age, arranging his apprenticeship at Staithes and supporting his career move to Whitby, James Cook, now a warrant officer and sailing master in His

Majesty's Navy, stayed at the manor house when visiting Great Ayton. I have no evidence of this, but surely, given that Thomas Skottowe lived until 1771, it is a possibility. Even so, it is true to say that he certainly would have visited the cottage.

Cook's father died, aged 85, in April 1779 (eight months before his son's death in Hawaii) at Marske-by-the-Sea, near Redcar, some 20 kilometres from Great Ayton. He had been living there with his daughter Margaret and her husband, James Fleck, and their five children since 1772. It is believed that his son James visited him on his return from the *Endeavour* voyage and convinced him to move from the cottage and live with Margaret's family.

Given that James Cook junior was married for seventeen years and only managed to spend less than five years actually living with his wife, Elizabeth, in London, the rest of the time being spent at sea, visits to Great Ayton or Marske-by-the-Sea would have been infrequent at best.

All that can be said, with certainty, about the cottage in Fitzroy Gardens is that it was built ten years after James Cook left home and was the home of both his parents and at least one of his sisters for about ten years . . . and his father's home for seventeen years . . . and James Cook certainly visited and probably stayed there on several occasions.

The ruined cottage where he was born was demolished around 1793, when the Rudd family bought the land and erected Marton Lodge. They marked the site of the famous explorer's birthplace cottage with cobblestones. Marton Lodge was destroyed by fire in 1832 and the property was purchased in 1853 by the first mayor of Middlesbrough, the German-born industrialist Henry Bolckow, who built a grand house known as Marton Hall. He removed the stones and marked the site of the long-gone humble cottage with an enormous granite vase. An inscription reads: 'This granite vase was erected by H.W.F. Bolckow of Marton Hall, A.D. 1858 to mark the site of the cottage in which Captain James Cook the world circumnavigator was born October 27, 1728.'

Bolckow became an avid collector of Cook memorabilia and owned the 'Holograph Journal' of the *Endeavour* voyage, which he bought at an auction held by book dealers Puttick and Simpson in London in 1868.

Marton Hall changed hands and fell into a neglected state after the dispersal auction of Bolckow's collection by Sotheby's in 1923, at which the National Library of Australia bought the 'Holograph Journal' and other letters and papers for £6000.

The local council ordered the demolition of the derelict Marton Hall in 1960 and it caught fire and burned down during the process. It is now the site of the Cook Birthplace Museum, erected in 1978, to celebrate the 250th anniversary of Cook's birth.

The enormous granite vase is still in place. Marton is now a suburb of Middlesbrough.

WHAT THE JOURNALS DON'T TELL US

There are two more elements of the 'Captain Cook and the *Endeavour*' story that are worth consideration. Both are the subject of extremely contentious claims about James Cook hiding knowledge and altering his journal retrospectively. The evidence upon which these claims are based is revealed by Margaret Cameron-Ash in her meticulously researched book *Lying for the Admiralty*. I will give only a short synopsis here.

Hiding Sydney Harbour

Cook spent eight days in Botany Bay (29 April to 6 May 1770) and went exploring on at least three of them. Given that he was known to walk briskly and climb hills to survey the land, and given that we know he went up Cooks River on Monday 30 April and walked northwards (and then went over to the north shore again the next morning and explored), there is every chance he saw Sydney Harbour.

Before the city of Sydney was developed, it would have been possible to see the harbour after a 2-mile walk from Cooks River and to actually reach it in less than 4 miles. Thus, an easy 45–60 minute walk would have given Cook a view of the 'finest harbour in the world'. There was a well-trodden path used by the locals, called the Bulanaming Track, from Cooks River to present-day Pyrmont. If he walked north on the Tuesday along the coastal cliff top, he could have reached Bondi in under three hours and seen the harbour from there.

If this happened, why is it not mentioned in any of the journals or logbooks?

Well, if you choose to believe that it happened, you have to accept that Cook deliberately kept the information to himself and those accompanying him were sworn to secrecy. His journal entries for those days do seem strangely devoid of any information and the phrase that he used, 'met with nothing extraordinary', was used in other places in his writings, as well as 'met with nothing remarkable', to hide valuable information.

Margaret Cameron-Ash makes a very good case for the theory that Cook did see Sydney Harbour and kept the discovery secret, which is why he sailed out to sea when he passed it after leaving Botany Bay.

The most compelling evidence to support this theory is to be found in the diary of Arthur Phillip some seventeen years later. Phillip wrote that, should Botany Bay prove unsuitable for settlement, he should: 'go to a port a few leagues to the Northward, where there appeared to be a good Harbour, and several Islands—as the Natives are very expert in setting fire to the grass, then having an island to secure our Stock, would be a great advantage'.

As the only view you get of Sydney Harbour as you pass the heads 3 miles out to sea, as Cook did, is the entrance, Middle Head and little else (no Sydney Harbour, no Middle Harbour, no Manly Harbour and certainly no islands), how was this information gained, to be then passed on to Arthur Phillip by Sir Philip Stephens at the admiralty in 1787?

If the information was not gained on Cook's walks northward from Botany Bay and later passed on to Stephens, where on earth *did* the information come from?

Changing 'Passage' Island to 'Possession' Island

The most contentious conspiracy theory proposed by Margaret Cameron-Ash is the possibility that the possession ceremony described in Cook's journal on 22 August 1770 never took place.

The assertion is that Cook went ashore in order to climb to the highest hilltop and find a passage through to the Timor Sea. Shots were exchanged from muskets on shore and guns on the ship to indicate that a passage could be seen. This was the cause of some jubilation and Cook named the island 'Passage Island'.

On their arrival in Batavia, they became aware that Bougainville had been there some months previously and had with him a native similar in looks and dress to Tupia, the Tahitian accompanying Cook.

This caused a panic. Had Bougainville already made some claim on the east coast of New Holland?

Cook's solution was to rewrite the four pages of his journal that included the 'Passage Island' activities, change the name of the island to 'Possession Island' and claim that he had performed the ceremony there. This would have been an easy task as the journal was compiled four pages at a time by doubling over folio paper to make four pages and placing them in order between boards.

The circumstantial evidence that this occurred is based on the following.

Joseph Banks, who often used Cook's journal to write his own, writes, 'The island was called Possession or Passage Island', with 'Passage' crossed out.

No other journals, apart from those that would have copied Cook's, mention 'Possession Island' or a possession ceremony.

As Cook acknowledges Dutch claims to New Holland west of Cape York, it seems very odd that he takes possession of the east coast after he has left it.

Cook uses the word 'passage' seven times in his journal entry for 22 August, but doesn't mention 'Possession Island' until the ship was leaving the following morning.

Cook makes sure that he covers himself by stating that he has already taken possession of New South Wales several times:

> . . . notwithstanding I had in the Name of his Majesty taken possession of several places upon this Coast, I now once More hoisted English Colours, and in the Name of His Majesty King George the Third took possession of the whole Eastern coast from the above Latitude down to this place by the Name of New Wales.

Yet, although there are several mentions of taking 'possession' of parts of New Zealand, there is no other reference in the journals of this occurring in New South Wales.

THE JOURNALS

It may surprise many readers to learn that Cook's original journal, the one he wrote in his own hand (which is known as the 'Holograph Journal' i.e. 'wholly' the work of James Cook), was not properly edited, published and available to researchers until 1955. The charts and maps that accompanied Cook's original journal were kept by the admiralty and only published as a complete set in 1988.

For well over a century after Cook's death, the only official account of the voyage available was the one by Dr John Hawkesworth, published in June 1773 in three volumes and titled *Voyages to the Southern Hemisphere*. The first volume concerns the earlier voyages of Byron, Wallis and Carteret, while volumes two and three contain Hawkesworth's retelling of Cook's voyage using whatever censored version of the admiralty's copy of the journal he was given, as well as the journals of Banks and Solander.

Hawkesworth made the decision to tell the entire story of the voyage in the first person, as though he was James Cook. The result of this decision is that the entire narrative is a combination of Cook's writings, Banks' and Solander's observations, and Hawkesworth's own thoughts written as if Cook is narrating them. The situation was made worse by the fact that many of Cook's descriptions and decisions puzzled Hawkesworth, as he was obviously not given certain parts of Cook's journal because the admiralty did not want certain things known.

When Cook became acquainted with Hawkesworth's efforts, on his return from the second voyage of discovery, he is reported as being 'mortified'. John Beaglehole, who had access to his letters and writings as well as his handwritten original journal, quotes Cook as writing: 'How these things came to be thus misrepresented, I cannot say, as they came not from me.'

Nevertheless, for the next 120 years, this version of the voyage was the only one available and it was much quoted as if it was Cook's original voice.

Hawkesworth's account of the voyage has been much criticised. Parts of the account were considered obscene at the time of publication due to the fact that the sexual activities on Tahiti are described in some detail. As well as this, for the next century and a quarter, many historians pondered on some of the obvious errors and omissions that became more apparent as maps of the world became more accurate in the years following Cook's death.

Poor old Hawkesworth, who had to work with what he was given, was obviously only partly to blame for this confusion. As he died shortly after the book's publication, in November 1773, he was thankfully spared the ordeal of having to read most of the many criticisms of his work.

William Wharton, who produced the next edited compilation of Cook's journals, 120 years later in 1893, tried to be fair and acknowledged that at least Hawkesworth's effort 'gave a clear description of the events of the voyage in a connected manner, and was accepted as sufficient'. Wharton, however, also echoed the thoughts of many historians when he stated that Hawkesworth:

... not only interspersed reflections of his own, but managed to impose his own ponderous style upon many of the extracts from the united Journals; and, moreover, as they are all jumbled together, the whole being put into Cook's mouth, it is impossible to know whether we are reading Cook, Banks, Solander, or Hawkesworth himself.

Wharton had access to three versions of Cook's journal, and these were all copies of the original 'Holograph Journal', to which Wharton did not have access. Indeed, he doubted whether it even existed.

Ships' captains were required to keep a daily journal and send copies home to the admiralty every six months. Obviously this was not possible on the *Endeavour*. It wasn't until the ship reached Batavia that Cook had the first opportunity to meet this obligation. His clerk, Robert Orton, made a copy of Cook's journal, corrected and edited by Cook, and it was sent home with the Dutch East India Company fleet, which departed while the *Endeavour* was delayed in Batavia, being repaired and refitted.

The manuscript was, of course, secured with the admiralty wax seal but, even if the Dutch did manage to read it, Cook had included a sentence politely acknowledging the Dutch claims to New Holland: 'on the Western side I can make no new discovery, the honour of which belongs to the Dutch Navigators'.

This sentence also appears in the 'Holograph Journal' (22 August 1770).

There is no evidence that anyone attempted to break the international code of honour (or the seal) and read the journal, but the comment was deleted from whatever copy was given to Hawkesworth. Obviously the admiralty did not think it necessary or wise to acknowledge any Dutch claims in the official account of the voyage.

Captain William Wharton (later Admiral, Sir), preparing the second published account of the journals in 1893, doubted that the original journal still existed or was anything more than notes and jottings. He knew that there were three versions of Cook's journal in existence and was obviously excited to have access to all three of them to work with.

There are, in fact, four copies of Cook's journal and at least three copies of the ship's log.

1 The 'Holograph Journal'

This is Cook's own handwritten original, complete with crossings out, corrections, amendments and retrospective changes. He took it to the admiralty on his return, straight from the ship. After the admiralty had studied and copied it, Cook asked Sir Philip Stephens if he could have it as a souvenir of the voyage. Stephens apparently agreed, on the proviso that it never be published.

Elizabeth Cook outlived her husband and all her children and some sources say she left the journal to her cousin Rear-Admiral

Isaac Smith. However, as Elizabeth outlived Isaac by four years, this seems a very odd claim to make. Nevertheless, it appears the journal was passed down through Smith's family until it was offered for sale, along with another ten volumes and a collection of maps, as Lot 277, in a sale conducted by book sellers Puttick and Simpson that ran for four days commencing on 10 March 1868.

The sale was advertised as containing:

> the library of the famous poet Samuel Rogers, the manuscript journals, log books, charts and papers of the celebrated navigator Captain James Cook, collections of maps and manuscripts relating to Kent Berkshire and Gloucestershire, books in all classes of literature . . .

In spite of the Cook collection getting second billing in the advertising, it constituted merely one lot from a total of 1764 lots offered for sale.

Henry Bolckow purchased Lot 277 for £14 and 15 shillings, and the material became part of his James Cook collection, in a room at Marton Hall, Middlesbrough, on the estate where Cook was born.

Bolckow was proud of his collection and it was certainly not kept secret, but for many years historians and researchers seem to have missed the fact that it actually contained the 'Holograph Journal'. Wharton, writing in 1890, certainly seems to have no knowledge of the Puttick and Simpson sale, or the fact that the original journal was sitting in a room dedicated to the great navigator's memory in a grand house at Middlesbrough.

When Wharton was first given the task of editing the journals, in 1890, he evidently advertised seeking any information or knowledge of any original James Cook material. He was successful in unearthing some lost material, but completely missed the 'Holograph Journal' and therefore based his 1893 edition on the three copies of the original, plus Banks' journal.

The 'Holograph Journal' and other papers and letters were acquired by the National Library of Australia at a Sotheby's sale in 1923, when the collection from Marton Hall was sold by Bolckow's great-nephew.

There had been attempts by institutions in Australia to buy parts of the collection before the auction and the Mitchell Library in New South Wales had offered £5000 prior to the auction. At the auction the Australian government made the top bid of £5000 and secured the journal along with four other lots for the National Library of Australia.

In 1955, New Zealand historian John Beaglehole was the first editor to use the 'Holograph Journal' to produce a comprehensive, edited version of Cook's written narrative of the voyage.

2 The 'Batavia' copy (aka the 'Corner' copy)

This copy, written by Cook's clerk, Robert Orton, with some corrections by Cook, ends on 23 October 1770, at Batavia. It is the one sent home with the Dutch East India Company fleet. Both the 'Holograph Journal' and the admiralty copy have the following entries for 1770:

> Oct 24—In the p.m. I went up to town in order to put on board the first Dutch ship that sails a pacquet for the Admiralty, containing a copy of my journal, a chart of the South Seas, another of New Zealand, and one of the east coast of New Holland . . .
>
> Oct 25th—In the evening I sent the Admiralty packet on board 'Kronenberg', Captain. Frederick Kelger, Commodore, who together with another ship, sail immediately for the Cape, where he waits for the remainder of the fleet.

This copy was kept by Sir Philip Stephens, Secretary of the Admiralty, and passed down through his daughter to her husband Thomas Jones, 6th Viscount Ranelagh, and then to Thomas Heron Jones, the 7th viscount, who sold it to a Mr Cosens in 1868 for £14. Cosens sold it to a wealthy admirer of Cook, Mr John Corner, for £31 in 1890.

Not long after he negotiated the sale, Mr Corner became aware of Wharton's search for Cook's journals and contacted him, stating that he wished him to have access to the journal he had just purchased. Odd as it may seem, Corner handed the journal to Wharton, who visited his home for the purpose, and died the following day!

This journal was purchased at some point by British Liberal politician and businessman Sir Leicester Harmsworth, who collected historic documents relating to Australia. In 1932, five years before his death, Harmsworth offered to sell his collection to the Mitchell Library and the Batavia copy and other Cook papers and letters, along with a log kept by the ship's master on the *Endeavour*, Robert Molineux, became part of the collection held by the Mitchell Library at the State Library of New South Wales.

3 The admiralty copy

This is a copy made by Robert Orton from the 'Holograph Journal', expressly to be kept as a record of the voyage by the admiralty. After the *Endeavour* left Batavia she sailed to Cape Town, arriving on 14 March 1771. Cook stayed a month and took on new crew members, having lost 26 men to malaria and dysentery. He intended to sail home in convoy with twelve British East Indiamen who were to be escorted through the Atlantic by the warship HMS *Portland*. He left Cape Town and met up with them at the British East India Company base at St Helena.

At St Helena it became apparent that many officers on the East Indiamen knew far more about the *Endeavour* voyage than they should. Information had been leaked during the month at Cape Town and the five days at St Helena, possibly by Orton, who was unreliable and prone to drunkenness, but any of the crew could have been responsible.

When the *Endeavour* struggled to keep up with the convoy Cook, keen to ensure that any information known to those in the fleet should not reach Britain before the admiralty were aware of it, signalled the *Portland* and recorded, on the morning of 11 May, off Ascension Island:

> Captain Elliott himself came on board, to whom I deliver'd a Letter for the Admiralty, and a Box containing the Ship's Common Log Books, and some of the Officers' Journals, etc. I did this because it seem'd probable that the Portland would get home before us, as we sail much heavier than any of the Fleet.

This box probably contained the admiralty copy of Cook's journal.

Many years later this copy of the journal went missing and was lost for a few decades. As reported by Wharton: 'The other and complete copy is still in possession of the Admiralty, though in some unexplained manner it was absent for some years, and was only recovered by the exertions of Mr. W. Blakeney, R.N.'

It was quite common practice for admiralty staff to 'borrow' journals, take them home to read and forget to bring them back, and this may have been the case with the admiralty copy of the journal. Mr Blakeney, it seems, was asked to track it down for Wharton to use, and successfully did so.

This copy is now in the British Public Records Office.

4 The royal copy

This is a copy of the Batavia copy, written neatly in several different styles of handwriting, possibly by clerks at the admiralty, and presented to George III, who ordered the voyage and had a huge library of maritime books and charts. It still belongs to the royal family.

Ships' logs and officers' journals

A ship's log and its captain's journal are two very different things. The log contains the technical and navigational information and any official goings-on that occur on board. The log was used to write the journal and included any 'remarkable events', which meant anything worthy of note. Captains were expected to write the journal in diary form each day and include their observations and opinions of each place they visited.

There are at least three copies of the *Endeavour* log. The original was given to Joseph Banks and he later presented it to the British Museum. A rather sketchy copy, made later and kept at Greenwich, where Cook was officer in command after his second voyage, also includes extracts from the 'Holograph Journal'.

Another copy, made for Sir Hugh Palliser, was in 1890 in the possession of a descendant of Palliser's wife, Mr Hudson of Sunderland. When Hudson replied to Wharton's inquiries, in a letter to *The Times* of 1 October 1890, he included an extract from the log and Wharton wondered if what Hudson had was the 'Holograph Journal'. He later realised it was a copy of the ship's log and, in the preface to his 1893 publication *Captain Cook's Journal during His First Voyage Round the World*, he notes:

The ship's Log Book of the Endeavour is in the British Museum. Mr. R.M. Hudson of Sunderland possesses Cook's own log, not autograph however, presented by Cook to Sir Hugh Palliser, the ancestor of his wife.

The Journals of all the officers of the Endeavour are preserved at the Public Record Office. There is, however, nothing to be got out of them, as they are mainly copies one of the other, founded on the ship's log.

The portion of Mr. Molineux's, the Master's, Log that exists (at the Admiralty) is a most beautifully kept and written document, enriched with charts and sketches that attest the accuracy of Cook's remark, that he was a 'young man of good parts'.

Cook does, indeed, say that in his journal entry of 16 April 1771, when he notes Molineux's death at Cape Town. What Wharton omits is the next part of the sentence, in which Cook notes that the death was alcohol related and Molineux 'had unfortunately given himself up to Extravagancy and intemperance, which brought on disorders that put a Period to his Life'.

Journal keeping being a compulsory requirement of being an officer, these men were allowed access to the ship's log in order to write up their own journals. So, there could be quite a few copies of parts of the log of the *Endeavour* in existence. Most of the officers' journals were kept at the admiralty and are now in the British Public Records Office.

Unofficial publications
The three-volume account of the voyages of Byron Wallis and Cook by Hawkesworth was commissioned by Lord Sandwich, First Lord of the Admiralty, in late 1771 and efforts were made to prevent any other accounts being published.

Less than three months after the *Endeavour* returned, an unofficial, brief and anonymous account of the voyage appeared, published by Becket and de Hondt. It carried a dedication to the lords of the admiralty and Joseph Banks, which the publishers were forced to remove. Translated into French, it was published in Paris in 1773 with Bougainville's account of his 1766–69 circumnavigation.

The author was undoubtedly the *Endeavour*'s American midshipman James Matra, who later proposed a settlement in New South Wales

for Americans who remained loyal to Britain after the American War
of Independence, and after whom the Sydney suburb of Matraville
is named.

Joseph Banks was the subject of two other, potentially embarrassing, attempts to publish information about the voyage before the
official, admiralty-sanctioned account could be published.

In the spirit of scientific brotherhood, Banks had written a brief
account of the voyage in a letter to a French friend living in London.
The letter was forwarded to the Academy of Sciences in Paris and
Banks learned it was about to be published, as a book, in London.
Luckily he was able to buy the prepared page plates before it was
printed and destroy them.

Banks had lent the journal of the artist Sydney Parkinson, who died
after leaving Batavia, to Sydney's brother Stanfield as a courtesy. The
journal was Banks' property as Parkinson was in his employ during
the voyage. He also paid Stanfield the £500 wages owed to his deceased
brother.

Stanfield Parkinson, who was declared insane not long afterwards,
accused Banks of keeping specimens and drawings that were rightfully
his (these are now in the British Museum) and used the £500 to print
and attempt to publish his brother's journal. Banks and Hawkesworth
were able, through the Court of Chancery, to prevent publication
of this journal until after Hawkesworth's version was published in
June 1773.

CONCLUSION

James Cook was an intrepid explorer, a great navigator, a stern but fair leader of men and a very competent captain. Relative to the times in which he lived, he was as decent a human being as you could hope to find leading a European expedition into uncharted territories. It is hard to imagine a better example of a European explorer of his era to choose as the discoverer of Australia's east coast.

It is, however, important to understand Cook in the context of the time, the political situation and the attitudes of the Age of Enlightenment in which he lived. He was, above all else, a servant of the admiralty and a subject of the king. If we attempt to impose 21st century sensibilities and attitudes on his actions, we cannot but fail to understand his motivation, limitations and achievements.

That he kept secrets and told lies as part of his job and sense of loyalty to his country and his employer is patently true. He hid information and lied about Point Hicks and Stewart Island, and possibly about taking possession of New South Wales.

He is not, however, responsible for the mythology perpetrated about him by writers, publishers, officials and school curricula.

He was not 'Captain Cook' when he sailed around New Zealand and up the east coast of Australia. He did not choose the *Endeavour*, or decide where she should sail. He did not believe New Holland was the Great South Land, and he wasn't the first European navigator to find the east coast of Australia. He didn't give a member of his wife's family the privilege of being first to set foot ashore at Botany Bay, he never discovered a cure for scurvy, and he never lived in the cottage that now stands in Fitzroy Gardens in Melbourne.

As well as all those things we were told as kids being untrue, I can also find no evidence that he ever chased a chook all around Australia.

ADDENDUM: THE TRANSITS OF VENUS EXPEDITIONS

O stensibly, the *Endeavour* voyage was all about observing the transit of Venus across the face of the sun. Why was this so important?

Venus can be observed crossing the face of the sun from Earth only rarely, but the phenomenon is predictable. Four transits occur every 243 years. The pattern of these four events is that two transits occur eight years apart, separated by gaps of 121.5 years and 105.5 years. What this means is that the phenomenon can be observed from Earth twice within eight years, but only every 105 or 121 years! The transits can last up to six or seven hours. Transits of Venus were due to occur in 1761 and 1769.

In 1677, the brilliant scientist, mathematician and astronomer Edmond Halley, who was all of twenty years old at the time, observed the transit of Mercury across the face of the sun from the island of St Helena. He realised that accurate observations and timing of the transits of the two planets between Earth and the sun from different parts of the globe could help calculate the distances between planets, the size of the solar system and our distance from the sun.

The French astronomer Joseph-Nicolas Delisle improved the theory by adding that, if the different observers knew their exact positions on Earth, they would only need to accurately time the moment when the edge of the planet touched the edge of the sun to make a valid measurement.

Transits of Mercury across the face of the sun are far more common than those of Venus. After that observed by Halley in 1677, there would be ten more in the intervening 92 years before James Cook and the astronomer Charles Green, having observed the transit of Venus from Tahiti on 3 June 1769, took their instruments ashore on the North Island of New Zealand to observe the transit of Mercury across the face of the sun on 9 November 1769.

Halley, who was a professor of geometry at Oxford University, was appointed Astronomer Royal in charge of the observatory at Greenwich upon the death of John Flamsteed, the first Astronomer Royal, in 1720. As early as 1714, Halley (who died in 1742) had calculated the best places on Earth to observe the transits of Venus across the sun in 1761 and 1769.

The 17th and 18th centuries were the Age of Reason, the Enlightenment, and these astronomical events were much anticipated by the scientific community across Europe and plans to observe them were put in place well in advance. In Britain, members of the Royal Society, along with many other astronomers, wished to conduct accurate observations of the two transits, which would not occur again until 1874.

The Royal Society planned two expeditions to observe the transit of Venus of 1761: one to Sumatra and one to the South Atlantic. The French Academie Royale organised three: one to India, one to Siberia and one to an island near Madagascar.

In 1761 a few obstacles stood in the way of scientific cooperation between the two nations most able to make the observations and share their results. The main problem was that they were at war with each other.

The Seven Years War between France and Britain, and their allies on both sides, was raging in Europe, the Americas, Asia and Africa. This severely hampered one of the British expeditions attempting to observe the transit, and completely scuppered one French expedition.

Two official British expeditions were organised by the British Royal Society in conjunction with the British East India Company. The intended suitable locations were two British East India possessions: the island of St Helena, in the South Atlantic, and Bencoolen, on the island of Sumatra.

Unfortunately, Bencoolen had been captured by the French in April 1760 and the alternative site of Batavia, on the Dutch-controlled island of Java, could not be reached in time, due to the expedition vessel, the *Seahorse*, being attacked and damaged in the English Channel by a French warship. As a result, the second expedition was forced to observe the transit from Cape Town, which was not really far enough from St Helena to be of much use.

The rather unsuccessful Bencoolen expedition was, incidentally, led by the British astronomers Charles Mason and Jeremiah Dixon, later to become famous for surveying the disputed borders between Maryland, Virginia, Delaware and Pennsylvania and thus delineating the 'Mason–Dixon Line', which, in 1820, became the border between the slavery and non-slavery states of the USA.

The observation on St Helena went ahead as scheduled and another, organised and financed by the British colonial government of Massachusetts and Harvard University, observed the transit from Newfoundland.

One French team, with Russian cooperation, made its way to Tobolsk in Siberia and made a partly successful observation. A second French team, operating from an island near Madagascar, failed to make a successful observation. The third French attempt, led by the unfortunate astronomer Guillaume Le Gentil, who had spent years preparing on Mauritius, headed to the planned observation site in the French colony of Pondicherry in India only to find it blockaded by the British. Le Gentil missed the first transit completely and then, eight years later, again in Pondicherry, missed the second transit when clouds obscured the entire event.

One of the best places to observe the second transit, in 1769, was the middle of the South Pacific Ocean. As the British East India Company did not sail in those waters, the astronomer Professor Thomas Hornsby of Oxford University proposed that the Royal Society and the admiralty might join forces in order to facilitate the observation. King George III, a keen amateur astronomer, liked the idea and the admiralty, keen to explore the Pacific ahead of the French (and also to support scientific research that might aid navigation and astronomy), agreed to provide a ship (or ships) and to help find an island in the Pacific Ocean where the observation could occur. The king ordered £4000 'clear of fees' be provided to finance the expedition. The Royal Society directed the Astronomer Royal, Nevil Maskelyne, who was a member of the society, to prepare the necessary instructions for the observers.

The Royal Society arranged, planned and financed three other observations for 1769. Astronomer William Wales, assisted by Joseph Dymond, was sent to Hudson Bay; Jeremiah Dixon and William Bayly went to Norway; and a Mr Call, who lived in Madras in India and had observed the earlier transit in 1761, was directed to make an observation with the help of officers of the British East India Company.

The planning for the Pacific expedition began in 1766 and, in December 1767, Alexander Dalrymple was chosen to lead the expedition. He insisted that there should be only one ship, arguing that two ships could become separated and slow down the operation. In March 1768 the vessel was chosen and sent to be refitted. As it would have to carry everything the expedition required, it also needed alterations below decks.

In the first week of April 1768, Dalrymple was sacked and James Cook was suggested as his replacement. After meeting with members of the Royal Society and being accepted as a suitable leader, Cook was officially appointed on 25 May 1768.

Up until three months before the *Endeavour* was due to sail, and just five days before Cook's official appointment to lead the expedition to the Pacific, there was no specific destination for the voyage. On 20 May 1768 HMS *Dolphin* arrived back in London after circumnavigating the globe on a second secret mission for the admiralty, and Captain Wallis informed his superiors that he had found the islands of Tahiti and claimed them for Britain. The members of the Royal Society rejoiced, for now there was a known destination, claimed by the British, which was the perfect place for observing the transit of Venus. Several members of Wallis's crew joined the crew of the *Endeavour* and Cook had the official report of Wallis's journey and probably met with him before departing.

Charles Green was appointed to the *Endeavour* expedition as astronomer and he and James Cook were paid to make the observations and record them for the Royal Society. Cook had a fort built at Matavai Bay in Tahiti that he called 'Fort Venus' and he, Green and Dr Solander all made separate observations there. Cook also sent small groups led by lieutenants Hicks and Gore to outlying islands to make separate observations.

When the *Endeavour* reached New Zealand, Cook and Green took the opportunity to set up the instruments again and observe the transit of Mercury across the sun on 9 November 1769. The place on the North Island where they did this has been known ever since as Mercury Bay.

Green died on the return voyage, nine days out of Batavia, either of pleurisy or a 'flux'. Cook noted that he was 'indefatigable' in making his observations and measuring latitude and longitude, and often left the ship's day-to-day navigation duties to Green, who he praised for his excellent observations and calculations. However, Cook was also critical of Green's lifestyle. When Green died on 29 January 1771, he noted: 'He had long been in a bad state of health, which he took no care to repair, but, on the contrary, lived in such a manner as greatly promoted the disorders he had had long upon him; this brought on the Flux, which put a period to his life.'

It was left to Cook and the Astronomer Royal, Nevil Maskelyne, to decipher Green's notes when it came to writing up the observations made on the voyage. Evidently he was rather less meticulous in recording than he was in observing. Maskelyne was critical of his work and Cook was forced to admit that Green's notes and papers were 'in a disorganised state'.

PART FOUR
FALSE WORD DERIVATIONS

'When I use a word,' Humpty Dumpty said in a rather scornful tone,
'it means just what I choose it to mean, neither more nor less.'

Through the Looking-Glass, Lewis Carroll, 1871

WORD WATCH

There are no better examples of furphies than the stories that are passed around to explain the derivations of words and phrases in our everyday language. While the evolution of language is an extremely complicated business (and a minefield for scholars and researchers), there are some glaringly obvious examples of popular word origins and derivation beliefs that can easily be proven to be wrong.

Usage often changes the meaning of words over time, making a nonsense of the original, perfectly logical meaning. There is no better example of this over the last few decades than the use of the word 'decimate' to mean 'annihilate' or 'wipe out'. Inherent in the word's Latin origin is the concept of ten per cent (*decim*) being lost and the word really means exactly that. If the Romans wanted to punish a rebellious group or population, they would kill one in every ten of the male population. To the Romans, a loss of ten per cent of soldiers in a battle was considered a disaster and thus 'the army was decimated'. The way the word is often used today is actually contradictory to its logical meaning.

The good old Anglo-Saxon four-letter 'vulgar' words can be easily traced back many centuries to their Germanic origins, yet many people perpetuate the nonsense that some are acronyms, such as 'store high in transit' for 'shit'. Supposedly this came from the sailing days when manure was being transported in a ship's hold—and could internally combust if compressed deep in the hold.

The probability (or common-sense) test tells you that the value of a cargo of manure would hardly be worth the cost of transporting it and, if it was being used as ballast, as some versions of this furphy claim, it would have to be stored low in transit, making the whole story nonsense! This is apart from the fact that the word has been used for many centuries to mean exactly what it has always meant.

'For unlawful carnal knowledge' is another example of this ridiculous nonsense. Just a moment's thought should be enough to make us realise that there are probably no acronymic derivations of words that have been around in our language, and others, for many centuries.

Words derived from acronyms are now common in any language (NASA, AWOL, UNESCO etc.), but they are all relatively modern words.

One of the most popular urban myths in the English language about a word's origin is the often-repeated story about the word 'posh'. This word is erroneously believed to be an acronym, but it isn't.

The Peninsula and Orient Steamship Company (P&O) have consistently and vigorously denied, for more than a century, that the word was ever used to denote a return passage to India where a cabin could be booked on the port side of the ship on the outward leg and the starboard side on the return voyage in order to avoid the heat of the sun. Yet the myth continues to be spread and it is widely believed—even today.

There is no evidence whatsoever that 'POSH' was ever written on a shipping ticket; indeed, there is plenty of evidence to say that it was not.

The true derivation of the word 'posh'—to mean 'privileged' or 'smart and classy'—probably evolved from the Romany (Roma or Gypsy) word that meant 'petty cash', 'ready money', 'real money', the stuff in your pocket or under the mattress in the caravan. It was popularised in the British military, where it evolved into 'posh up', meaning 'having the ready cash to dress well and attend exclusive events'.

Here are some glaringly obvious Aussie examples of these urban myths about word derivations being popularly believed.

POM

I was recently rather surprised to be admonished by a radio listener for using the word 'pom' to denote English migrants in Australia. The listener assumed that the word was derogatory, which, I must say, had never occurred to me. Both my parents were 'poms' and often referred to themselves as such, although they were, in temperament, both proudly Australian, and Australian citizens. In our house the word implied no disrespect and simply identified where you came from.

Once again, the 'acronym brigade' are to the fore, claiming such derivations as 'prisoner of His (of Her) Majesty' or 'prisoner of Mother England', from the convict days (supposedly stamped on the convicts' clothing), or 'Port of Melbourne', or 'permit of migration' for later free settlers. All of which are complete nonsense.

Common sense would tell you that a term like 'Mother England' would hardly be used formally to denote Britain, and two minutes research would tell you that convicts wore their own clothing for the first two decades of transportation to New South Wales. When clothing was provided for convicts it was marked with the broad arrow, denoting the monarch's property, and, at times, with the letters 'PB' for 'prisoners' barracks'.

The broad arrow, taken from the coat of arms of Edward III, had denoted the monarch's property since the year 1330.

Apart from any of that, there is no evidence to support the Port of Melbourne or permit of migration nonsense, and there is no evidence of the word 'pom' being used to denote a British (or specifically English) migrant before 1912.

There is evidence, however, that, from around 1870, British immigrants were commonly referred to in Aussie slang as 'Jimmy Grants', rhyming slang for 'immi-grant'.

In his 1923 novel *Kangaroo*, D.H. Lawrence explained that 'pommy-grant' was being used in Australia as 'almost' rhyming slang for an immigrant. This had the added cachet of referencing the word 'pomegranate' to refer to the ruddy complexion of many English migrants, by comparing it to the reddish colour of the fruit of that name. Evidently the term was then abbreviated (a common process in Aussie slang) to 'pommy' and then to 'pom'.

DINKUM

A furphy has developed, in the last 30 years or so, that dinkum is derived from the Cantonese term for 'real gold' or 'top gold', and was borrowed by the diggers on the Australian goldfields during the goldrushes of the 19th century, and used to mean 'the real thing'.

Perhaps this is a belated attempt to reverse the harsh racial discrimination of that time, or to be overly politically correct, or to make us seem retrospectively multicultural.

It's complete rubbish.

My Chinese-Australian friends tell me that the closest sounding Cantonese term for 'pure gold' or 'real gold' or 'best gold' or 'top gold' would be pronounced 'seong gam'—and that's a long way from 'din kum'.

Anyway, it's all irrelevant, as the term was actually recorded as being used to mean 'hard work', or 'a due share of work', in Derbyshire and Gloucestershire before the First Fleet departed, and 'fair dinkum' was recorded as an old Lincolnshire term by Joseph and Elizabeth Wright in their *English Dialect Dictionary*, compiled between 1896 and 1905.

DIGGER

While on the subjects of gold and the Chinese, let's consider the case of the word 'digger'.

Although noting that 'digger' originated on the goldfields circa 1855, Eric Partridge, in his *Dictionary of Slang and Unconventional English* (1937–61), defines the word as a 'military term'. He implies that the revised sense of the word in World War I refers to those who 'shovelled Gallipoli into sandbags'.

I would argue, however, that digging trenches in World War I has little to do with the word 'digger' being used to imply mateship, as it had already been used in that sense for 60 years.

The diggers who stood united under the Southern Cross at the Eureka Stockade made their stand for 'a fair go' against what they saw as the overzealous enforcement of oppressive regulations. They were all white men of European descent, united in mateship and, demanding to be treated as free men in a new country, they wanted democracy. There were distinct overtones of the French Revolution and the American War of Independence at play. There was a new flag without a Union Jack in the corner.

There were also very definite racist overtones in this new idea of mateship that certainly did not include the Chinese.

The unpopularity of the Chinese on the goldfields was a major factor in uniting the native-born white Australians and the British,

American, German, Italian, Hungarian, French and other European migrant miners in bonds of mateship as diggers.

The Chinese usually came to already established goldfields and often 'worked over' the abandoned mullock mounds that had been dug and left by the white diggers. There was resentment when the more meticulous and 'group' methods of the Chinese extracted gold missed by the previous miners.

The diggers accused the Chinese of polluting the water supplies on the goldfields by 'puddling' over the material left behind by those who dug the original mineshafts. This was, of course, mostly due to the fact that the Chinese were unable to make new claims.

Dislike of the Chinese was mostly due to paranoia about the 'unknown'. They worked as teams, they were 'different', their customs were a mystery, there were no women, they smoked opium, they were 'cheap labour' at a time when unionism was in its infancy, and they were not Christian. They returned to China with their gold, they were not part of Australian society, etc. etc.

Of course, the Chinese were not allowed to stay, even if they wanted to (although surprisingly many did!), and most of the fear and hatred was just 'cultural' ignorance. It was enough, however, to lead to shameful racist attacks and killings, like those at Lambing Flat. It was the fear that this resentment and violent behaviour would become part of our way of life, as well as pure racism, that led to the legislation that was called the 'White Australia policy'.

So, there are definite overtones of mateship and the desire for democracy and equality implied in the term 'digger'. There are also strong overtones of blatant racism and white supremacist ideology.

It is not exactly accurate to claim that the origin of 'digger' is purely military and began in Gallipoli. There is evidence that it was used between Australians in the Boer War—and there was a very limited amount of trench-digging in that war.

In my opinion, it is far more likely that it was used as a term of recognition, respect and affection between white Australian males from the 1850s onward and was carried over into World War I, where it became recognised as a military term only because large numbers of Australian men were serving together, and using the term, in overseas locations.

CHUNDER

This uniquely Australian term for regurgitation can be easily proven to derive from a hugely popular, long-running series of advertising cartoons that appeared in *The Bulletin* magazine from 1909 to 1920.

However, before we demystify the weird and wonderful (and magnificently politically incorrect) history of Chunder Loo of Akim Foo and Cobra boot polish, we need to dismiss the far more recent attempt to explain the origin of the term, which is a pathetically obvious furphy.

Since the 1960s a story has circulated that 'chunder' is an abbreviated version of an old sailing days warning, 'watch under', that was yelled by sailors who were about to vomit while working aloft in a sailing ship's rigging.

Even at first glance this derivation seems highly unlikely to be valid. Firstly, sailors develop their 'sea legs' relatively quickly and, secondly, they would be unlikely to go aloft feeling obviously nauseous. Then there is the fact that regurgitation usually comes on rather suddenly and the victim is highly unlikely to take the time to shout a warning. Opening the mouth to shout anything would, in all likelihood, precipitate involuntary vomiting.

Although I have no definite proof, I suspect that this story is the work of Barry Humphries who, in the 1960s, invented Bazza McKenzie, a cartoon caricature who represented the ultimate extreme example of the crude Aussie 'ocker'.

The cartoon strip, which was suggested to Humphries by Peter Cook and drawn by Nicholas Garland, began in *Private Eye* magazine in 1964. It was a highly satirical send-up of the uncultured, sex-starved, boozy Australian ex-pat living in London's Earl's Court.

The character became enormously popular, because the idea appealed on so many levels. British readers loved the 'put down' of the stupid Aussie, many Aussies enjoyed the satire and laughed affectionately, recognising an exaggerated version of people they knew. In many ways Bazza was an assertion of 'Aussieness' over English pomposity. On a completely different level, many young Aussie males identified with the character as a role model and hero!

Two movies, *The Adventures of Barry McKenzie* and *Barry McKenzie Holds His Own*, were made and there were popular songs, like 'Chunder in the Old Pacific Sea', 'The Adventures of Barry McKenzie', 'Washed Down the Gutter' and 'Give Her One for Christmas Underneath the Christmas Tree'.

As part of the satire, Humphries invented colourful, pseudo Aussie colloquialisms, such as 'point percy at the porcelain' for urination; 'technicolour yawn', 'rainbow laugh' and 'liquid laugh' for vomiting; and supposedly common Aussie curses like 'May your chooks turn into emus and kick your dunny down.'

(I had the opportunity recently to ask Barry Crocker, who played the part of Bazza McKenzie in the movies, whether it was true that, when the film was shown in the USA, there were sub-titles to explain the Aussie jargon, and the phrase above was sub-titled 'May your fowls turn into large Australian native birds and kick down your outhouse.' Barry confirmed that it was the case!)

In one adventure from the comic strip, Bazza vomits from an upper deck of a ship over a woman on the deck below, who is holding a chihuahua. He rushes down to apologise, sees the tiny vomit-drenched dog and exclaims, 'Struth, I don't remember eatin' that!'

Along with all the newly invented pseudo Aussie terms, Humphries was also responsible for bringing back into popularity genuine Aussie slang words like 'chunder' and phrases like 'up shit creek without a paddle'.

The obviously phony story of the derivation of chunder has a very 'Humphries-like' flavour.

The real derivation is an even better story.

Blyth & Platt Ltd was an English firm, owned by the Rowe family, that manufactured boot polish and various other products very successfully in the UK, at first in Cheshire and later at Watford. One member of the family, Samuel Rowe, was a successful furniture and textile designer of the Arts and Crafts movement who migrated to Australia in 1899 at the age of 29 and became the founder of what is today the National Art School.

Samuel saw opportunities for expanding the family business into Australia and, due to the high protective tariffs on imported products, encouraged the family to set up a factory in Australia in 1908, at Waterloo in Sydney, to manufacture their Cobra brand boot polish.

In 1909 the company began an advertising campaign in the hugely popular *Bulletin* magazine, which involved the artist brothers, Lionel and Norman Lindsay, drawing a full-page cartoon each fortnight, with an accompanying rhyming verse, written by the short-story writer and regular *Bulletin* contributor Ernest O'Ferrall.

As bizarre as it may seem, in the heyday of the White Australia policy, the hero of the cartoon series was an Indian who worked shining shoes at Circular Quay. His heroic exploits were all due to his use of Cobra boot polish. The hero's name was 'Chunder Loo of Akim Foo'. The name sounded vaguely Indian and amusing, and 'Akim Foo' was actually a failed campaign battle in the Ashanti War!

For the first two years, 1909–11, the cartoons appeared fortnightly, drawn by either Norman or Lionel, whose drawing styles were almost indistinguishable.

(Norman's professional drawing career had begun in 1896, when he was seventeen. His older brother Lionel had taken two jobs illustrating, sketching and cartooning for two Melbourne magazines, *Free Lance* and *Hawklet*. When Lionel could not cope, he had young Norman sent to Melbourne from the family home in Creswick and paid him 10 shillings a week to draw what he didn't have time to draw. Norman drew them and Lionel signed them! In 1901 Norman moved to Sydney to work for *The Bulletin*, which he did for more than 50 years.)

The Chunder Loo cartoons became phenomenally popular and *The Bulletin* was the most successful magazine in the land (it was known as 'The Bushman's Bible'). By 1912 the cartoons were appearing weekly.

The 22 October 1912 edition showed Chunder Loo dreaming of winning the Melbourne Cup on a horse named 'Cobra'. The verse by Ernest O'Ferrall read:

> Chunder Loo of Akim Foo goes to sleep as others do.
> Dreams he sees the Melbourne Cup, 'COBRA' winning—Chunder up.
> Shining like a victor's shield, 'COBRA' leads the thund'ring field
> Past the packed and cheering host, up the straight and past the post.
> Chunder with a beaming face, wakes and cries, 'I've won the race!
> Of all dreams, that was a gem! Get my boots and COBRA them!'

The Lindsays and O'Ferrall cleverly made the weekly cartoons topical and amusing. At the start of World War I, Chunder Loo went to war and gave the enemy hell! By this time he had acquired two companions, a koala and a Jack Russell terrier. This was probably Norman's idea, as nobody drew koalas, dogs or cats better than Norman Lindsay.

There were more than 500 Chunder Loo cartoons created and today the originals are collectors' items worth thousands of dollars.

All bushmen, working men and soldiers knew the cartoons and, somewhere along the way, Chunder Loo became universal Aussie rhyming slang for 'spew' and was used by Australian soldiers in World War I. As is usually the case with such colloquialisms, it was soon shortened to just 'chunder'.

PART FIVE

EDWARD HARGRAVES—WHO DIDN'T DISCOVER GOLD IN AUSTRALIA

'If it was so, it might be, and if it were so, it would be: but as it isn't, it ain't. That's logic.'

Through the Looking-Glass, Lewis Carroll, 1871

LIES WE LEARNED AT SCHOOL

One of the greatest lies we were ever told in primary school was that Edward Hargraves was the man who first found gold in Australia and should be regarded as a hero because this wonderful discovery was responsible for a giant leap forward in the history of civilisation—as we know it in Australia.

It simply isn't true. Hargraves was a con man who cheated and betrayed his friends, not once, but many times. He also had no intention of being the first to discover gold in Australia; his plan was only to claim the government's generous reward. In this popular story of our colonial history the hero was, in fact, a villain.

THE OPPORTUNIST

E dward Hammond Hargraves was born at Stoke Cottage in the
village of Alverstoke, near Gosport in Hampshire, on 7 October 1816.

Edward was the third son in a family of fifteen children. His father
was a low-ranking military officer and it seems that young Edward
spent some time being educated at Brighton Grammar School and
Lewes Old Grammar School before going to sea as a cabin boy at the
age of fourteen.

He was tall, strong and robust, and evidently made a good sailor. As
an adult he stood at least 6'3" (some reports say 6'6") and weighed up
to 18 stone in later life. He arrived in Sydney in 1832 aboard Captain
Lister's ship *Wave*. He had served with Captain Lister for a considerable
time and was friendly with the captain and his wife and young son. In
Sydney Hargraves joined the crew of the ship *Clementine*, which headed
north to collect bêche de mer and hunt turtles in Torres Strait.

During this voyage the ship's captain, David Parry-Okeden,
inherited a large sum of money and left the ship to buy property and
become a pastoralist.

The voyage ended in Batavia (modern-day Jakarta), where the ship
was sold and most of the crew, 20 of the 27, died of typhus (some
reports say yellow fever). Hargraves, however, was possessed of a
strong constitution and, having survived the rigours and dangers of
life at sea, returned to Sydney as a crewman on the *Red Rover*, via
London, Cape Town and Hobart, in 1834.

Back in New South Wales he made his way across the Blue Mountains and worked for some time on Captain Hector's property 8 miles from Bathurst before deciding to follow the example set by Captain Parry-Okeden by taking up 100 acres (40 hectares) of land near Wollongong and attempting to become a farmer.

Although he never stuck at anything for very long, Hargraves was, it seems, possessed of a good deal of self-confidence and had the ability, as do many successful people, to make his own luck—often by making good use of people he met throughout his life.

While he was no great success as a farmer he was, evidently, 'lucky in love', for, in 1836 at St Andrew's Cathedral in Sydney, he married Elizabeth Mackay, who came with a substantial dowry that included a number of cottages at East Gosford, a privately developed township north of Sydney, in which Elizabeth's father had invested.

The happy young couple then secured a small place in Australian colonial history by establishing the first general store ever set up south of Wollongong, which they sold in 1839 when they decided to move to East Gosford and establish another business—a general store that also operated as an agency for the General Steam Navigation Company.

Hargraves used part of his wife's dowry to build a pub, The Fox Under The Hill, and became a publican as well as a storekeeper and agent for the General Steam Navigation Company.

By 1843 Edward and Elizabeth had four children and perhaps the tall opportunist was finding family life rather tedious. The pub had failed and he was forced to forfeit the property, leave Elizabeth to run the store, and take up land in the Manning River district further north.

Apparently he was back with Elizabeth by the beginning of 1849—not for long but at least long enough to father the fifth and last of their children, Emma Maria, named after Edward's favourite sister who had died a decade earlier.

By the time baby Emma was born in September 1849, her footloose father had already sold up most of his property, paid some of his debts, and departed for the California goldrush, leaving his pregnant wife to mind the store—and look after the other four kids.

Hargraves left Sydney on a British ship, the *Elizabeth Archer*, in July 1849, and returned from San Francisco in November 1850 aboard a ship called the *Emma*.

Perhaps the more observant readers among you may have noticed a certain wistful irony in the fact that Hargraves chose to return to Australia on a vessel that shared its name with the daughter he had never seen and that he left on a ship that shared the given name of his wife.

But it was not a desire to see his new daughter and be reunited with his family that brought Edward Hargraves scurrying home from California after just sixteen months.

He had left Australia determined to make his fortune on the goldfields but found the work hard for a man of his size and admitted himself that he had little aptitude for the actual work of mining. He had, however, found some friends whose willingness to share their knowledge and skill with him was to prove very useful. Big Edward always did have a way of making good use of his friends.

The two friends in question were fellow passengers on the *Elizabeth Archer*. One of them, Simpson Davison, was an experienced miner with a good understanding of geology. The other was Enoch Rudder, who was travelling to California with his two sons in the hope of making his fortune by way of a new gold-washing machine that he had invented and designed.

The men teamed up for a time and travelled together to the diggings on the Sacramento River, Marysville and Foster Bay. Hargraves tried his luck at several of these places with no success; he was far more successful in getting his two experienced and knowledgeable companions to share their understanding of the geology and mineralogy involved in the business of finding gold. Perhaps more importantly, they had a lot to tell him about the history of gold discoveries in the Blue Mountains area of New South Wales, an area with which they were somewhat familiar. They also showed Hargraves how to construct and operate a cradling machine, the device that uses a plentiful supply of water to wash alluvial gold from soil.

All this information was to be very useful to Edward Hargraves in the not-too-distant future.

What brought him hurrying home from California wasn't homesickness or a desire to see his family, or even the fact that he had failed to find any success on the goldfields.

What brought him back was the knowledge that the New South Wales government had changed its attitude towards the possibility of the existence of large amounts of payable gold in the colony.

Previous to 1850 the colonial administration had suppressed any news of gold discovery for fear of convict riots, uncontrollable population movements and civil unrest.

Transportation had ended in 1840, however, and there was a recession in the colony in the 1840s. And now thousands of men were leaving the colony for the California Rush, which began in 1848. Perhaps it was time for a change of policy. In 1849 the government asked the Colonial Office in England to allow exploration to begin with the purpose of exploiting any mineral resources that could be found in New South Wales and requested a geologist be sent to supervise the process.

The Colonial Office agreed and a reward was then offered for the first person to find 'payable gold' in New South Wales.

Samuel Stutchbury, who had been in the colony previously as a naturalist to the Pacific Pearl Fishery commercial expedition to New South Wales and the Pacific Islands, was appointed as the colony's geologist and arrived in November 1850.

As soon as he heard the news, Edward Hargraves knew where his fortune lay—and it wasn't in California. He had a plan and he took the first available ship home, which happened to be the *Emma*. He left on 23 November 1850 and arrived in Sydney in January 1851, just two months after the arrival of Samuel Stutchbury.

Edward Hargraves had no intention, after leaving California, of making his fortune by finding and mining gold. He only ever intended to make his fortune by claiming to be the first person to discover the precious mineral. He later wrote: 'It was never my intention ... to work for gold, my only desire was to make the discovery, and rely on the Government and the country for my reward.'

In the process of achieving this ambition he lied, exaggerated, twisted the truth and ruthlessly befriended, manipulated and used people whom he later betrayed and cast aside. In the end the part he played in 'discovering' gold was insignificant but he managed to claim the reward and the fame—it was actually a clever con job.

You see, it was a well-known fact that there was 'gold in them thar hills' west of Sydney and the Great Dividing Range. It had been a very poorly kept secret since the 1820s.

Let's take a look at the evidence.

WHO KNEW ABOUT GOLD?

There are accounts of convicts finding traces of gold along the roads they were building across the Blue Mountains as early as 1814 and later in the 1820s, but these are unsubstantiated.

A Russian naturalist named Stein, part of the Bellingshausen scientific expedition that visited New South Wales in 1820, made a twelve-day trip to the Blue Mountains and claimed to have found gold-bearing ore.

James McBrien, the colony's assistant surveyor, made notes in his journal in February 1823 stating that he had found alluvial gold while exploring and surveying along the Fish River to the east of Bathurst.

In 1837, newspapers reported that a Russian stockman had found gold and silver ore 30 miles (50 kilometres) from Segenhoe in the Hunter Valley.

In 1839, the Polish count, explorer and geologist Paul Strzelecki reached Sydney via New Zealand and spent four years making a geological survey zig-zagging back and forth across the colony as far as the Southern Alps, where he climbed what he took to be the highest peak and named it after the Polish democratic leader, Tadeusz Kościuszko.

In 1845 Strzelecki became a British subject, and published in London his *Physical Description of New South Wales and Van Diemen's Land*, for which he received the founder's medal of the Royal Geographical Society.

Strzelecki reported later that when he told the governor, Sir George Gipps, of his discovery of alluvial gold near Hartley in the Blue Mountains and at Wellington in the central west, Gipps 'frightened' him into 'saying nothing about it'.

Strzelecki took mineral samples to show English geologist Sir Roderick Murchison, who examined them and concluded that gold 'would be found in the Eastern Cordillera of Australia'. When he was made president of the Royal Geographical Society in 1844, Murchison, in his first presidential address, predicted the existence of gold in Australia's Great Dividing Range. His ideas were published in a feature in the *Sydney Morning Herald* on 28 September 1847, paraphrased as 'gold will be found on the western flanks of the dividing ranges'.

Another geologist and friend of Murchison's, Reverend William Branwhite Clarke, also arrived in the colony in 1839. He was headmaster of The King's School for two years and then ministered to parishes in the Parramatta, Hawkesbury and Campbelltown districts, before becoming rector of St Thomas' Church in North Sydney, where he died and was buried in 1878. While prospecting between Hartley and Bathurst, Clarke found numerous samples of gold-laden quartz and reported his finds to some members of the New South Wales legislative council. While giving evidence before an 1861 parliamentary inquiry, he stated that, when he showed the samples of gold to the governor, Gipps evidently responded by saying, 'Put it away, Mr Clarke, or we shall all have our throats cut.'

After a government inquiry was held in 1853 into the management of the Australian goldfields and the legitimacy of Hargraves' and others' claims, Clarke was awarded £1000, followed by another £3000, after the inquiry in 1861, and he is credited as the 'scientific discoverer of gold in New South Wales'.

In an area known as Lewis Ponds or Yorkie's Corner, where two creeks converge 10 miles east of the township of Orange, there was local knowledge of gold being discovered by shepherds over many years. One shepherd, the eponymous 'Yorkie', had his hut there and found a nugget that was displayed around the district. There is some suggestion that this was the nugget later shown to Colonial Secretary Edward Deas Thomson by an amateur geologist and mineralogist with the delightful name of Mr William Tipple Smith, though Smith claimed he found the nugget himself.

At least two other shepherds working in the area, a Mr McDonald, working on property owned by William Lane, and a Mr Delaney, working for Henry Perrier, were known to have found gold in the area.

In December 1845, a shepherd arrived at the George Street jewellery shop owned by goldsmith Mr E. Cohen and sold him a 4-ounce (115-gram) gold nugget embedded in quartz, which was, for quite some time, displayed in the window of Cohen's shop.

This prompted William Tipple Smith, who owned an iron foundry and lapidary business in George Street, to make a few trips west of the mountains.

Smith sent mineral samples he had obtained to Sir Roderick Murchison early in 1848 and Murchison contacted the secretary of state, Earl Grey, suggesting a mineral survey of the area where the samples had been taken. It was felt, however, that a goldrush would threaten the colony's economy, especially the lucrative wool trade.

Smith then went to see the colonial secretary in Sydney. He showed Deas Thomson the rock samples and a nugget weighing more than 3 ounces and promised to tell the administration the location of the find in return for a reward. When Governor Charles FitzRoy was informed about the offer, he declined to take it up.

The *Bathurst Free Press* reported, in May 1850, that a shepherd named M'Gregor had found a considerable amount of gold at Mitchell's Creek, near the town of Wellington, over the past several years. The paper was adamant: 'Neither is there any doubt in the fact that Mr M'Gregor found a considerable quantity of the precious metal some years ago, near Mitchell's Creek, and it is surmised he still gets more in the same locality.'

Mr Deas Thomson features again in the saga in 1849. Just after his interview with Mr Smith he was a guest of Thomas Icely, an influential landowner who had property at Carcoar, near Blayney southwest of Bathurst.

The property was being mined by the Belubula Copper Mining Company and the copper miners had discovered samples of gold several weeks before. These were also sent off to Sir Roderick Murchison, who had become convinced, as early as the mid-1840s, that gold could be found west of the mountains in New South Wales and had suggested the idea of sponsoring Cornish miners to migrate to the colony to search for gold in the area.

Ironically, there were already Cornishmen there who would have a part to play in the events that were to follow.

So, who knew there was gold to be found west of the Great Divide before 1851?

Well, various governors certainly knew. Charles FitzRoy, the incumbent at the time, knew, as did his predecessor George Gipps. It is more than likely that Richard Bourke, Ralph Darling and Thomas Brisbane also knew, because James McBrien, the colony's assistant surveyor, knew in 1823, which meant that John Oxley, the surveyor general at the time, must have known too.

Landowners like Thomas Icely, William Lane and Henry Perrier knew.

Explorers and fossickers like Strzelecki, the Reverend Clarke and William Tipple Smith knew.

Shepherds like 'Yorkie', McDonald, Delaney and M'Gregor around Wellington, Orange and Bathurst knew.

Lots of locals in those areas knew and that's probably how Hargraves' Australian friends in California, Simpson Davison and Enoch Rudder, knew (and they told Hargraves what they knew).

Anyone who looked in Cohen's jewellery shop window in George Street knew.

Colonial Secretary Edward Deas Thomson certainly knew, as did famed British geologist Sir Roderick Murchison and the British secretary of state, Earl Grey.

You might be tempted to ask, 'Who didn't know?!'

GOLD FEVER

So, how did a man like Edward Hargraves, a man whose knowledge of geology and mining was very limited and all second-hand (as was his knowledge of the discoveries made over the previous decades just west of the mountains), manage to claim the reward and the fame for 'discovering' gold in Australia?

It's a very good question.

The answer is a little complex.

As soon as Hargraves disembarked on 17 January 1851 he began lobbying the colonial administration for government funding to finance a gold prospecting expedition across the mountains.

Not only did he want the reward from the colonial government for finding the gold—he wanted the colonial government to pay him to find it!

Ever the optimist, Hargraves had boasted, 'There is as much gold in the country I'm going to as there is in California, and Her Most Gracious Majesty, the Queen, God bless her, will appoint me one of her Gold Commissioners.'

The response from the FitzRoy administration to Hargraves' request for funding was a resounding 'no'. The newly appointed Inspector General of Police, William Spain, called the concept 'a wild and unprofitable undertaking'.

Hargraves later reflected on the whole exercise of seeking government assistance by saying, 'One and all, however, derided me, and treated my views and opinions [as those] of a madman.'

Not everyone thought him mad, however, and he did have friends in Sydney.

Always adept at using others, especially friends, to gain his own ends, Hargraves raised enough money for a one-man expedition. Chief contributor was an old friend, William Northwood, who threw in £100.

Equipped with a horse and supplies, and an invitation to visit Thomas Icely at Carcoar (and without bothering to visit his family at Gosford), Hargraves wasted no time in crossing the Blue Mountains. He kept going past Bathurst and met Icely near Blayney.

Hargraves had decided to start his quest by following up information he had gleaned about the shepherd M'Gregor's finds near Wellington. He told Icely his plan and the two men discussed possibilities.

As Hargraves seemed in a great hurry to achieve his goal, Icely suggested that he head straight to Lister's Inn, at the small settlement at Guyong 8 miles (13 kilometres) to the north of Blayney, rather than staying with Icely at Carcoar.

This was an attractive option for Hargraves—for several reasons—but unfortunately he got lost for several days and didn't manage to reach the hotel until 10 February.

One reason Hargraves was happy to head north to stay at Guyong was that it put him much closer to Lewis Ponds, or Yorkie's Corner as it was known locally, and he knew gold had been found there in the past.

The main reason he liked the plan, however, was that it put him back in contact with some old friends—who were sure to come in useful. Based on Icely's description of the pub at Guyong, Hargraves thought he might find a welcome there.

The owner and licensee of the inn was none other than Mrs Susan Lister, wife, and now widow, of Captain John Lister, for whom Hargraves had worked as a cabin boy and sailor.

Hargraves, as we have seen, had first arrived in Sydney as a crewman on Lister's ship the *Wave* and knew the family, having sailed with Mrs Lister and her young son on board on several voyages, including the one to Sydney.

Most accounts of Hargraves' discoveries mention that he was assisted by a young man, John Lister, who he met at Guyong. Those accounts fail to make the connection—John Lister was a long-lost 'friend' whom Hargraves had played with and told yarns to when he was a toddler on his father's ship.

Here was somebody else to use and manipulate!

In 1838, the Listers had settled in Sydney and embarked upon a number of unsuccessful business enterprises.

The first was a shipping agency, which went bankrupt. That was followed by a stint as captain of a coastal trading vessel that foundered in Moreton Bay. The crew were rescued by Aboriginal people, but the vessel was lost.

Then, in 1846, the family took up the licence of a pub on the Wellington road out of Bathurst with the rather long-winded name of the 'Robin Hood and Little John Inn'.

Just six months before his old cabin boy arrived back from California, however, Captain Lister was killed by a fall from his wagon and his widow had taken the family a little further west to run the pub at Guyong, which was rather confusingly named the 'Wellington Hotel', although it was 60 miles from the town of Wellington, which was of course named after the Duke of Wellington . . . as was the pub at Guyong.

Once Susan Lister had recognised and welcomed Hargraves, and Hargraves had chatted to young John about some of the rock samples he noticed around the pub, the intrepid explorer and fortune-seeker decided to postpone his trek to the town of Wellington to follow up leads about M'Gregor's finds, and stay a while at the pub, which was close to the area he had heard so much about—Lewis Ponds or Yorkie's Corner.

This seemed a good plan because, oddly enough, the hotel just happened to be run by the widow of his old boss, who just happened to have a son aged 23, who just happened to know quite a lot about fossicking for gold in the local area.

Within two days the change of plans was proved to be a stroke of sheer genius—or incredibly good luck.

On 12 February John Lister guided Hargraves down Lewis Ponds Creek to a place called Radigan's Gully, some 2 miles from Yorkie's Corner. It was here that the supposedly 'amazing' discovery was made.

In fact, the reason for choosing this site was merely that the summer had been so hot there was little water around and this was the only place that provided sufficient water for Hargraves to do some panning. Apparently Hargraves went through the process six times and on five occasions tiny specks of gold were found.

This was enough for the ever-optimistic Hargraves to proclaim to his young companion, 'Where you walk over now there is gold.'

On a piece of paper torn from the corner of the *Empire* newspaper he wrote, 'Gold discovered in the alluvial at Lewis Ponds Creek this 12th day of February, 1851' and added his signature.

Quite carried away by this rather insignificant find and an overwhelming sense of his own importance he then, apparently, proclaimed to his audience of one, 'This is a memorable day in the history of New South Wales: I shall be a baronet, you will be knighted and my old horse will be stuffed, put in a glass case and sent to the British Museum.'

Hargraves was well aware of the fact that a few tiny specks did not constitute 'payable gold', but he had found something, and that was the main thing. He had a credible witness, although it no doubt also occurred to him that he now was in partnership with the Listers, who had provided horses, equipment and local knowledge for the day's expedition.

He could deal with that problem later. For now he had evidence, a witness and the plan.

He planned to cheat.

He had to make it appear that he'd found substantial amounts of gold at one location and he knew how he could do that. He had to find significant amounts from as many places as possible and put it all together and say it came from the same place.

Hargraves had an idea that the best place to search locally was along tributaries of the Macquarie River, one of which was the Fish River where Assistant Surveyor McBrien had found gold in 1823.

John Lister suggested that they enlist the help of the Tom family, who lived in the nearby Cornish settlement.

James Tom joined the prospecting team and Hargraves headed north to try his luck in the creeks around the township of Wellington, as he had originally planned.

None of the fossickers had any luck and, on his return, Hargraves showed James's brother William Tom, a carpenter, how to construct a 'California-style' cradle to speed up the process of washing earth to find alluvial gold.

William built the cradle in the front room of the family home and Hargraves demonstrated how to use it, then the four men made a verbal pact that no one would say a word until they could produce convincing evidence of a find that produced £1 worth of gold a day. They also agreed that any profits would be shared equally.

Sadly, none of the agreements were made in writing.

Hargraves and John Lister then went east and panned along the Fish and Campbell rivers unsuccessfully. Lister then returned home and Hargraves made his way back to Sydney, leaving the other three to search and cradle the local creeks while he, supposedly, set off for Moreton Bay in Queensland to try his luck there.

While Hargraves and Lister were away, James, William and a third brother, Henry Tom, tried out the cradle successfully, obtaining sixteen grains of gold for three days work.

A LIAR AND A CHEAT

B ack in Sydney, Hargraves immediately broke the solemn promise he had made to Lister and the Tom brothers and visited Colonial Secretary Edward Deas Thomson, asking for £500 as an advance on the reward and claiming to have found payable gold. He was asked to put his request in writing, which he did (neglecting to mention his three 'partners').

Deas Thomson's reply, dated 5 April, said in part: 'I am directed by the Governor to inform you that His Excellency cannot say more at present than that the remuneration of the discovery of gold on the Crown Lands, referred to by you, must entirely depend on its nature and the value when made known . . .'

Hargraves also broke his promise of secrecy by sharing the news of his discovery with his friend from California days, Enoch Rudder, who wrote to the *Sydney Morning Herald* on 4 April 1851, announcing that 'someone' had discovered a goldfield 'extending over a tract of country about 300 miles [480 kilometres] in length'. Hargraves had plans that included the involvement of Mr Rudder, but whether he approved the leaking of the news or not is uncertain.

Meanwhile, west of the Great Divide, events were moving forward very satisfactorily.

On 7 April, John Lister and William Tom, acting on local information about the location of the find made by the shepherd Delaney, panned at the junction of Lewis Ponds Creek and Summer Hill Creek, in other words right 'in' Yorkie's Corner, and William Tom found a nugget weighing more than half an ounce (14 grams).

Over the next five days they used the cradle and found around 2 ounces. Then John Lister walked down the creek a little way and found a nugget weighing 2 ounces in the submerged roots of a tree. They also found a heart-shaped nugget weighing a quarter of an ounce.

John Lister wrote to Hargraves telling him the news and Hargraves returned to Guyong on 5 May. The 4 ounces of gold, worth about £13, was shared equally between the four men and then Hargraves said he wanted it all in his possession when he represented the partnership to the colonial officials—so he paid the three other men for their share of the gold, promising that they would be included as equal partners in his dealings with the government.

The next day Hargraves' friend Enoch Rudder arrived and melted and combined some of the gold to make a larger nugget.

The Tom brothers and John Lister begged Hargraves not to disclose the find until they could stake some official claim and ensure their right to work the area but, on 8 May, Hargraves made his way to Bathurst and met with some of the town's influential citizens and showed them the gold—the larger natural nuggets and the one created by Rudder.

He referred to the gold as 'his' find and officially made the discovery public.

He then waited until the government geologist, Samuel Stutchbury, arrived three days later and took him to the creek, where he was able to produce twenty grains of fine gold from three hours cradling.

The *Bathurst Free Press* reported on 17 May as follows:

> ... the existence of gold is therefore clearly established, and whatever credit or emolument may arise therefrom, Mr. Hargraves is certainly the individual to whom it properly belongs.

The goldrush era had begun.

Stutchbury wrote to the colonial secretary on 19 May:

> ... gold had been obtained in considerable quantity. The number of persons at work and about the diggings (that is occupying about one mile of the creek) cannot be less than 400, and of all classes ... I fear,

unless something is done very quickly, that much confusion will arise in consequence of people setting up claims.

Hargraves was awarded £10,000, appointed as a special commissioner of Crown Lands, and given the use of a covered wagon, two horses and two policemen.

Not to be completely outdone by New South Wales, the new colony of Victoria, which had come into existence on 11 November 1850, also decided to award Hargraves £5000, and actually paid him £2381 of the money. The reason they stopped paying was that news began spreading that the Tom brothers and John Lister were hotly disputing the validity of Hargraves' claim. The remainder of the reward was never paid.

It was, however, all rather late. Hargraves had been too clever for his partners and the horse, as the saying goes, had well and truly bolted.

Hargraves travelled to Britain, where he gave talks as an expert on geology and gold discovery, was made a member of the Royal Society and met Queen Victoria in 1854. He produced a book, *Australia and its Goldfields*, that sold very well, as did life-sized prints of the imposing 'discoverer of gold' painting by T. Balcombe (at 3 bob a print!). The book—except for the parts about Hargraves and his wonderful achievements—was almost certainly ghost-written by his far more knowledgeable friend Simpson Davison.

The City of Sydney gave him an official reception at which he was presented with a 'pure gold cup' supposedly valued at £500. The money for the cup was raised by public subscription, to which Hargraves had donated substantially himself.

In a fitting and hilarious footnote to that affair, Hargraves later melted down the cup and found it to consist mostly of lead and copper!

Hargraves' effrontery knew no bounds. He even claimed to have given the goldfield its name, Ophir, when it was actually William Tom Senior, who was a Wesleyan lay preacher, who suggested the name, which was taken from the name of King Solomon's legendary mine in the Old Testament and related to the First Book of Kings, chapter 9 verse 28—'They came to Ophir and they fetched from thence gold.'

Hargraves not only lied and betrayed and cheated his partners, it seems he could not stand anyone else being credited with any part of the 'discovery'.

He even had the audacity to ask John Lister to sign the following letter and send it to the *Sydney Morning Herald*:

Gentlemen—A report having been spread abroad by some malicious person who evidently is jealous of Mr. Hargraves' great discovery to the effect that I was the party who made it and communicated it to him, I beg leave most unreservedly to contradict this false report, although having been upwards of two years searching for it at one time with two geologists, and mineralogists who told me there were indications but could not find the gold. Mr. Hargraves, during his explorations, called on me as an old friend of my late respected father, and in course of conversation he told me this was a gold country, and if I would keep a secret, he would combine [with] me. This I agreed to—he was as good as his word, and scarcely ever made a failure,—where he said gold was to be found, he found it. I neither understand geology or mineralogy—but I was convinced my friend Mr. Hargraves knows where and how to find gold, and all honour and reward in the late discovery belong to him alone. Indeed, few men would have done what he has, intersecting the country with blacks, sometimes alone, sometimes with my friend Mr. James Tom, and during his explorations, had rain set in, from the imperfect manner in which he was equipped, starvation and death must have been the result. Trusting you will give this publicity in the columns of your valuable journal.

I am, Gentlemen,
Your most obedient servant,
John Hardman Lister

P.S.—I have also heard it reported that Mr. Hargraves had not acted fairly towards me,—I beg most distinctly to state that in all transactions with that gentleman, he has acted strictly honourable with me and friends in the secret of the great discovery. Mr. Hargraves is now no longer connected with me or my party at Ophir, and wherever he may go he has my best wishes, and I believe of all who have known him in the district of Bathurst.

Naturally John Lister not only refused to sign the letter, he openly refuted the claims it made and sent it on to the *Bathurst Free Press* with the following reply:

> I could not subscribe my name to the untruths it contained . . . I also assert in plain words that Mr. James Tom and I never travelled with Mr. Hargraves with any other understanding than that we were his prospecting colleagues and concerned equally with himself in any favourable results that might accrue from our journey or journeys.

I find it puzzling that a man as cunning and manipulative as Hargraves could be so deluded about his own wickedness and besotted with his own sense of importance that he would think that a man he had betrayed and cheated would help him to establish himself in the position he had cheated the other man to gain!

It took 40 years for the other partners in the discovery to gain any real justice. But it was too little too late.

William Tom had, on their behalf, written to the colonial secretary, in June 1851, but all Deas Thomson could say was that Mr Hargraves had made no mention of any partners at any stage in his communications with the government.

They wrote again in December directly to Governor FitzRoy.

Both letters were published in the *Bathurst Free Press* in January 1853, together with an article that made certain accusations.

Finally a government select committee, chaired by the colonial secretary, addressed the claims during June and July 1853.

Hargraves gave evidence, as did the other partners, but by this time Edward Hargraves was acknowledged as a hero of almost legendary status in the colony and Deas Thomson was very sympathetic to his version of events.

Nevertheless, John Lister, William Tom and James Tom were awarded a £1000 reward to be shared between them for 'having played a part' in Hargraves' discovery of payable gold.

Simpson Davison and Enoch Rudder (who had played a part in the 'deception' regarding the amount of gold found) were also 'forgotten' in Hargraves' version of events and did not remain his friends for long. Both published their own accounts of their adventures in

California, in which they claimed that Hargraves' specious claim—that he recognised the similarity in terrain and geology between California and the district around the Ophir Goldfield and knew there was gold there—was, in fact, based on their knowledge of geology, their knowledge of both areas and their observations, which they had discussed with Hargraves while in California.

In his 1860 book *The Discovery and Geognosy of Gold Deposits in Australia*, Davison questioned the integrity of the colonial secretary and questioned why he was so slow in considering evidence that cast doubt on Hargraves' claims.

Hargraves revelled in his fame and celebrity status. Some 20 miles from East Gosford he built a grand house that was partly a replica of Stoke Cottage, where he was born. When he was staying at the house, which he called 'Noraville', rather than his other residence at Forest Lodge in Sydney, he flew a flag to indicate he was 'in residence' like a member of the royal family.

His travels and lavish lifestyle saw him practically broke in less than ten years, so he used his Masonic connections to attempt to get the remainder of the Victorian reward and to lobby the New South Wales parliament to pay him an annuity—and was finally granted £250 a year in 1877.

Invited by the Western Australian government in 1862 to advise them on finding gold in that colony, he explored and confidently reported that gold would never be found there.

(Between 1892 and 2012, more than ten thousand tons of gold were mined in Western Australia, which still produces 70 per cent of Australia's gold each year.)

The controversy about Hargraves' claim never went away and finally, in August 1890, a second select committee was appointed to again investigate the affair. John Lister and the Tom brothers were now old men and John Lister died from influenza on the day he was to give evidence. His son, daughter and sister all died of the same disease within the following week.

Lister's other sister, Mrs Bates, said in her evidence that the gold her brother and Hargraves found in 1851 consisted of 'three specks and they were so small I could not see them distinctly with the naked eye'. The gold found between 7 and 12 April by John Lister and William

Tom, on the other hand, amounted to more than 4 ounces.

In December 1890 the second select committee into the claims made by Lister and the Tom brothers announced that they were 'undoubtedly the first discoverers of payable gold in Australia', and that given the 'substantial improvement in trade in the colony' their discovery had brought about 'the petitioners had not been adequately rewarded'.

While their claims were finally justified, the New South Wales parliament did not give assent to the committee's findings and no additional reward was paid.

A memorial column, unveiled at the Ophir Goldfield by the minister for mines in 1923, states that those responsible for the discovery of payable gold in Australia were Edward Hammond Hargraves, John Hardman Australia Lister, James Tom and William Tom.

Hargraves died at Forest Lodge in Sydney on 29 October 1891 of pneumonia. Although he had received more than £12,000 in rewards and an annuity of £250 yearly, he left an estate of just £370. Even in death he was the subject of publicity-seeking sensationalism, with a story being circulated that he had died in a riding accident.

The Tom brothers made some money exhibiting the original 'California-style' cradle and the heart-shaped nugget at agricultural shows for a time. The heart-shaped nugget is now owned by the Orange Historical Society.

As late as 1924 the younger sister of the Tom brothers, Selina Webb, who had been a witness to many of the events and conversations as a fifteen-year-old girl, was still writing to the press telling their side of the story.

In the meantime, millions of little Australians learned that 'Edward Hargraves discovered gold in Australia'.

It was all so much simpler in primary school.

PART SIX

THE MYTH OF NED KELLY'S REPUBLIC AND REBEL HERITAGE

'Consider your verdict,' the King said to the jury.
'Not yet, not yet!' the Rabbit hastily interrupted. 'There's a great deal to come before that!'

Alice's Adventures in Wonderland, Lewis Carroll, 1865

WHEN TRUTH IS LESS WELCOME THAN FICTION

I t is a furphy that Ned Kelly had an Irish rebel heritage or any notion of leading an uprising to form a republic in North East Victoria.

Attempting to unearth the truth about the Kelly Gang is a risky business. It's much easier to repeat and promote the myths, as most biographers have done in recent times, or to create new myths by fictionalising the story even further, as writers like Peter Carey and Peter FitzSimons and artist Sidney Nolan have done, with great success. I think the fact that the world's first multi-reel feature film, *The Story of the Kelly Gang*, which premiered at the Athenaeum Theatre in Melbourne on Boxing Day 1906, has a lot to do with it. The first time most Australians became aware of the story was through the powerful new medium of the cinema—and it was a fictional account.

The truth lies somewhere between the extreme opinions about Ned expressed over the last 140 years.

For example, Peter FitzSimons claims that:

All of the contemporary accounts of Ned [are] that he was the best rider, the best bushman, the best fighter, the best leader of men . . . the strongest . . . the complete package . . .

Promotional video for *Ned Kelly*, 2014

On the other hand historian Malcolm Ellis, in *The Bulletin*, 31 December 1966, calls Ned:

> . . . one of the most cold-blooded, egotistical and utterly self-centred criminals who ever decorated the end of a rope in an Australian jail. His . . . utter vengefulness, his cruelty, his cold-blooded lack of regret at the wiping out of the lives of decent men can only repel.

I would dispute FitzSimon's claim on the grounds that many 'contemporary accounts' actually painted Ned as a despicable thief and murderer, and his fighting reputation (Ned claimed to be the boxing champion of North Eastern Victoria) was based on a boxing match against his friend Isaiah 'Wild' Wright, a fellow member of the Greta Mob.

Malcolm Ellis, on the other hand, certainly cuts Ned no slack in terms of his background, or his heroism in saving another child's life when he was eleven years old.

To add to the almost religious fervour of the 'Ned Kelly as Hero of the Downtrodden' myth is the belief, propagated by some writers and believed by some Australians, that, at the time of the 'Kelly outbreak', there was an uprising of poor, decent folk imminent in North East Victoria, and that it aimed to establish a new republic and overthrow the colonial government.

To many of us, who have seen the impact of fake news over the past decade, this sort of thing, although it is bewildering, is not surprising.

Only a fool would plunge headlong into the 'Ned Kelly hero or villain' debate. However, it was something that I did, albeit in a light-hearted fashion, at the Port Fairy Folk Festival in 2011.

As part of the festival's spoken-word program, which it has been my pleasure and privilege to help organise for more than 25 years, myself and my good friend, author, performer and folklorist the late Dennis O'Keeffe, invented an event called the 'True Blue'. This was a light-hearted two- or three-sided debate (or argument) in which the audience was invited to vote and comment.

The 'True Blue' was designed as entertainment rather than a serious insight into our history and we argued such things as 'Who was the most *Australian* poet—Paterson, Lawson or C.J. Dennis?' That year Henry Lawson, represented by local boy Dennis O'Keeffe, won easily on the audience vote; C.J. Dennis, represented by C.J. Dennis authority Dr Stephen Whiteside, was a respectable second audience choice; and poor old Banjo Paterson, represented, obviously not too well, by myself, received hardly a vote.

In 2011 the 'True Blue' was a two-hander between myself and Dennis. The topic was 'Ned Kelly—Hero or Villain?'

I should point out, for those who do not know that part of western Victoria, that Port Fairy was once called 'Belfast' and the nearby town of Koroit, which conducts an annual Irish festival, calls itself 'the most Irish town in Australia'. The census figures for the district's main city of Warrnambool show that, of those professing to be Christian, the Catholics easily outnumber the non-Catholics, and the percentage of Catholics in the population of Warrnambool is almost 50 per cent greater than the national average.

In retrospect it's easy to see my foolishness in accepting the challenge to take the 'villain' side of the Ned Kelly argument—in fact, I would have been happy to take either side—but my mate and Warrnambool-born-and-bred Dennis gave me no option. Needless to say, the result was an overwhelming victory for Ned Kelly as a hero. My arguments were so loudly and regularly 'booed' that I felt like an AFL footballer from a non-Victorian team, taking a set shot for goal against Collingwood at a packed MCG (or, more appropriate to the district, against Geelong at Kardinia Park)!

Until that time I had never researched or explored the Ned Kelly story in any depth. As a member of a 'bush band' in the 1970s and 1980s I had often sung the Redgum song 'Poor Ned', and had even co-written a song about Ned's last stand at Glenrowan called 'Fire in the Heart'.

The small amount of research I did for that event brought me into contact with some of the less savoury hard facts and undeniable truths of the Ned Kelly story and gave me an understanding of why some historians opposed the notion that Ned was some sort of hero.

I have no intention of revisiting the 'villain or hero' debate in full here in print. Space does not permit and there have been many millions of words written, presenting both sides of the story, in hundreds of books, newspaper articles, academic papers and website blogs. Also, I am still mentally scarred and bruised from the hammering I received from Dennis and the Port Fairy Folk Festival audience in 2011.

However, the recurring myths of the 'Kelly republican uprising' and Ned's supposed 'rebel heritage' cannot be allowed to go unchallenged.

THE CREATION OF THE 'REPUBLIC' MYTH

The myth of the 'Kelly Republic' is based partly on a mischievous media furphy that began twenty years after the event in *The Bulletin* magazine of 9 June 1900. The furphy was itself a kind of amalgam of previous newspaper and magazine comments and articles. In other words, the sort of thing the media has always done.

Having fun at the expense of the Kelly Gang, and the police, was nothing new.

On 27 March 1879, while the gang was still on the run, *Melbourne Punch* published what was obviously a 'joke letter' from Ned, 'per Dan', under the heading 'LATEST FROM MR. KELLY'. The letter gave the return address of 'Wombat Ranges' and claimed the gang had kidnapped Police Commissioner Standish and 'two other perlice' who, if the gang didn't receive free pardons, 'will be killed without fear or favor, and the lord hav mercy on there soles'.

The postscript to the letter reads:

Ain't this a prime game, old Punchey? The govment darn't let 'em be killed in coled blood, and there is no alternatif but to give us al a pardon, and let us clear out of the coloni with our swag like gents. Dan says he'll go to Urope, and do the 'gran tour'. I shall make for Texas, 'osses is plentiful th'are. Hart is agoing to turn parson, and preche agin bushranging, and Byrne is agoing to jine the Perlice force in the old country.

Not all the fake news surrounding the gang, however, was so obviously a send-up, joke or spoof.

Let's try to follow the 'paper trail' that led, twenty years later, to *The Bulletin*'s article and the subsequent myth of the Kelly Republic.

On 2 July 1880, five days after the siege at Glenrowan and the capture of Ned, the *Sydney Evening News* reported:

> It is rumoured that in Ned Kelly's possession [after his capture] was found a pocket book, containing a number of letters, implicating persons in good positions, and the name of one Member of Parliament is mentioned. The authorities will give no information on the subject. Ned Kelly is said to be very anxious to see representatives of the Press.

The report was picked up and published by several other newspapers in the colony of New South Wales but, as Dr Stuart Dawson of Monash University quite rightly states:

> It does not mention any republican document or sentiments. Given that Kelly made no political statements when he was interviewed at length by reporters shortly after his capture, it is likely—if the rumour was true—that the letters were rambling self-justifications like those he sent to parliamentarian Donald Cameron MLA after the Euroa bank robbery . . . and tried to have printed at Jerilderie.

Three months before the siege, on 8 April 1880, the *Ovens and Murray Advertiser* ran an article on the failure of the reward offered by the colonies of New South Wales and Victoria to have any effect on finding the gang, and launched an outraged attack on the locals who remained silent through fear or tacit support:

> And then this hero Kelly—the monster not only shot Kennedy through the heart; but, like the commonest thief, rifled his pockets, and stripped the very rings from the fingers of his dead companions. It is almost impossible to conceive how such a butchery should be condoned, or such a miscreant forgiven; and yet he has not only sympathisers amongst the ignorant who would not touch the money

placed on his head, but intelligent apologists who, it is true, may be influenced more by fear than favor. It is not in the least too much to say that nine out of ten bush-hands and swagmen heartily applaud every act of the gang.

Twenty years later *The Bulletin* apparently used these two newspaper references to help construct an item for the magazine's 'Aboriginalities' page. 'Aboriginalities' began as 'Bush Pars' when the magazine came into existence in 1880.

Patricia Rolfe, in her comprehensive history of *The Bulletin, The Journalistic Javelin* (1979), describes 'Bush Pars' as 'anecdotal paragraphs' about life in the bush, mostly sent in by readers. Often paragraphs were added by staff writers to fill out the page. Often the page was omitted altogether, due to lack of contributions. Rolfe tells us:

In the first years something called Bush Pars appeared and disappeared . . . Aboriginalities made its first appearance in the late 1880s but it was clearly impossible to find enough material each week so it came and went.

On 9 July 1900, the 'Aboriginalities' page included this 'par' (paragraph or pithy short article). It was the only one without a contributor's name attached:

If certain statements contained in reports in the Vic. Police Department anent the Kelly Gang are to be believed, that crowd narrowly escaped making a political landmark in Australian history. These reports indicated the existence of such a widespread state of disaffection in N.E. Victoria owing to what was called the 'remand-ring' as applied to persons 'guilty' of being Kelly sympathisers, that the Kellys had determined to take advantage of it for their own purposes. They had resolved, it was said, after having upset the special train containing the police from Melbourne, to make a cut across country from Glenrowan to Benalla, destroying bridges and telegraph lines en route, and there to have proclaimed N.E. Vic. a republic with Benalla as capital. This move was stopped by the failure of the effort to

destroy the train, owing to a miscalculation of the time at which it was
to arrive. But for this hitch, it is asserted, nothing could have averted
the railway catastrophe as a prelude to the Presidency of Edward Kelly,
Esq., supported by nine men out of every ten in the disaffected district.

The reference to the 'remand-ring' concerns the fact that 23 'known
Kelly Gang sympathisers' were arrested and held in remand for as
long as three months while the gang was at large. The arrests began on
3 January 1879 and the last of those arrested was released on 22 April
1879. It is true that many people saw this as a serious breach of normal
justice. The suspension of *habeas corpus* in Ireland in 1866, in order
to prevent the Fenian uprising, was fresh in the minds of many in the
Australian colonies in 1879, and still remembered in 1900.

The Bulletin's concoction of two twenty-year-old newspaper references to make a furphy to fill the 'Aboriginalities' page was described
as 'a bit of mischief' by Kelly researcher and historian Doug Morrissey
in his 2015 book *Ned Kelly—A Lawless Life*. It was, however, the sort
of thing *The Bulletin* did regularly, and the items on the 'Aboriginalities' page were never guaranteed, or indeed expected by readers,
to be 100 per cent true.

The 'Kelly Republic in North East Victoria' furphy reached its most
'accepted as history' level four decades later, and the perpetrator was
a well-known broadcaster and author of books of Australian folk tales
and oddities: Bill Beatty.

Beatty was born in Paddington in 1902 to Irish-born Catholic
parents and attended Christian Brothers School in Waverley. He was
an excellent pianist and worked as a piano teacher and clerk before
joining the Catholic radio station 2SM in 1936 as a pianist and host of a
light-hearted Australiana program called *Cuckoo Court*. He joined the
Australian Broadcasting Commission in 1941 and wrote and hosted
almost 500 weekly programs of historical curiosities and amazing facts
called *Australoddities*. His popular historical anecdotes appeared as an
illustrated weekly column called 'Believe Bill Beatty' in the *Wireless
Weekly* (1939–41) and the *ABC Weekly* (1941–43).

The first of his many published collections of folk tales and anecdotes, gleaned from old magazines and newspaper articles, *This
Australia, Strange and Amazing Facts,* appeared in 1941. It contained

this 'story', which he repeated in various forms in subsequent collections:

> Did you know that had not a certain train been running late, in one
> period of our history we might have had an Australian Republic with
> Ned Kelly as the President? After the Kelly Gang had been broken
> up, certain papers and documents were found which indicated that
> Ned went close to altering the whole political history of Victoria. It
> is stated that if Ned had succeeded in wrecking the police train he
> intended proclaiming north-eastern Victoria a republic, with Benalla
> the capital city and himself as first President. Only the fact that the
> train was running late put the knocker on the gang's plans and hopes.
> Had the plan carried, it is certain large numbers would have flocked to
> the banner of the Kellys, for their sympathisers were legion through-
> out Australia.

Among other publications, the story was repeated in the very popular *A Treasury of Australian Folk Tales and Traditions*, which was first published by Ure Smith in 1960 and ran to second, third and fourth impressions (i.e. republished) in 1961, 1963 and 1965.

The idea was subsequently picked up and inserted into Kelly mythology by biographers, as early as Max Brown, in *Australian Son* (1948), then John Moloney, *I Am Ned Kelly* (1980), and Ian Jones, *Ned Kelly: A Short Life* (2003).

By the time the idea had passed from *The Bulletin* to Beatty to Brown it had become:

> In the first hour of his capture, the police took from Kelly's pocket
> a declaration for a republic of north-eastern Victoria.

It is amazing how this notion, once generated, slips into the 'history'. It becomes part of the Kelly legend and evidence is then found to corroborate the furphy, in retrospect, as biographers begin to reassess the events and Ned's dictated letters looking for hints of republican sentiments.

In the letter written at Euroa to Member of the Legislative Assembly Donald Cameron, Ned, dictating to Joe Byrne, states:

I have no intention of asking mercy for myself or any mortal man, or apologising, but wish to give timely warning that if my people do not get justice, and those innocents released from prison, and the police wear their uniform, I shall be forced to seek revenge of everything of the human race for the future.

This demand appears in both the Euroa letter to Cameron and the later Jerilderie letter and 'my people' has been fancifully misinterpreted as meaning those supporting Ned's fabled political aims.

The 'innocents' referred to are not 'freedom fighters' or even Kelly sympathisers. The arresting and remanding in custody of the 23 men regarded as 'sympathisers' had not occurred when this letter was written.

'Innocents' here obviously refers to those arrested in relation to the Fitzpatrick shooting (Ned's mother, Ellen, Ned's sister's husband, William Skillion, and their neighbour Brickey Williamson) and those receiving horses known to be stolen by Ned and Dan (the Baumgarten brothers). 'My people' simply refers to Ned's family and close friends.

In the Jerilderie letter Ned demands that the authorities 'give those people who are suffering innocence, justice and liberty'. The only way this makes any sense is that Joe Byrne misspelled 'innocents' as 'innocence'. In other words, it's the same demand as the one in the Euroa letter.

Although the 23 sympathisers had been arrested by the time the Jerilderie letter was written, this is not a demand to release them as some have implied. In fact, Ned never mentions them at all in any interviews or letters.

Ian Jones was so keen to imply that the phrase 'give those people who are suffering innocence, justice and liberty' is a republican demand that, in at least one publication, according to historian Stuart Dawson, Jones inserted the word 'in' and claimed the text of the Jerilderie letter reads 'give those people who are suffering *in* innocence, justice and liberty'.

Jones, in *Ned Kelly: A Short Life*, claims the Jerilderie letter 'contains the only available fragments of a rebel manifesto that underlay the attempt to proclaim a republic in the north-east'.

John Moloney, in *I Am Ned Kelly* (1980), declares that Ned's diatribe about his family and friends being mistreated is an indication that the gang's battle with the law represents evidence that a 'far wider circle of people in the northeast . . . felt that in some way the struggle . . . was the struggle of them all'.

It is drawing a very long bow to claim that, in among the rants against the police, interspersed with tangential uninformed views of history, racist remarks and egotism, there is any evidence that Ned is calling for a republic in the Jerilderie letter. It's much easier to see the letter as an illogical tirade of self-justification by a man who has murdered three policemen.

Time and again the letter begins some bizarre argument about imaginary situations, demonstrating a complete ignorance of any real grasp of history or general knowledge, that quickly turns into 'poor me', 'it's all about me' egomaniacal ravings:

> What would England do if America declared war and hoisted a green flag as it is all Irishmen that has got command army forts of her batterys, even her very life guards and beef tasters are Irish. Would they not slew round and fight her with their own arms for the sake of the color they dare not wear for years and to reinstate it and rise old Erin's isle once more from the pressure and tyrannism of the English yoke, and which has kept in poverty and starvation and caused them to wear the enemy's coat. What else can England expect, is there not big fat necked unicorns enough paid to torment and drive me to do thing [sic] which I dont [sic] wish to do without the public assisting them.

There's a lot about Ned's friends and family being innocent, revenge, self-justification and a personal vendetta and there's a lot about 'old Erin' and convicts, but nothing at all about the idea of an uprising to form a republic. As Stuart Dawson points out, genuine republican and Irish uprisings in colonial history, like the Vinegar Hill rebellion and the Eureka Stockade, don't seem to exist in Ned's fantasy world of anecdotal generalisations about the convict days and the troubles of 'Old Erin'.

On 2 January 1914, the *Jerilderie Herald and Urana Advertiser* ran an article about the letter and quoted the town's schoolteacher, William Elliott, the man who read the letter and wired a precis to the *Melbourne Argus*. Elliott is quoted as saying that, in general, the letter was, in his opinion, 'little better than emanations of wild fancies from a disordered brain'.

Personally, I fail to see how anyone can disagree with Dawson's conclusion that:

> There is no support for the Kelly republic theory in the Jerilderie letter. The claim is built on the false hypothesis of its being a precursor document for a 'declaration of a republic' that never existed.

It is hard to calculate just how much support Ned *did* have before the myth grew larger than the man and Ned Kelly became a symbol of 'Australianness', gameness and republicanism.

The sarcastic and derogatory editorial 'aside' in the *Ovens and Murray Advertiser* on 8 April 1880 that 'nine out of ten bush-hands and swagmen' in the local area covertly took pleasure in the Kelly Gang's exploits is nowhere near being accurate. In fact, the detailed demographic analysis undertaken by Doug Morrissey for his Honours thesis in History at Latrobe University in 1977, 'Ned Kelly's Sympathisers', calculates that less than two men out of ten in the parishes of Greta, Lurg and Glenrowan were Kelly sympathisers.

Morrissey found that the support for Kelly has generally been exaggerated by his sympathetic biographers (and by outraged newspaper editors at the time). Much of the 'support' was also obviously based on fear and a desire to be 'left alone' by the gang. Stuart Dawson summarises Morrissey's findings this way:

> The nucleus of this support was the Greta Mob, the group of bush larrikins (hooligans) who accepted Ned Kelly as their leader. Numbering about forty, 83 per cent of its members were the Australian-born sons of Irish-born parents, and 56 per cent had been convicted for criminal offences, mostly horse-stealing. If we take the wider group of 124 people identified by the police as active Kelly supporters, 78 per cent were of Irish birth or parentage.

About a hundred people attended Dan's funeral after his death at Glenrowan, which seems to tally with Morrissey's assumptions about local support and the police calculations. There was no trouble at the funeral.

Many local settlers were fed up with the government's poor efforts at policing and an inept, underfunded police force. To them the Kellys were highlighting a problem. Some selectors, but certainly not a majority, had gripes against the system of land distribution but this was not a case of the 'poor' against the 'ruling class', or the persecuted Irish against authority, as Ned attempted to make out in the letters.

Similarly, Kelly sympathisers point to the 34,434 signatures collected to have Ned's death sentence commuted. On the other hand, that campaign was mostly conducted by the Society for the Abolition of Capital Punishment. It was more about opposition to capital punishment than it was about Ned Kelly. Of course, the conservative press claimed many in 'Kelly Country' were forced to sign it and the *Sydney Morning Herald* pompously reported, on 9 November 1880, that:

> An examination of the petitions showed that they were signed principally in pencil, and by illiterate people, whilst whole pages were evidently written by the one person.

Some wag also apparently pointed out that at least 245,566 citizens out of Melbourne's 280,000 residents had chosen *not* to sign it!

As far as being truly representative of the poor battlers and free selectors, who supposedly saw Ned as a leader who was 'just like them' and would trust him to create a new republic, the Kellys, especially after the death of father and husband John 'Red' Kelly, were far from being 'typical' battlers or free selectors.

A year after Red's death, matriarch Ellen moved the family to a derelict hotel building in Greta in May 1867. They shared the dwelling with two of her sisters, who had married the two Lloyd brothers, and their children. The two husbands were in prison for horse theft. On 27 January 1868, Red's brother, James 'Jim' Kelly, recently released from prison, set fire to the building after a drunken argument with Ellen. The three sisters and their families (sixteen people in total) survived the fire. In April the following year Jim Kelly was convicted of attempted murder and sentenced to death, commuted to fifteen years in prison. He spent most of the rest of his life in Ararat and Beechworth lunatic asylums.

By the time Jim was sentenced Ellen had moved the family onto an 88-acre (36-hectare) selection at 'The Eleven Mile', 5 kilometres west of Greta and about 8 kilometres south of Glenrowan. Her brothers and sisters lived in this area and her father, James Quinn, had taken a lease on the nearby Glenmore Run in the King Valley in 1864, after he sold a property in Wallan.

The Glenmore Run was a perfect conduit for stolen horses and cattle between the colonies of Victoria and New South Wales. It was also a safe haven for the notorious escaped bushranger Harry Power, a family friend of the Quinns and Lloyds. Ellen and her sons never made any attempt to farm the selection; Ellen turned it into a 'sly grog' shanty and primitive doss house. The floor of the rough slab hut was dirt, the walls were hessian.

The Quinn clan arranged for Ned, from the age of thirteen, to help Harry Power in his highway robberies as a sort of apprentice. Ned's first arrest, however, was for assaulting a Chinese miner and peddler, named (hilariously) Ah Fook. The case was unproven.

These are the police court records for Ellen and her three sons:

Ellen Kelly

1867	Abusive and threatening language—£2
1870	Illegally selling alcohol—Discharged
1871	Furious riding in a public place—Discharged
1872	Stealing a saddle—Discharged
1878	Aiding and abetting attempted murder—3 years

Edward 'Ned' Kelly

1869	Assault and robbery—Discharged
1870	Robbery in company; robbery under arms (twice)—Discharged
1870	Violent assault—3 months; sending an indecent letter— 3 months (this was the result of sending calves' testicles to the childless wife of a family enemy)
1871	Horse stealing and receiving—3 years

| 1877 | Drunk and disorderly—1 shilling; assaulting police— £2 and 5 shillings; resisting police—£2 |
| 1880 | Horse theft, attempted murder and murder—Death |

Dan Kelly

1871	Illegal use of a horse—Discharged
1876	Stealing a saddle—Discharged
1877	Violent assault; breaking in and stealing; wilful damage—Discharged
1880	Horse theft and murder—(Died at Glenrowan)

Jim Kelly

1871	Illegal use of a horse—Discharged
1873	Cattle stealing (two counts)—5 years
1878	Horse stealing—3 years

When Ned was arrested at age fifteen for 'Robbery in company' he was held until he gave information that helped the police find and arrest Harry Power. Although it was Ned's uncle, John Lloyd, who led the police to the bushranger's hide-out, Power never forgave Ned and openly accused him of treachery for the rest of his life, both in and out of prison. Power outlived Ned by eleven years and was never backward in coming forward to blacken Ned's reputation with accusations that he was betrayed by Ned.

Even some within the Quinn/Lloyd/Kelly mob, along with others in the district, were treating Ned as an outcast. At age fifteen Ned wrote to the police asking for help. The note ended in a poorly punctuated plea:

Every one looks on me like A black snake send me
An answer as soon possible

When the police arranged for Ned to go and work on a sheep station over the border, Ellen vetoed the idea.

Between 1860 and 1879 seven of Ellen's brothers, brothers-in-law and nephews were charged with a total of 42 crimes and convicted of 16 including assault, wilful damage, indecent assault, bodily harm, murderous assault, horse and cattle theft and maliciously killing horses.

While running the 'sly grog' shanty Ellen became pregnant to a man named Frost and successfully took him to court for maintenance of the child. That court victory resulted in the drunken ride through town for which she was arrested but discharged. While Ned was in prison in 1872, she met a 23-year-old American named George King and had his child. They married in 1874 and she eventually bore him three children.

Ned claimed he went 'straight' after his release and for a brief time he worked cutting timber and in a sawmill, but then became a self-confessed systematic horse thief in collaboration with his stepfather, brother Dan, uncles and cousins.

When the whole operation was beginning to be exposed in early 1878, warrants were issued for the Baumgarten brothers, who were receiving the stolen horses on the other side of the Murray River. Later warrants were issued for the arrest of Dan and Ned for horse stealing and this led to policeman Alexander Fitzpatrick's ill-advised attempt to arrest Dan, the event that triggered Ellen's arrest and the outlawing of the gang.

One thing that is rarely explored in depth is the disappearance of Ellen's second husband, George King. This occurred around the time of the Baumgarten arrests. There is no evidence of an American aged around 30 anywhere in the colony after 1878. There are two theories.

The first is that, with the criminal operation exposed, King, who had married Ellen and fathered her last three children, deserted her, 'shot through' and changed his name.

The second is that King was beating Ellen (there were rumours of repeated domestic violence) and he and Ned went for a ride to look at some horses and only Ned returned.

Whatever the truth is, the Kellys never mentioned him again. Ellen was always referred to as 'Mrs Kelly' although she was actually 'Mrs King'. George King's children were raised as 'Kellys'.

Ned ended the Jerilderie letter with the famous line 'I am a widow's son, outlawed and my orders must be obeyed.' Although the letter is full of egotistic, self-justifying nonsense, I can't help wondering whether that statement was, technically, true—and Ned knew it.

To claim that the Kellys, Quinns and Lloyds were 'typical Aussie battlers' is an insult to the real battlers who settled in the bush and built a decent life there.

Under the revised *Land Acts* of the 1860s, almost 80 per cent of selectors in the Greta district successfully gained freehold of their selections within the required ten years. About half of them achieved this result purely by farming and the other half by working at other jobs and farming.

Only 10 per cent of selectors regularly defaulted on their payments and one of those was Ellen Kelly, who took 23 years to satisfy the requirements for the selection at The Eleven Mile.

The rest of the story has been written a thousand times; it goes like this.

A warrant was issued for the arrest of Ned and Dan for horse stealing. A policeman named Fitzpatrick foolishly attempted to arrest Dan at The Eleven Mile hut. Dan and Ellen attacked him. Ned, who claimed he was not there, shot him in the wrist. Ned and Dan fled into hiding in the Wombat Ranges. Ellen was arrested and sentenced to three years. A party of four police was sent to track down gang members Dan, Ned, Steve Hart and Joe Byrne. The gang ambushed the police and killed three of them at Stringybark Creek.

The four fugitives then held up and robbed the towns of Euroa in Victoria and Jerilderie in New South Wales and planned a showdown by murdering a former gang member, Aaron Sherrit. This, as expected, brought a train load of police to Glenrowan. The gang forced fettlers camped near Glenrowan Station to tear up the tracks and then held more than 30 locals prisoner in Anne Jones's hotel for 24 hours while they waited for the train. The plan was to kill all the police, either in the train wreck or by shooting the survivors.

The siege occurred when the train arrived safely after Ned allowed a schoolteacher named Curnow to leave the pub to attend to his supposedly sick wife. Curnow stopped the train at 2.30 a.m. on 27 June 1879. The siege began at 3 a.m. The four outlaws donned their heavy armour and went onto the verandah and invited the police to shoot. A gun battle ensued in which two hostages were killed by stray police bullets.

Ned left the hotel wounded and, unable to mount his horse, lay in the bush until 7 a.m. He then attacked the police and was shot down and captured. Joe Byrne was shot through the groin under his armour and died. The last of the hostages were released at 10 a.m. Dan Kelly and Steve Hart refused to surrender. The police set fire to the hotel at 4 p.m. Dan and Steve possibly suicided, or were burned to death in the fire.

It has been proposed that members of the Greta Mob were to be called by Ned to help hunt down any survivors of the train wreck and the signal was the firing of two rockets. When the train wreck never happened, there were reports that two rockets were fired from the besieged pub, but the only ones to arrive were two of Ned's sisters and Greta Mob member Isaiah 'Wild' Wright, who were on their way anyway and made no attempt to interfere with the police.

The supposed rallying of an army of sympathisers, predicted in some accounts to occur at Glenrowan once the train was wrecked, never happened. Neither, of course, did the train wreck. The story that Ned left the hotel to ride off and turn back a large group of supporters is pure fantasy. The timeframe from the verandah gun battle from 4.30 to 5 a.m. and Ned's surprise appearance out of the mist to attack the police at 7 a.m. doesn't fit. While awaiting execution, Ned told another prisoner that, badly wounded and weighed down by 90 kilograms of metal, he couldn't even mount his horse after leaving the hotel.

Ned was tried, and hanged in Melbourne Gaol on 11 November 1880.

THE TRUE STORY OF
JOHN 'RED' KELLY

The second furphy that props up the notion that the Kelly uprising was about republicanism, the rebel spirit and a consequence of persecution of the Irish derives from misinformation about Ned's father, John 'Red' Kelly, and claims that he was an 'Irish rebel'. He was, in fact, convicted of stealing pigs.

In 1929 a book called *The Complete Inner History of the Kelly Gang and their Pursuers* was published at Moe in Victoria by The Kelly Gang Publishing Company Pty Ltd.

In effect, The Kelly Gang Publishing Company was also the author, Catholic schoolteacher, trade unionist and Labor Party stalwart J.J. Kenneally, and the book was a defence of the Kellys against what Kenneally believed to be the lies told by other historians.

The book was also Kenneally's reaction to the sectarian antagonism towards Catholics in Victoria, which was keenly felt in the 1870s debate over state aid to Catholic schools, Bishop Mannix's opposition to conscription in World War I and the attempt by Catholics to take over the Labor Party.

Bob Reece, in his article 'Ned Kelly's Father' in *Exiles from Erin*, notes that Kenneally's response to the claim that the Kellys were nothing more than poor, habitual or even hereditary criminals was:

> ... not to investigate John Kelly's Irish background more closely, but
> to invest him instead with an Irish nationalist pedigree at a time when

memories of Easter 1916 were still fresh and the Irish Free State was just eight years old.

Kenneally certainly did that. Here is his description of Ned's father:

> John (Red) Kelly, the father of Ned and Dan, was born in Co. Tipperary, Ireland. He was a fearless young man of some education and outstanding ability. He was the type of young Irish patriot who was prepared to make even the supreme sacrifice for his country's freedom. He was a man whom the landlords and their henchmen regarded as a menace to the continuation of injustices so maliciously inflicted on the people of Ireland.
>
> Like other patriots, he was charged with an agrarian offence (but not assault or murder as falsely stated by the royal commission after Ned Kelly's execution). With jury packing reduced to a fine art, the ruling class in Tipperary had no difficulty in securing his conviction, and transportation to Van Diemen's Land.

It is true that Ned's father was never charged with assault or murder and it is true that the royal commission wrongly surmised that he was charged with those crimes, when it was, in fact, another convict called 'John Kelly'. The convict records clearly identify Red—by his description and Irish court records—as the pig-stealing John Kelly. The other man had black hair, for a start! John Kelly was a very common name.

It is false to claim that Red Kelly was charged with an 'agrarian' crime.

Agrarian crimes were rebellious protests involving murders, shootings, threats and destruction of property carried out from about 1790 to the 1880s against tenants deemed to have secured small holdings unfairly from Protestant landlords, and later against the landlords themselves. For the first few decades of the struggle, these crimes were carried out at night by local secret societies with names like 'Magpies', 'Rockites', 'Whiteboys' and 'Jays'.

Red Kelly's crimes were, however, merely agricultural, rather than 'agrarian': he stole, or attempted to steal, pigs and cattle.

The son of Thomas Kelly and Mary Cody, who reared a family of seven on less than half an acre of land at Clonbrogan, near the village of Moyglass, which is 8 miles (12 kilometres) from Cashel in County

Tipperary, John Kelly was baptised on 20 February 1820 in Moyglass Church in the parish of Killenaule.

Today there is nothing left of the Kelly home, clearly marked on maps in the 1840s near Slievenamon Mountain, but the records contained in *Ireland, County of Tipperary, South Riding, Barony of Middlethird, Unions of Callan, Cashel, Tipperary and Clonmel, Primary Valuation,* published in Dublin by Her Majesty's Printers in 1850, tell us it stood on 'one rood and twenty-three perches of land, rented from Jeremiah Scully Esq. for six shillings per annum' and that rent on their dwelling (a one-room, mud and thatch cabin) was valued at 7 shillings per annum.

In 1841 Red was convicted of pig stealing. Irish police records show that, on 4 December 1840, 'John Kelly' stole two pigs, 'value about six pounds', from James Cooney, a labourer living at Ballysheehan, near Cashel.

The police report, written by Sub-Inspector Cox of New Park Police Barracks (the closest police station to Ballysheehan), states:

> Cashel 7th Decr, 40.
> Have to report, that on the 4th inst. about 4 A M two pigs, valued about six pounds, the property of James Cooney, were stolen by one John Kelly who drove them to Cahir Market (distance 14 miles) and there sold them to a person named Flood, who afterwards on the same day sold them to a pig buyer from Carrick on Suir. The Police, hearing of the occurrence, were on the alert and Conble. Hallam assisted by H. Johnston succeeded on same night in arresting Kelly in a Lodging house in this city and placing him in Bridewell. Hallam proceeded by order of Captain Haugh on the morning of the 5th to Carrick accompanied by Flood and returned on last night having discovered and brought back the pigs.
> Informations were this day sworn agt. Kelly for the offence and he stands committed for trial. This Kelly, who is a notorious character, is the person alluded in my report of the 19th ulto. as being an accomplice of Regan's who was wounded by Mobaman Police. I have not visited Cooney's place as I would gain no information by so doing.
> Joseph Cox
> 1st Sub Inspr.

This crime was not an isolated incident. There is more to the story, and it's of particular interest in terms of the sort of role models Ned had from his father's side of the family, as well as his mother's side.

The sub-inspector's claim that John Kelly was 'a notorious character' (at the age of 21) is an indication that he was at least suspected of a number of other crimes and misdemeanours. The incident of the '19th ulto' refers to the theft of seven cows several weeks earlier, and John Kelly's involvement is of particular interest.

The trials resulting from these two alleged crimes were held at the Cashel Quarter Sessions on 6 and 7 January 1841. The first trial, on 6 January, concerned the theft of the cows. The British archive trial record states:

> Pat Regan, a notorious character, was put to the bar, charged with stealing 7 fat cows off the lands of Moyglass, the property of James Ryall esq. Constable Perry swore that in consequence of this information he received that an attempt would be made on the night of the 17th November to steal Mr. Ryall's cows, proceeded with 2 other policemen to the cross roads close to Moyglass, where he found the prisoner at the head of, or before, the cows (which were being driven by another man, whom he saw) to prevent them from turning to another road, seizing the prisoner, who placed a pistol on his breast, and snapped it at him. The prisoner then got from him among the cows, when the witness and his comrade fired at and wounded him, the prisoner effected his escape, but was next morning arrested in the house of a person named Maher, which was in the immediate neighbourhood. This witness knew the other man who was driving the cows. Constable Murphy proved that there was a third man concerned in driving the cows and added that the prisoner could not be secured without firing at him.

On 9 January 1841 the *Clonmel Herald* reported on the second trial, which occurred on 7 January 1841 the day after Regan's trial:

> John Kelly, indicted for stealing pigs, the property of James Cooney, was found guilty and sentenced to 7 years' transportation (this culprit was an accomplice with Patrick Regan, found guilty yesterday of

stealing Mr. Ryall's cows; it was he that gave information respecting Regan.)

So, Constable Perry recognised a second man involved in the theft of the cows and Constable Murphy stated that there was a third man. One of those was, obviously, Red Kelly, who had, when arrested, informed on Regan.

Kelly was found guilty only of the theft of the pigs and sentenced to seven years transportation to Van Diemen's Land. He was not tried for the theft of the cows, most likely because he had informed against Regan.

Regan was sentenced to ten years transportation, but died in prison six weeks later from the wounds received on the night of 17 November 1840.

As we have already discovered, the *Report of the Royal Commission into the Circumstances of the Kelly Outbreak* of 1881 made an error when it noted:

John Kelly . . . who was the father of the outlaws, was a convict, having been transported from Tipperary, Ireland, to Tasmania in 1841, for an agrarian outrage, said to have been shooting at a landlord with intent to murder.

The report is completely wrong with the 'said to have been' information. The convict records, as previously stated, identify the John Kelly charged with what was generally termed an 'agrarian outrage' as a different person.

There have been many attempts by authors to paint John 'Red' Kelly as an Irish rebel in order to give credence to the 'freedom fighter' myth that surrounds the Kelly Gang. The truth is that he was known to local police, by age 21, as a 'notorious character' who was, in the space of three weeks, involved in stealing two pigs and, in company with two others, attempting to steal seven cows. He then gave information to the police that led to the arrest and conviction of Pat Regan.

Red Kelly was merely a poor thief who stole from his neighbours.

The author Frank Clune, in his book *The Kelly Hunters,* implied that Red Kelly was unfairly victimised and treated as a rebel for an insignificant crime when he was merely a poverty-stricken victim of circumstance:

> Pig stealing, especially from a prosperous Irish farmer, was not a remarkable offence. It had no political implications.

It is true that the crime was not political, but Clune tries to make a case that the police treated Red Kelly *as if* he was a rebel. The problem with this assumption is the implication that James Cooney was 'a prosperous Irish farmer' when, in fact, he was nothing of the kind. Bob Reece, in chapter ten of his collection of essays *Exiles from Erin*, points out that:

> Cooney, far from being the prosperous farmer portrayed by Clune, was a landless labourer like Kelly's father.

Reece refers to a report to the Commissioners of the Poor Enquiry (Ireland) of 1836 that contains a witness statement that, in the barony of Middlethird, 'A man holding from 5 to 10 acres [2 to 4 hectares] is called a cottier; he is distinguished from a labourer who holds less or no land.'

In that same year, 1836, British liberal statesman Sir George Cornewall Lewis (best known for his efforts to keep Britain neutral during the American Civil War) remarked in a reply to the report of the Select Committee investigations into poverty and 'outrages' in Ireland, that: 'In a large part of Ireland there is less security of person and property than in any other part of Europe, except perhaps the wildest districts of Calabria or Greece.'

The one-room, mud and thatch cabin that John Kelly's parents and family inhabited was valued for rental at 7 shillings per year. To say that stealing pigs valued at £6 from a neighbour, whose circumstances were similar to your own, was 'not a remarkable offence' is true only in respect of the fact that Ireland, at that time, had the worst crime rate in western Europe, a situation that was exacerbated by the almost unimaginable state of poverty in which the bulk of the population lived.

To infer that stealing anything worth the price of fifteen years rent was not a serious crime is ridiculous. There is a photograph, taken in

1988, of Cooney's dwelling that shows it to be a small one-room stone cottage.

Ned's father was no Irish rebel. He never liked to talk about his past and, although he made some attempts to improve himself and build a decent life for his family, basically he was a semi-literate thief whose life was, sadly, blighted in his earlier years by poverty and criminal tendencies and, in later life, by alcoholism.

Red Kelly served two years in a convict work gang south of Hobart and was only in trouble once for absence and 'misconduct', which got him two months hard labour in chains. He was never flogged and behaved reasonably well. He was then assigned as a servant to a family near Launceston and obtained his ticket of leave in 1845, but could not depart the colony of Van Diemen's Land until his sentence expired in 1848.

He obtained work from a farming family and, in spite of being reported by them and fined 5 shillings for being 'drunk and disorderly' in 1847, he was given good reports as being 'quiet and orderly'. He was apparently working as a handyman and acquired some rudimentary building skills in this time. In 1848, like many other ex-convict 'Vandemonians', as they were known, he made his way to the mainland colony of New South Wales in what was known as the 'Port Phillip District' of that colony which, two years later, would become the separate colony of Victoria.

There is no evidence that Red Kelly was harassed by police at any time after leaving Ireland, as Kenneally claimed. In fact, he personally had no problems with the law for eighteen years, between 1847 and 1865. His contact with the police in Ireland was, it appears, due to his criminal tendencies and ended with him dobbing on his partner-in-crime, Pat Regan. There is no evidence of rebel activities.

The 'Vandemonian Trail' was a well-worn migration path that led from Hobart via Port Albert to Gippsland and on to the Victorian High Country, or via Beechworth and Mansfield to the developing grazing districts of the Riverina, or to the fertile areas being developed as cattle-raising districts in Gippsland or north of Melbourne to the west. Many ex-convicts, sons of convicts, ex-bushrangers, gold seekers and other 'Vandemonians' made their way along this trail to the cattle-grazing country and later to the various goldfields of Victoria during the boom years of the 1850s.

By 1850 Red was working just north of Melbourne, at Beveridge, as a timber getter, wood splitter, fencer and bush carpenter. There were many Irish Catholic families in the area, and many of them were families of ex-convicts from Van Diemen's Land who had followed the 'Vandemonian Trail' and settled in the district. Many other poor Irish migrants arrived as free settlers during the Great Potato Famine.

Kilmore is the oldest inland town in Victoria and the area, just to the north of Melbourne, from Donnybrook to Beveridge and Wallan and north to Kilmore, was very much an Irish Catholic community.

(Even today, in these secular, irreligious times, the latest census figures show Kilmore's population to be more than one-third practising Catholic, over 50 per cent more than the Australian average, and well ahead of the Anglicans at 13 per cent—and even ahead of 'no religion' at 30 per cent!)

Apparently Red met his future wife's father, James Quinn, in a pub in Donnybrook and, sometime later, looking for a secluded place to set up a still and start an illegal whisky-making operation, he visited the Quinn family's farm in Wallan to discuss the scheme.

The Quinns had emigrated as assisted free settlers from County Antrim in Ireland and settled in the Port Phillip District of the colony of New South Wales in July 1841. They arrived with ten children and another was added to the family after their arrival. They farmed firstly at Brunswick and then moved north to Wallan.

It appears that James Quinn, whose extended family were certainly not averse to illegal activities themselves, was suspicious of his fellow countryman, an ex-convict with alcoholic tendences, and rejected the plan to join him in the scheme.

It was on that visit, however, that 30-year-old Red Kelly made the acquaintance of Quinn's 17-year-old daughter, Ellen, and, much to her father's chagrin, Ellen became pregnant to Red in May 1850. Evidently this caused major rows and upheavals between father and daughter until, finally, James Quinn gave up the battle to keep his daughter from marrying the ex-convict and agreed to let Kelly build a hut for himself and his bride on the Quinn property after they were married in Melbourne in November 1850.

Red worked for Ellen's father and the child, Mary Jane, was born in February 1851, but died in infancy before the end of the year. In June and July 1851, gold was discovered in the newly created colony of Victoria, near Clunes and Castlemaine and later Ballarat. Red spent most of 1853 at the goldfields and managed to find enough gold to buy a 40-acre farm at Beveridge, a little closer to Melbourne. He moved Ellen and their second-born, a daughter named Anne, to their new home and Ned was born there in 1854.

The Kelly family fortunes ebbed and flowed for ten years at Beveridge. Red purchased a half-acre block in town, built a house on it and even became a landlord for a time. Later he mortgaged the farm for £200, then sold it at a loss, along with half of his town block. He built a shack on the other half of the block and the family lived there until Red purchased a smaller farm and another town block. Finally, in 1864, he sold up all his property at Beveridge for £80 and moved the family 75 kilometres north to Avenel in the Strathbogie Ranges, where he rented a farm for £14 a year. There were now six children, and a seventh was born after Red moved the family to Avenel in 1865.

Red and Ellen were 'semi-literate', being able to read but not write. During their time at Beveridge, the three oldest children attended the local school at a cost of four pence each per week. This meant that Anne, Ned and Margaret, unlike their parents, were able to both read *and write*. Ned excelled at sport and was, apparently, an athletic boy and an average student.

Ned attended school until he was at least eleven. At sixteen he was literate enough to write a badly spelled letter to the police asking for help. Later in life, however, he dictated letters for Joe Byrne to write and a note attached to a letter from Police Superintendent Edmund Fosbery to NSW Premier Henry Parkes, as part of their discussions about the Kelly Gang reward, states:

> My dear Sir Henry, Neither Ned nor Dan Kelly can write—that is, that they can scarcely write their names. The Victorian Constable states that they get sympathisers to write letters for them.

This is, obviously, a misunderstanding, based on Joe being the gang's 'scribe' or simply a lie told by the police.

Ellen's sister Margaret and her husband, Patrick, also lived in Beveridge with a large family and appear to have been well-respected law-abiding people. Margaret's husband came from Galway during the goldrushes and, although he and Margaret shared the same surname, he was no relation to her family. The fact that Margaret was a Quinn by birth and a Quinn by marriage was pure coincidence. (Ellen and Margaret also had an older brother named Patrick Quinn.)

It has been conjectured that Red moved Ellen and their children to Beveridge *away* from the criminal influence of the family at Wallan, or that Ellen wished to be near her sister at Beveridge, or that the move was a compromise, but such assumptions are nothing more than guesswork.

Also during the Beveridge years, 1856 to be exact, five of Red's siblings, James (Jim), Edward, Daniel, Ann and Mary, having survived the Great Potato Famine that devastated Ireland between 1845 and 1852, emigrated to Victoria on the *Maldon*, arriving in Melbourne in July 1856. Red's brother James, known mostly as 'Jim', who was fifteen years younger than Red, came to live with Red's family at Beveridge.

In April 1863, at the age of eight, Ned Kelly had his first experience of the criminal justice system, and his first experience of lying in a court room, when he gave evidence at the Kilmore General Sessions trial of his uncle Jim Kelly, who was charged with cattle theft. Ned's evidence, that he had been at home with his uncle when the cattle were stolen, did not convince the police magistrate, who subsequently convicted Uncle Jim and sentenced him to three years hard labour. Jim Kelly had been arrested three times for cattle theft before being convicted.

All his life Ned Kelly would be surrounded by members of his mother's extended family, and their friends and in-laws, who were habitual criminals. From the age of six, he was also under the permanent 'bad influence' of two male role models, his paternal uncle Jim and his alcoholic father Red.

The family move to Avenel in 1864 may have been due to the failing financial situation, or Red's alcoholism, or a desire to get away from a growing reputation in the district for criminal activities after the arrival of Red's younger brother. There is certainly no evidence of police harassment as has been suggested by Kenneally.

It was at Avenel, in 1866, that eleven-year-old Ned saved the life of seven-year-old Richard Shelton. Richard, who could not swim, was on his way to school when his hat blew into the creek and, in trying to retrieve it, he fell in. Ned jumped in and saved his life. Richard's father, a local publican, presented Ned with a green sash at a school ceremony as a reward for his brave act. Ned cherished the sash (possibly as a reminder of his humanity as a youngster, as well as his bravery and athleticism). He wore it under his armour at Glenrowan and, stained with Ned's blood, it is on display in the Benalla Museum.

At Avenel, Red Kelly, after eighteen years, was finally again in trouble with the police, in May 1865. Accused of stealing a calf from a neighbour, he was found guilty only of being in possession of the hide of a stolen beast. It is plausible to assume that the Kellys, or someone they knew, had eaten the rest of the evidence.

Red did not appear in court to answer the charge. The fine was £25. It is, perhaps, evidence of the family's descent into poverty at this time that Red could not pay the fine and served about four of the 'six months hard labour' sentence in Pentridge in lieu of payment. He was certainly free by 3 October 1865 when he registered the birth of his last child, Grace, at Campion's store in Avenel, listing his birth-place as 'Clonbrogan, Moyglass, Co. Tipperary, Ireland' and his age as 45.

Red died just over a year later, on 27 December 1866, of what was then called 'dropsy', possibly oedema of the kidneys or liver, one of the complications of sustained alcohol abuse. His death was reported by his son Edward (Ned) Kelly, who was eleven years of age. John 'Red' Kelly was buried in an unmarked grave in Avenel Cemetery, Victoria, on 29 December 1866.

With his father dead and his uncle in prison, Ned was now the oldest male in the household, but it was his mother, the matriarch Ellen, who was the unchallenged head of the Kelly family.

Red Kelly was, according to J.J. Kenneally, a victim of 'the campaign of anti-Irish hatred so well organised in the Colonies' where 'Irish patriotism was such an unforgivable crime in the eyes of the British Government officials in the Colony of Victoria, that even the serving of a savage sentence would not wipe [it] out'.

This statement needs serious analysis. It's nonsense.

Firstly, it was written by an Irish Catholic schoolteacher and political activist almost 50 years after Ned was hanged. Kenneally had lived (and taught in Catholic schools) throughout the decades of heated debate that followed the withdrawal of colonial government aid to Catholic schools in 1873 and had, no doubt, been subjected to the vitriol and sectarian hatred that was part of the conscription debate in World War I.

The 'campaign of anti-Irish hatred' that Kenneally claims the colonial government aimed at Red Kelly is a retrospective invention that reflects Kenneally's struggle against the anti-Catholic sentiments that were a part of his own lifetime—not Red Kelly's.

Secondly, it is really distorting the truth to call Red's convict experiences 'the serving of a savage sentence'. The convict system was harsh, it is true, but of the 162,000 convicts transported to the Australian colonies, Red appears to have been one of the luckier ones. He arrived in Hobart in January 1842, not on a brutal convict ship but with a small group of eleven convicts on the merchant ship *Prince Regent*. He was never flogged, he was reasonably well behaved, apart from one misdemeanour, and he was described as 'quiet and orderly'. He served almost exactly two and a half years of his seven-year sentence before being released, on a ticket of leave, to live freely and seek work within the colony of Van Diemen's Land.

Thirdly, the suggestion that Irish patriotism was an 'unforgivable crime in the eyes of British Government officials in the Colony of Victoria' really needs some scrutiny. It's rubbish.

John O'Shanassy, the undisputed leader of the Irish Catholics in Victoria, was premier of that colony three times between 1857 and 1863. He was a proud Irishman born in Tipperary two years before Red Kelly. O'Shanassy migrated to Melbourne with his new wife in 1839, again about two years before Red Kelly arrived in Hobart. All men in the colony of Victoria, including Irishmen, were granted the right to vote in 1857 regardless of land possession or wealth.

The minister for lands in the colony of Victoria (twice during the last decade of Red's life) was Charles Gavan Duffy, an Irish Catholic who revised and improved the selection acts and brought into law the act that made it easier for landless Victorians to gain land and thus a degree of independence. That act bears his name, the *Duffy Land Act of 1862*.

In 1871 and 1872, when Ned was in prison for horse stealing, Duffy was the premier of Victoria. During the three years 1877 to 1880, when Ned was outlawed, Duffy was the speaker of the house in Victoria's colonial government.

The problem with Kenneally's assertion that Irish patriotism was an 'unforgivable crime' in Victoria is that Duffy was something that Red Kelly never was and never had been—an *Irish rebel*.

Charles Gavan Duffy was born in Monaghan in 1816. As leader of the Young Ireland Movement, he was active in the rebel movement with Daniel O'Connell and set up the weekly *Nation* newspaper to promote Irish culture and emancipation and defend Catholicism.

Duffy was imprisoned and tried five times under the *1848 Treason and Felony Act*. After his release, Duffy represented New Ross in the British House of Commons from 1852 to 1855. Disillusioned after failing to achieve land reforms in Ireland, he migrated to Victoria, set up as a barrister and was elected into the first Victorian colonial legislative assembly. He was the only member of the assembly to have served in the British parliament and was therefore a great asset to the government and a much respected figure.

It seems to me that Kenneally's view of Victoria's history is a little distorted by the political struggles in which he was involved in his own lifetime and his assumptions lack any historic perspective or 'balanced view' of the past.

In his tirade about the colonial government, in the Jerilderie letter, just after a reference to the 'tyrannism of the English yoke', Ned raged about politicians as 'big fat-necked unicorns paid enough to torment and drive me to do thing [sic] which I dont [sic] wish to do . . .'

Ned was possibly ignorant of the fact that at least one of those, the speaker of the house, was a genuine Irish rebel. If he had known, he wouldn't have cared. It wouldn't have fitted into his fantasy world.

Ned's letters, those dictated at Jerilderie and Euroa and those sent to Victorian premier Graham Berry and his New South Wales counterpart Henry Parkes, reveal no real understanding of colonial politics or history. They are all about Ned himself and how specific acts by authorities had impinged on his activities.

Constable Bracken, one of the hostages at the siege at Glenrowan, reported: 'When we were held prisoners in the hotel Ned Kelly began talking about politics.' When Bracken asked Ned's opinion of the premier, the constable reported that Ned replied, 'I have written to Berry and he would not publish my letter and he gave too much money to the police for my capture.'

There is no 'big picture' or informed opinion, just a subjective, rather simple-minded reaction to two specific items relating to Ned.

Bracken claims that Ned then declared that the Berry government were '... all damned fools to bother their heads about parliament at all for this is our country'. Even this, the childish dismissal of the need for any government at all, coming from a stressed and desperate man who had not slept for days and had no real understanding of how the government worked or what it could and couldn't do, has been seen as a call for a republic.

If Ned's throwaway comment meant anything at all, it obviously was intended to mean something like 'Who needs parliament, anyway?' It cannot, by any stretch of the imagination, be interpreted to mean 'I am, however, going to bother my head about creating a republican government in this part of the colony.'

Perhaps the last word should be from the final interview with Ned's mother, Ellen, conducted by Bartlett Adamson and published in *Smith's Weekly* on 7 April 1923, a week after Ellen died, aged 91. Describing the room in which the interview took place, Adamson noted:

The kitchen was decorated with various photos. One was of the late historic Kate, who became Mrs Foster, while another was that of her son, Fred, who was killed in the Great War. There was also the large photo of Ned Kelly, black hair and luxuriant black beard, taken the day before his execution. Opposite to this, whether in symbolic defiance or as a sign of amity it is difficult to say, was a picture of King Edward, now some time deceased.

PART SEVEN

ICONIC FOLKLORE FURPHIES

'As to poetry, you know,' said Humpty Dumpty . . . 'I can repeat poetry as well as other folk, if it comes to that—'
'Oh, it needn't come to that!' Alice hastily said, hoping to keep him from beginning.

Through the Looking-Glass, Lewis Carroll, 1871

FACTS EVOLVE INTO FOLKLORE

I must say, when it comes to folklore, folk songs and bush verse I can understand Alice's apprehension only too well. In my time, I have sat through quite a few over-long and badly recited versions of 'The Man from Snowy River' at bush verse competitions and events. And, as a member of the long-gone Aussie folk band Bandy Bill & Co for more than ten years, there are a few songs about sheep and cattle that I don't miss having to sing or listen to.

It's in the nature of folklore and folk songs to evolve and proliferate into various 'versions', with different verses, tunes and claims of origin. When we are too lazy to find out the truth, we say what we'd like to be true—and call it 'folklore'.

I remember, only too well, that when I was compiling and editing the *Australasian Post* magazine's bush verse page twenty years ago, and compiling anthologies of bush verse for publication, I would come across verse labelled 'anonymous' that I knew was written by popular verse writers like Bruce Simpson, Col Wilson, Wilbur Howcroft, Grahame Watt and others. Even worse, authorship was often wrongly claimed, knowingly or inadvertently, by others. It was not uncommon for family members to find a book of handwritten verse after Granddad passed away and assume he wrote the verse, when it was in fact a collection of verse written by others that he'd written out by hand and often recited.

DAD AND DAVE

W here a story or folk tale begins its life and where it ends up are often a long way apart. A good case in point is the saga of 'Dad and Dave'.

The characters were created by Arthur Hoey Davis, the eighth of thirteen children of a Welsh blacksmith and ex-convict father and an Irish mother who fled the Great Potato Famine. The family grew up on a selection at Emu Creek on the Darling Downs near Toowoomba. Arthur left school at age twelve and worked as a stock rider before joining the public service in Brisbane at fifteen and making a career in the sheriff's office.

He sent his first story to *The Bulletin* in 1895, his first collection of 26 stories, *On Our Selection,* in 1899, and *Our New Selection* followed in 1903. The stories were whimsically humorous accounts of the hard life of a family on a bush selection and the characters of Dad, Dave, Mum, Mabel and the rest of the family became incredibly popular. So much so that Davis, who wrote under the pen name of 'Steele Rudd', retired at the age of 35 and lived from his writing income for the rest of his life. He produced volumes of stories and even had his own magazine, *Rudd's Magazine*, which ran successfully for four years at sixpence a copy.

Dad and Dave, Mum and Mabel became iconic Aussie characters. They were used as the protagonists in every 'yokel' joke and smutty joke told in every Australian playground and pub. The original stories were, however, anecdotal accounts of bush life.

If you ask any older Aussie where Dad and Dave live, however, they will not say 'on the Darling Downs', they will say 'Snake Gully', and some may also know 'it's near Gundagai'. This is because, through a hugely popular radio serial version of the stories, the family became associated with the mythical town of 'Snake Gully', set near the New South Wales town of Gundagai; you'll even find statues of the family in the park in Gundagai.

Naturally the style of the stories was altered somewhat by the radio scriptwriters. The musical theme of the radio series was the well-known popular tune 'Along the Road to Gundagai', written by prolific songwriter Melbourne's Jack O'Hagan.

This, naturally, cemented the idea in Australian minds that the family lived near Gundagai, and their 'selection' was down there at 'Snake Gully'.

What makes the whole business even more fascinating and amusing is that Jack O'Hagan's famous song, written in 1922, was only about Gundagai because the Murrumbidgee River, which flows through the town, has four syllables. O'Hagan began writing a song called 'Along The Road to Bundaberg', but the river at Bundaberg, the Burnett, has only two syllables and Jack wanted four syllables, without using the word 'river', to make one line scan and sing nicely. So he looked for a town with the same number of syllables (three) situated on a river with four syllables (Murrumbidgee)—and found Gundagai. O'Hagan also wrote the popular song 'Where the Dog Sits on the Tuckerbox', often known as 'Five Miles from Gundagai', which places one of the characters from the stories, Mabel, in the same location.

When he was invited to be the special guest at Gundagai's centenary celebrations in 1951, Jack revealed the truth about his famous song and admitted that he had never been to Gundagai in his life until that day.

So, although the incredibly popular 'Dad and Dave' stories were set in Queensland and the author's personal experiences and reminiscences were all of the Darling Downs district and trips to Brisbane, the radio serial, statues and songs have put Dad, Dave, Mum and Mabel well and truly in 'Snake Gully'—near the southern New South Wales town of Gundagai!

WHO WROTE OUR UNOFFICIAL ANTHEM?

In his twenties Andrew Barton Paterson, aspiring writer, was partner in a law firm with John Street, who had a cousin named Sarah Riley.

Paterson was not known as 'The Banjo' in those days; his friends and family called him 'Barty' from his middle name Barton. He and Sarah became engaged in 1887—and remained so for eight years.

A few months after the shearers' strikes and unrest in Queensland in 1894, Sarah and Barty visited her brother's property, Vindex, near Winton in Queensland.

Sarah had been educated at Oberwyl Ladies College, in Melbourne, and her best friend at school was Christina Macpherson, one of the eleven children of Ewan Macpherson, who owned Peechelba, a 150,000-acre (60,700-hectare) property near Wangaratta. He also owned Dagworth, which adjoined Vindex, near Winton.

When Ewan took his unmarried daughters Christina and Jane to visit Dagworth in early 1895, the two old school friends were delighted to be staying so close and many house parties were arranged.

At one of these parties Christina played a tune on an auto harp. It was one that she had heard played by a band at a race meeting in May the previous year while visiting her married sister at Warrnambool.

The tune was from a Scottish song, 'Ye Bonnie Wood O' Craigielea', which Christina learned by ear. Her version of it became the original tune to some words written by Paterson about the shearers' struggle with landowners.

In September 1894 a group of striking shearers had burned the Dagworth shearing shed, which contained 150 lambs. This act caused police to be sent to the area and they hunted for the culprit with the station manager, Ewan Macpherson's son Robert.

The man accused of lighting the fire, Samuel Hoffmeister, was found dead in a dry billabong. The inquest said 'suicide', but many thought otherwise.

As Paterson was often a guest in the house of the man who may well have been an accessory to the murder, he had to be circumspect and the lyrics he wrote were more allegorical than factual.

The collaboration between Christina and Paterson evidently developed into far more than a song-writing exercise. It seems there was a strong romantic bond—flirtation and possibly more—between the two, which led to the breaking of Paterson's engagement to Sarah Riley and eventually led to the end of the law firm partnership as well. Neither Sarah Riley nor Christina Macpherson ever married.

The song?

Oh yes, it was 'Waltzing Matilda'.

Paterson wrote four simple verses. In the first, the swagman is camped in the dry section of the billabong boiling his billy for tea. In the second verse, a sheep comes to drink and the swagman grabs it and turns it into 'tucker' (i.e. slaughters it for food). Then, in verse three, the squatter arrives with the police and accuses the swagman of stealing the sheep. Finally the swagman suicides by drowning in the deeper part of the billabong, which is then haunted by his ghost.

Into this simple story of an iconic Aussie figure killing a sheep and being harassed into suicide by a landowner and the police, Paterson wove echoes of the shearers' strikes and struggles against authority. He also suggested that the repercussions would haunt us for some time to come.

The chorus of the song was totally unrelated to the storyline. It implied that there were many stories to be heard in the bush and wandering the outback like a swaggie, with someone you loved, was a thing to be desired and enjoyed. It seems to put the verses into the realm of 'folklore', and the original idea for a title was 'Carrying a Swag', which was used as a subtitle to the lyric when it was written as verse.

Certain historians have argued that the verses contain a relatively 'harmless' allegorical version of the struggles of the shearers' strikes, while the chorus suggests a flirtation between the lyricist and the composer.

Here is the original lyric, as written by Banjo Paterson:

Oh, there once was a swagman camped in the Billabong,
Under the shade of a coolibah tree;
And he sang as he looked at his old billy boiling,
'Who will come a-waltzing Matilda with me?'

In the original manuscript Paterson wrote: 'Who'll come a-roving Australia with me?' He then crossed out 'roving Australia' and substituted 'waltzing Matilda' and used it for the rest of the lyric. The words then continue:

Who'll come a-waltzing Matilda, my darling,
Who'll come a-waltzing Matilda with me?
Waltzing Matilda and leading a water bag—
Who'll come a-waltzing Matilda with me?

Down came a jumbuck to drink at the water-hole,
Up jumped the swagman and grabbed him in glee;
And he sang as he put him away in his tucker-bag,
'You'll come a-waltzing Matilda with me.'

Who'll come a-waltzing Matilda, my darling,
Who'll come a-waltzing Matilda with me?
Waltzing Matilda and leading a water bag—
Who'll come a-waltzing Matilda with me?

Down came the Squatter a-riding his thorough-bred;
Down came Policemen—one, two and three.
Who's [sic] is the jumbuck you've got in the tucker-bag?
You'll come a-waltzing Matilda with me.

Who'll come a-waltzing Matilda, my darling,
Who'll come a-waltzing Matilda with me?

Waltzing Matilda and leading a water bag—
Who'll come a-waltzing Matilda with me?

But the swagman, he up and he jumped in the water-hole,
Drowning himself by the coolibah tree,
And his ghost may be heard as it sings in the Billabong,
'Who'll come a-waltzing Matilda with me?'

Who'll come a-waltzing Matilda, my darling,
Who'll come a-waltzing Matilda with me?
Waltzing Matilda and leading a water bag—
Who'll come a-waltzing Matilda with me?

The chorus refers to dancing. 'Matilda' was a term for a swag, a blanket rolled and containing a swagman's belongings, that he carried slung over his shoulder, either across his chest or on his back.

The term 'Waltzing Mathilde' was originally German and referred to soldiers carrying their belongings while on campaigns. On long treks between battles the army would be followed by large numbers of 'camp followers' in wagons. These various 'entrepreneurs' provided services such as food and supplies that were not part of standard army provisions. One of the services offered was, of course, sex for profit and the women who provided such things were universally referred to as 'Mathilde'. Thus, 'Waltzing Mathilde' was German army slang for being on the march and having no female companion to dance with or sleep with—just your blanket roll to keep you company on the road and in camp at night. The blanket roll became your 'Mathilde', a substitute for what you could not access—or afford! The term was brought to Australia by German migrants during the goldrushes.

'Leading a water bag' is also a dancing reference. The billy and water bag usually hung from the swag at the back. Thus a swaggie 'led' the dance and the water bag 'followed'.

Banjo was always rather publicly dismissive of the song, which no doubt was a source of sadness and embarrassing memories for him. The evidence inclines me to think he wanted to forget the whole thing. In his 1944 publication *The Story of Waltzing Matilda*, Sydney May referred to Paterson having 'sad memories' of his stay in Winton.

Clement Semmler, in *The Banjo of the Bush* (1966), states: 'Paterson had a greater affection for this ballad than most of his others; others have mentioned that Winton and Dagworth had sad memories for Paterson. The reason, then, is purely simple. He did not marry Sarah Riley.'

Eight years later, in April 1903, Paterson married Alice Walker of Tenterfield Station near the town of the same name in northern New South Wales. The couple had met the previous year, when he visited the property. Towards the end of 1902, possibly needing cash for the impending wedding, Paterson arranged to sell the copyright of his latest book of collected verse, *Rio Grande's Last Race and Other Verses*, to his publisher Angus & Robertson.

At the same time he also sold the copyright of some unwanted verses and unpublished verse and sketches to Angus & Robertson, and among the discarded writing was 'Waltzing Matilda'. The amount received for these 'bits and pieces' is usually reported to be £5 or £10.

Angus & Robertson now owned the lyric, and they then leased the musical rights to James Inglis and Co., who owned the Billy Tea Company. James Inglis and Co. had the rights to set the words to music and publish the work as a song. Their intention was to do that and use the song as an advertising tool for their tea. Several tunes were tried and finally the wife of the managing director of James Inglis and Co., Marie Cowan, composed the jaunty march tune that we all know today.

There is some suggestion that Paterson sent her a copy of the tune that Christina Macpherson had played. In a letter, written in 1931, Christina explained that Paterson wrote to her several years after they had created the song together, asking her for a copy of the tune, and he then passed it on to 'a musical friend'. Others think the 'musical friend' was Harry Nathan, whose version of the song, published by Palings, appeared very late in 1902. There are no known copies of the sheet music of Nathan's version in existence. So we cannot compare his version of the tune or the words until a copy is found under the lid of some old piano stool.

Banjo certainly was sent, as a courtesy, the final version of the Marie Cowan song. He is reported to have said, in a telephone conversation, that she had done a 'good job' and wished the company 'good luck' with the project.

However, Marie Cowan, or somebody else, also changed the words, quite significantly. In one of his radio talks, in 1936, Banjo said, 'Miss Macpherson used to play a little Scottish tune on a zither and I put words to it and called it "Waltzing Matilda".' Banjo said he liked the 'whimsicality and dreaminess' of the tune and thought it would be nice to set some words to it.

There is very little 'dreaminess' in Marie Cowan's tune and Paterson's 'whimsicality' in the chorus is completely lost, with three of the four choruses reinforcing the idea of the billy and the tea!

Once a jolly swagman camped by a billabong
Under the shade of a Coolibah tree
And he sang as he watched and waited 'til his Billy boiled
You'll come a-waltzing Matilda with me.

Waltzing Matilda, Waltzing Matilda
You'll come a-waltzing Matilda with me
And he sang as he watched and waited 'til his Billy boiled
You'll come a-waltzing Matilda with me.

Down came a jumbuck to drink at that billabong
Up jumped the swagman and grabbed him with glee
And he sang as he shoved that jumbuck in his tuckerbag
You'll come a-waltzing Matilda with me.

Waltzing Matilda, Waltzing Matilda
You'll come a-waltzing Matilda with me
And he sang as he watched and waited 'til his Billy boiled
You'll come a-waltzing Matilda with me.

Up rode the squatter mounted on his thoroughbred
Down came troopers one two three
Whose [sic] that jumbuck you've got in the tuckerbag?
You'll come a-waltzing Matilda with me.

Waltzing Matilda, Waltzing Matilda
You'll come a-waltzing Matilda with me

And he sang as he watched and waited 'til his Billy boiled
You'll come a-waltzing Matilda with me.

Up jumped the swagman and sprang into the billabong
You'll never catch me alive said he
And his ghost may be heard as you pass by that billabong
You'll come a-waltzing Matilda with me.

The swagman has become 'jolly' (not Paterson's idea at all). The swagman is camped 'by' the billabong, rather than 'in' it. (A billabong is formed when a river that meanders over flat terrain forms a new channel in a flood and cuts off one of its own 'bends', which then becomes a small lake of still water.) 'In the billabong' is a more genuine bush saying than 'by a billabong'.

Other changes to the actual verses include the policemen becoming 'troopers', which gives the song a much older context than 1894 and dilutes the connection to the shearers' strikes. Paterson's swagman 'looked at his old billy boiling' while Marie Cowan's character 'watched and waited' for his Billy (with a capital B for the company name) to boil.

Paterson's swagman 'put him [the jumbuck] away' in his tuckerbag, after the butchering has been done, obviously. In Marie Cowan's version he shoves him (sometimes 'stows' him) in the tuckerbag after grabbing him. Her version implies that a live sheep is being shoved into a tuckerbag before it has been turned into tucker, which makes no sense in real bush terms.

Finally, Paterson's swaggie is 'drowning himself' in the 'water-hole'. This is seen by some researchers as a reference to the often queried verdict of 'suicide' in the Hoffmeister case. Marie Cowan's swaggie jumps up and 'springs' into the billabong yelling, 'You'll never catch me alive.'

These changes are all in the verses, but the most important changes occur in the chorus. The dancing imagery and suggestion is almost gone, and only 'Waltzing Matilda' remains; 'leading a water bag' is lost and so is 'my darling'. And the words 'Waltzing Matilda' are repeated and placed in a strong march tempo, rather than the more graceful and gentle original tune, which suggests romantic dancing.

Marie Cowan's version also introduces the repetition of 'And he sang as he watched and waited 'til his Billy boiled' in the chorus and first two verses.

In general her version has less feel of the bush and the time of the events, while Paterson's original has a more genuine bush feel and uses bush terminology. Marie Cowan's words are what you might expect from someone in the city writing about the bush from lack of first-hand experience, someone not properly understanding the original sense of the story. Someone who thinks being a swaggie is 'jolly'.

There is also a suggestion that Marie Cowan's version was actually influenced by another version of Paterson's original set to music.

It appears that she was not the first one to attempt the exercise. Harry Nathan was a Sydney singer and musician and grandson of the flamboyant English composer Isaac Nathan, who had taught singing to the royal children and collaborated musically with Lord Byron before emigrating to Sydney and composing Australia's first opera, *Don John of Austria*, in 1847.

Writing in the *Sydney Morning Herald* on 14 August 2015, when a fuss erupted about the copyright ownership of the song, Greg Pemberton correctly stated that, as there was no Commonwealth copyright law until 1905, state laws still applied in 1903 and Nathan's version, published by Palings in December 1902 and crediting Banjo with the lyrics, was copyrighted in Queensland in March 1903.

Pemberton mistakenly assumes that Nathan found the poem in *Rio Grande's Last Race and Other Verses*, the copyright of which Paterson sold to Angus & Robertson in January 1903. Pemberton is correct when he says that the copyright transfer 'was registered in NSW on January 12, 1903 as No. 03/1725'. Paterson sold the copyright for a lump sum, outright, and thus gave up his ownership of the lyric.

Unfortunately, Pemberton wrongly assumes that 'Waltzing Matilda' was published in *Rio Grande's Last Race and Other Verses*. It was not. The first publication of 'Waltzing Matilda' as a poem did not occur until 1917, in *Saltbush Bill JP and Other Verses*. There is no version of 'Waltzing Matilda' in *Rio Grande's Last Race and Other Verses*. However, it was part of the 'bits and pieces' also 'sold' to Angus & Robertson at the same time as that collection of verse.

So, while Pemberton makes a simple error in claiming that anyone could have seen the lyrics in *Rio Grande's Last Race and Other Verses*, it is true that Angus & Robertson now had the right to sell or lease the musical rights to use the words as song lyrics. It appears that they sold the musical rights to Palings, as well as James Inglis and Co.

Pemberton is quite right to say that other versions of the song had been around before 1903, reportedly in the Boer War, possibly sung to a well-known folk tune called 'The Bold Fusilier'.

It is not true, however, that others 'could not have known Christina Macpherson's unpublished tune from Dagworth'. The song was very popular around the Winton and Longreach districts, and there are reports that 'the whole district was singing it' in the late 1890s.

Not long after the song was written, Paterson and Christina sang it, using a piano, in the parlour of the North Gregory Hotel in Winton. They also visited nearby Oondooroo Station, where the song was sung by the gifted and trained baritone Herbert Ramsay (later Sir Herbert Ramsay), who was a cousin of the owners. Apparently he also sang it at the Post Office Hotel in Winton. The song spread by word of mouth throughout the district and, on 25 September 1900, when the governor of Queensland, Lord Charles Lamington, visited Winton, Herbert Ramsay sang the song again at a banquet held in the governor's honour at the North Gregory Hotel.

In his book *Waltzing Matilda: The Secret History of Australia's Favourite Song*, folklorist and relentless Paterson researcher Dennis O'Keeffe wrote:

> The original song was also sung by soldiers at the Boer War. From there Waltzing Matilda found its way back to Sydney, either via soldiers who lived in Sydney, or via returned servicemen travelling through Sydney on their way back to western Queensland. Perhaps Marie Cowan had heard the song then.

In his attempt to make sense of the tangled history of the song's copyright in the *Sydney Morning Herald* article, Greg Pemberton explained some of the difficulties:

> Melbourne music publisher Messrs Allan & Co said they bought the words' copyright from Angus & Robertson in 1923 and paid royalties to

Cowan for the music, a claim they maintained when Banjo's daughter sought ownership. Yet, there is no record of this transaction, although registration was not mandatory.

Allan & Co claimed the exchange of copyright took place and they paid Marie Cowan's estate royalties on the strength of her son's word that the tune we know today was hers.

Later versions of the song lyrics altered the choruses, so that each chorus repeated the third line of the previous verse.

Paterson sold the words for a few quid and seemed glad to forget it. When it refused to go away, he gave it a few passing nostalgic thoughts. His family was always reluctant to deal with the song and its origin in biographies after his death, especially after their attempts to claim some royalties failed.

So, did Banjo write 'Waltzing Matilda' as we know it?

I would say he certainly did *not* write the version we sing with great gusto today, and the tune to which he set his version is nothing like the tune we know today. The words are *based* on some he wrote but the Marie Cowan words, which tell the story as a sort of folk tale for kids, are far closer to the way we understand the 'jolly' song we sing.

As to where the Marie Cowan words, and later versions of them, came from—who knows? Marie herself certainly wrote some of them, and perhaps soldiers in the Boer War, or Harry Nathan's version, provided others.

It's way too late to revert to the original, which is a shame. To me it has the loveliest 'whimsical and dreamlike' melody, with the best chorus of the lot.

Footnote

Oddly enough Christina Macpherson has a different 'claim to fame' in Aussie history. One that predates all this.

On 8 April 1865 the psychotic bushranger, arsonist and murderer Daniel 'Mad Dan' Morgan arrived at the Macpherson homestead Peechelba, near Wangaratta, and held the family and their employees hostage at gunpoint in the dining room.

Morgan was the most wanted man in the colonies at the time, known for his erratic behaviour and sadistic tendencies. He once held up a station and wounded a man, then apologised and allowed another to ride for the doctor, then changed his mind again and rode after the man and killed him.

On this occasion, having rounded up all the adults on the property as prisoners in the dining room, he allowed Alice Keenan, a nurse-maid, to go and attend to a crying infant in another room. The brave girl climbed through a window and ran to the next homestead, home of the Macphersons' relatives, the Rutherfords.

They notified the local police and a trap was set. Next morning as Morgan was leaving the homestead, a stationhand named John Quinlan, the best shot in the district, shot him in the back.

Morgan died of his wounds and the event was celebrated in the press with gruesome photographs of his body, mutilated by souvenir collectors, propped against the stable.

The infant whose crying caused Mad Dan Morgan to allow Alice Keenan to leave the room, and consequently bring his life to a bloody and gruesome end, was fifteen-month-old Christina Rutherford Macpherson.

Christina lived quietly as a spinster in Melbourne until she died aged 72 in 1936. Her relatives said Paterson's behaviour had scandalised the families involved.

THE MYTH OF THE DOG
ON THE TUCKERBOX

The evolution of verse, songs and bush folklore stories into more acceptable versions of the originals, that make more sense in a modern context or in a more contemporary vernacular, is probably not of any great importance in the big scheme of things. When the whole point of the story is lost, however, or the moral is 'reversed', we obviously lose the true sense of what the story was trying to tell us about the attitudes, humour and social beliefs of the time. Once again the tendency is to rewrite history to suit our contemporary attitudes and beliefs.

One of the most amusing Aussie examples of such a reversal in the real intent behind a story is the myth of the iconic 'Dog on the Tuckerbox' statue, just outside the town of Gundagai.

My mother often told me that the statue and the poem were a tribute to both the hard-working 'bullockies' and their brave and loyal dogs, who guarded their belongings as their owners slept beneath the wagon. The verse by Jack Moses, which led to the song by Jack O'Hagan and the famous statue, was about the trials and tribulations suffered by the bullocky and his faithful dog:

I've been jilted, jarred and crossed in love, and sand-bagged in the
dark,
Till if a mountain fell on me, I'd treat it as a lark.

It's when you've got your bullocks bogged, that's the time you flog and
  cry,
And the dog sits on the tucker box, nine miles from Gundagai.

This was based on an earlier poem by an anonymous poet calling
himself 'Bowyang Yorke'. Jack Moses's poem echoed the sentiments of
the earlier poem, which was about the hard life shared by the bullocky
and his canine companion, which guarded the precious tuckerbox.
Jack Moses's version of the verse ends with the dog being reverentially
buried in the tuckerbox.

Well, the truth of the matter is that an even earlier original poem,
on which Bowyang Yorke's verse was based, had a slightly different
theme. While it was about the hard life of a bullocky, the dog in the
original version was part of the problem rather than a loyal companion that alleviated some of the bullocky's hardships:

I'm used to punching bullock teams across the hills and plains.
I've teamed outback for forty years in blazing droughts and rains.
I've lived a heap of troubles down without a blooming lie,
But I can't forget what happened to me nine miles from Gundagai.
'Twas getting dark, the team got bogged, the axle snapped in two,
I lost me matches and me pipe, gawd, what was I to do?
The rain came on, 'twas bitter cold, and hungry too was I,
And the dog . . . he *shat* in me tucker box, nine miles from Gundagai!
Some blokes I know has lots of luck, no matter how they fall,
But there was I, Lord love a duck, no bloody luck at all!
I couldn't make a pot of tea or get me trousers dry,
And the dog *shat* in me tucker box, nine miles from Gundagai!
I can forgive the blinking team, I can forgive the rain,
I can forgive the cold and dark and go through it all again,
I can forgive me rotten luck—but hang me till I die . . .
I can't forgive that bloody dog—nine miles from Gundagai!

Another version differs slightly:

Good morning mate, you are too late, the shearing is all over.
Tie up your dog behind a log, come in and have some dover,

For Nobby Jack has broke the yoke, poked out the leader's eye,
And the dog *shat* in the tuckerbox, five miles from Gundagai.

(NB: author's italics. 'Dover' was a brand name of a bushman's clasp knife and thus became a slang term for any food, meat or damper, cut and eaten with such a knife.)

Various crude versions of this rhyme were popular among bullock-ies but could not be printed at that time. Some versions avoided the scatological reference by saying the dog 'sat in the tuckerbox', which would still have spoiled the food to an extent, but Bowyang Yorke's 'cleaned-up' version called 'Bill the Bullocky' reads:

As I was coming down Conroy's Gap
I heard a maiden cry:
'There goes Bill the Bullocky,
He's bound for Gundagai.'
A better poor old beggar
Never cracked an honest crust;
A tougher poor old beggar
Never drug a whip through dust.
His team got bogged at the five mile creek,
Bill lashed and swore and cried,
'If Nobby don't get me out of this
I'll tattoo his bloody hide.'
But Nobby strained and broke his yoke,
And poked out the leader's eye;
And the dog sat on the tucker box
Five miles from Gundagai.

In changing one letter—from 'shat' to 'sat'—obviously in an attempt to make the verse more marketable and acceptable in mixed company, Bowyang Yorke managed to change the entire meaning of the story and make the disgusting canine villain into a hero! It is also interesting to note that the various versions cannot even agree on the distance from Gundagai—is it five or nine miles?

There is a lesson there in just how quickly any 'facts' become clouded in uncertainty.

PART EIGHT

THE LEGEND OF BREAKER MORANT

'Who in the world am I? Ah, that's the great puzzle.'

Alice's Adventures in Wonderland, Lewis Carroll, 1865

THE MYSTERIOUS MR MORANT

The execution of lieutenants Harry Morant and Peter Handcock, and the circumstances surrounding the episode and the events that led to it, provide yet another example of myth building to the point where certain basic facts are completely overlooked. The plethora of books, articles, documentaries, mock re-trials, debates and a movie have, in a similar fashion to the Ned Kelly case, made the truth virtually irrelevant. The mythology is so powerful, and the mysteries surrounding insignificant aspects of the lives of the men involved are so argued over, that facts that would be otherwise glaringly obvious seem to be ignored or discounted as mere background details.

I am of the opinion that, if you step away from 'Breaker' Morant as the central figure and look at the bigger picture, certain facts become clear—and the legend unravels.

Firstly, Morant was not even Australian. The British military did not recognise him as Australian, nor did he think of himself as Australian. He actually claimed to be the son of a British admiral and maintained this claim until his death, apparently requesting in his last wishes that his belongings be sent to the admiral's family.

Morant was a mystery man of uncertain background. We do know that he was born in Somerset, England, though there are questions about who his father was (quite probably not the admiral he claimed), and that he was sent to Australia at the age of nineteen (possibly due to his misbehaviour surrounding unpaid gambling debts and a scandal involving a young woman). He spent fifteen years in the colony, trying his hand at a range of occupations involving horses, developing a reputation for his reckless daring and horsemanship, and becoming a well-known writer of verse for *The Bulletin* magazine. He also became well known for not paying his debts.

How he came to take part in the Second South African War is also unclear. Some historians say that Morant saw the war originally as his 'ticket home' to England, where he could redeem himself for his earlier disgrace that had him exiled to Australia. Whatever his reasons for joining a colonial regiment in Renmark, South Australia, at the outbreak of the war, it probably wasn't to 'fight for the empire'. Others believe that he only returned to the war and enlisted in the Bushveldt Carbineers on 1 April 1901 because of his friend, Captain Percy Hunt.

The infamous Bushveldt Carbineers regiment with which Morant served weren't all Australian. They were a British Irregular Regiment, and a mix of Australians, English, South Africans, Americans, New Zealanders, Canadians and even a German. However, the Boer War was the first war in which Australians fought together as a nation, and Australian soldiers did make a stand during the war, at the Battle of Elands River, that established their reputation for bravery, skill and irreverence, which has been their trademark ever since.

It is highly likely that Morant and Handcock were not the main targets of the investigation and court martial. British Army Intelligence probably constructed their case with an eye on removing one man, the disreputable Captain Arthur Taylor, from the army and possibly bringing the Boers to the negotiating table. Taylor was not even a member of the Bushveldt Carbineers, and there's evidence to show that he was protected by the military hierarchy to cover up their own disgraces.

In fact, Morant and Handcock should have been pardoned as a military matter of course. Regardless of whether they were guilty of criminal acts and murders, whether these were committed of their own volition for personal gain or under orders given from their superiors. Morant's and Handcock's heroism in the defence of the Pietersburg garrison during a raid by a Boer force 'saved the day'—and it happened during the trial, while they were prisoners! Their lawyer filed for clemency, but it was denied.

While Morant has been 'mythified' in folklore as the 'Aussie' underdog and scapegoat, it can be argued that it is Lieutenant Peter Handcock who was the real 'Aussie' victim of this saga. Handcock has been vilified by some as a disgraced war criminal who committed atrocities and does not deserve a place in any honour roll of those who served. There have been recent calls to have his name removed from the monument at Bathurst that lists those who served in the war. Handcock was a self-confessed killer, but he was provably, patently and obviously following a direct order given by an immediate superior officer, in every case. He was executed for obeying orders rather than refusing to carry out a direct order.

An honour roll records the men and women who enlisted and served without comment. It is not a record of an award. If you are going to remove the names of anyone accused of acting wrongly or possibly committing what we call 'war crimes', as Handcock was, then there are going to be a lot of investigations and removals of names to be undertaken. If you enlisted and served, your name should be there.

In order to show how these things played out, we need to take a look at the background to the war, Australia's involvement, and the strange way the war progressed. It began as the last conflict fought in a traditional manner by British troops but transformed into the first all-out guerrilla war where the British employed such tactics as a scorched earth policy, concentration camps for civilians, deportation of prisoners of war and the execution of 'suspected' enemies.

There's a lot more to the story than the mystery of Mr Morant.

BACKGROUND TO THE WAR

The first European settlement on the southern tip of Africa was set up by the Dutch East India Company in 1652, in order to serve as a staging post in the spice trade between Europe and the Dutch East Indies, where the Dutch had established control by defeating the Portuguese in a series of wars in the 17th century.

The population of the Cape Colony, 250 years after its beginning, consisted of a mixture of the descendants of Dutch settlers, along with some Protestant Germans and French Huguenots and many people of mixed race, descendants of the European settlers, Malay and Central African slaves imported into the colony over several centuries, and the many indentured servants from the local Khoi and San peoples. These people were often referred to as 'Cape Coloureds', although many of the rural-dwelling farmers of the colony, known as 'Boers', were also of mixed-race ancestry.

During the French Revolutionary and Napoleonic wars, factions developed in the colony supporting either side and this led the British to intervene and seize the colony in 1803, give it back in 1805, and finally take control in 1806. In 1815 the Dutch accepted a payment of £6 million for the colony and it became an undisputed British possession.

The British administration immediately banned the Dutch language and established British customs and this, in turn, led to many of the Boer colonists 'trekking' away to the northeast to be out of reach of the British administration. This movement increased after 5000 middle-class Britons migrated in the 1820s to help establish the colony as a British trading centre, and the 'trek' became a flood after Emancipation Day in 1838 when the British declared all slaves to be free. Boer farmers relied on slaves and many had purchased slaves on credit or used them as security for loans.

The treks resulted in the displacement of some African tribes from their homelands and led to the establishment of independent 'Afrikaaner' colonies, which became the Boer republics. The British recognised the Republic of South Africa (Transvaal) in 1852 and granted sovereignty of part of the expanded Cape Colony to the Boers, to become part of the Orange Free State, after a savage war with the Basotho people in 1854.

By the late 19th century 'South Africa' was made up of four major territories. The British Cape Colony extended along the western, southern and eastern coasts and up to the north, while the smaller British colony of Natal lay on the east coast. In between these British colonies were the land-locked Boer republics of the Orange Free State and, further north, the Transvaal (South African Republic).

The discovery of diamonds at Kimberley in the north in 1869 led to a dispute over the sovereignty of the area, which was settled in favour of the Griqua mixed-race colonists who had settled there in the late 1820s. Fearing the Boers, just across the border in the Orange Free State, the Griqua accepted British protection and the protectorate was then made part of the Cape Colony in 1871.

A British attempt to unite the colonies led to the annexation of the Transvaal in 1877 and a rebellion against British control three years later then led to the First South African War in 1880, which resulted in a British defeat and the republic regaining its independence in 1881.

The discovery of gold near Johannesburg in 1886 resulted in large numbers of British and other migrants heading north into the Transvaal and was an excuse for the British to interfere in the affairs of the republic on the pretext that migrants were being denied civil rights.

In 1895 an incident known as the 'Jameson Raid' occurred. It was an abortive attempt by 600 mercenaries employed by Cecil Rhodes—the prime minister of the Cape Colony, part-owner of a Kimberley mine and creator of the British colony of Rhodesia—to start an uprising on the goldfields in the Transvaal. It caused international outrage and led the Transvaal government, led by Paul Kruger, to form an alliance with the Orange Free State and seek help from Germany to arm the republic and prepare for war. A telegram of congratulations to Kruger from the Kaiser after the Jameson Raid had deeply offended the British and, later in the war, a German volunteer unit fought for the Boers, as did several units from the Netherlands.

In 1899, when Britain demanded that Kruger give the 60,000 foreign whites at the Witwatersrand Goldfields voting rights, he refused and demanded the withdrawal of British troops from the borders of the South African Republic. When the British ignored the demand, Kruger declared war on 11 October 1899.

The Boer troops were members of civilian militias, organised into military units called 'commandos'. They elected their officers and a leader, titled *Veldkornet*, who called the men to arms when required. In the early phases of the war, the artillery and state-of-the-art weaponry was provided by the governments of the Transvaal and the Orange Free State and mostly supplied by the German companies Mauser and Krupp.

At first the Boer 'army', which was made up of 25,000 Transvaal commandos, 15,000 Orange Free State commandos and 5000 Cape Colony Boers (later supplemented by 5000 European mercenaries), outnumbered the British troops—but enlistment in Britain was rapid and this soon changed. Eventually some 340,000 British and British Empire troops were involved in the conflict, including the first soldiers to fight as 'Australians'.

THE SECOND SOUTH AFRICAN (BOER) WAR

1st phase — October 1899 to January 1900 (three months)

The Boer commando forces of the Transvaal, comprising 25,000 trained men equipped with 55,000 Mauser rifles, 50 million rounds of ammunition and the latest heavy artillery and maxim guns, invaded the British colony of Natal to the east of the Orange Free State and laid siege to the town of Ladysmith. To the west Boer commandos from the Transvaal and the Orange Free State invaded Cape Colony and cut off the British garrisons at Kimberley and Mafeking. The British, under Commander in Chief Sir Redvers Buller and fighting mainly as infantry, won battles at Talana and Elandslaagte in Natal but suffered a series of defeats at Stormberg and Magersfontein in Cape Colony and Colenso in Natal during the second week of December 1899. At Spion Kop, in the British Natal colony, 8000 Boer commandos defeated 20,000 British infantry attempting to lift the siege at Ladysmith, in January 1900.

2nd phase — February 1900 to September 1900 (eight months)

Lord Roberts, with Lord Kitchener as his chief of staff, replaced British General Sir Redvers Buller and under his command British troops turned the tide of the war. The three major sieges were lifted: Ladysmith in Natal (28 February 1900), Cape Colony at Kimberley (15 February 1900) and Mafeking (18 May 1900). The retreating Boer armies were pursued and, in March 1900, the British took

Bloemfontein, the capital of the Orange Free State. In May the Orange
Free State was annexed as the British Orange River Colony and British
troops entered Johannesburg, in the Transvaal. Pretoria fell in June
and the Transvaal was annexed on 1 September 1900. Officially, as far
as Britain was concerned, the war was won.

3rd phase—September 1900 to May 1902 (21 months)

Due to continued guerrilla activities against British troops in the
Transvaal, Lord Roberts instituted a policy of burning farms and set
up concentration camps as a form of control of the families whose
farms were destroyed. Roberts then handed command to Lord
Kitchener, on 23 December 1900, and returned home.

Some of the Boers accepted British rule and became known
as 'hands uppers'. When the war was rekindled some of these men
switched sides, fought with the British, and were known as 'joiners'.
Others again took up arms against the British and joined those who
had refused to surrender and were known as 'bitter-enders'.

Boer leaders Christiaan de Wet, in the Orange Free State, and Louis
Botha, Jan Smuts, Koos de la Rey and Christiaan Frederik Beyers in the
Transvaal, set up small and mobile commando units to attack supply
depots, disrupt communications and make raids on outposts of the
British 'army of occupation'. Tactics were for the men to gather, make
a raid and then disappear back into the farming communities. Units of
the 250,000-strong British army would respond in force but, as soon
as the troops left the area, the British again lost control of the district.
This was especially the case in the frontier areas of the Transvaal. Each
commando unit was made up of men from the district who had local
support and knew the area.

The British response was to form 'irregular' mobile regiments
and establish outposts in forts and blockhouses protected by barbed
wire. The British then embarked on a scorched earth campaign to
deny support to the local commandos. Thirty thousand farms were
burnt, 8000 blockhouses were built and occupied by 50,000 troops,
and 25,000 captured Boers were sent overseas to POW camps in
Bermuda, Ceylon (modern-day Sri Lanka), India and St Helena to
prevent them escaping and rejoining the war. Then 200,000 displaced
members of Boer and African families were moved forcibly into more

than 60 concentration camps, where a quarter of them died. These harsh tactics finally prevailed and the last of the Boers surrendered in May 1902.

The peace terms offered by the British were surprisingly generous: £3 million was given for reconstruction and the Boer republics were promised and granted limited self-government within the British Empire in 1906 and 1907. Finally all the colonies and republics combined to become the Union of South Africa and remained part of the British Empire and, later, the British Commonwealth of Nations until voting to withdraw in 1960.

It was during the Second South African War that Australia became a nation, on 1 January 1901.

AUSTRALIANS AT THE BOER WAR: A NATION BORN IN WARTIME

Unlike many other nations, ours was not born out of conflict or disagreement with the 'motherland'. Quite the opposite is true, in fact—our nation formed at a time when support for Britain among Australians was at its absolute peak and men were clamouring to fight *for* the 'Old Country', certainly not against it!

In retrospect, it may seem odd to some that while the British colonies in Australia were in the process of becoming a nation and thus asserting some level of independence, the 'motherland' had never been more popular and Australians have, arguably, never been prouder of being British than they were in 1901. It is true to say that Australians then were, in general, 'more British than the British', and believed that the distant 'motherland' could do no wrong in world affairs.

The opposition to the war, much debated in British parliament and newspapers in Britain in the later stages, was far more muted in Australia, although any hint of discrimination against our troops by British officers was much debated in the Australian press.

The Second South African (Boer) War was the first time we fought as 'Australians', as our nation federated and was born during the course of the conflict.

The first contingents sent to fight in South Africa were raised by the Australian colonies in response to the outbreak of war in 1899. Mostly these contingents were men in the militia of the various colonial forces.

The next lot to go were what were called the 'Bushmen' contingents, recruited from more diverse sources and paid for by public subscription or by gifts from wealthy individuals.

The next groups to be recruited were the 'Imperial Bushmen' contingents, which were raised in a similar way but paid for by the British government in London. Then there were 'draft' contingents, which were raised by the state governments after Federation on behalf of the new Commonwealth government, which as yet didn't have the infrastructure to do so. These were, technically, the first 'Australian' military units to fight for their country—or, more accurately, fight on behalf of their country for the British Empire.

As far as the population of the Australian continent was concerned, there was no real distinction between being an Australian and being British. Australia may have been a nation in 1901, but her people were all subjects of the Queen (for 22 days at least, until Victoria died and we became subjects of the King). The Australian constitution does not mention the word 'citizen', referring only to the Australian people as 'subjects' of the monarch. Australian travellers all held British passports until the first Australian passports were issued in 1949 and it became possible to be an 'Australian' when overseas.

About 16,000 Australians fought in what was almost always called the 'Boer War' by Australians. They were under British command and contingents were often broken up and attached to British forces. Towards the end of the war, Australian Commonwealth mounted contingents fought through the guerrilla phases of the war, which lasted until 1902.

Few Australians, even today, have any idea how patently shameful and mercenary Britain's motives were in going to war in South Africa, or how brutal and inhumane were the tactics the British used to defeat the Boers.

During the war a total of 282 Australian troops died in action or from wounds sustained in battle, while 286 died from disease and another 38 in accidents or of unknown causes. Six Australians received Victoria Crosses during the fighting in South Africa.

In many ways Australia's participation in the Second South African War serves as a reminder of just how 'British' Australians were at the time we became a nation. It is interesting to consider just how much influence this had in shaping Australian attitudes to being an independent, indivisible nation.

On the other hand, the way the Australians fought in South Africa was an indication of just how different those men were from their British counterparts. One obvious reason for this difference is the fact that the British troops were all regular army, while the Australians were all volunteers and a large majority of them were bushmen. Our military history as a nation began in the Boer War.

During an engagement in the Orange Free State at Stinkhoutboom Farm on 24 July 1900, New South Wales Army Medical Corps' Captain Neville Howse rescued a young bugler who lay wounded without shelter in the field of fire, and was awarded Australia's first Victoria Cross. Neville Howse was elected to federal parliament in 1922, was knighted twice, and became the Australian minister for defence in the Scullin government. He died of cancer in 1930, aged 67. Although his act of bravery occurred before Federation, his Victoria Cross is regarded as Australia's first as it was officially gazetted on 4 June 1901, six months after we became a nation.

The stereotype of the Australian soldier as a fearless, laconic, reckless and extremely efficient fighting man with a wry sense of black humour, which would become a source of great pride to Australians in both world wars, had its foundations in the Second South African War. There is no better example of this than the now long forgotten Battle of Elands River.

During August 1900, a Boer commando force of around 3000 men surrounded and laid siege to a storage post, which was defended by 299 Australian militia fighting as the Australian Imperial Bushmen. These were all citizen militiamen, made up of 141 Queenslanders, 105 men from New South Wales, 42 Victorians, nine Western Australians and two Tasmanians, none of whom had ever been shot at before. They were joined by 200 Rhodesian volunteer militia.

The Boers had twelve modern artillery pieces, which pounded the post in its exposed position. They also had snipers positioned on three sides of the camp. The defenders had one Maxim gun and one old seven-pound muzzle-loader. Unfortunately, the supplies at Elands River post did not include ammunition.

A British force led by Major-General Sir Frederick Carrington attempted to reach the isolated outpost and save the day, but was repulsed and retreated. General Robert Baden-Powell assumed that the post had been taken by the Boers.

On 8 August Boer commander Koos de la Rey sent a messenger under a flag of truce and offered to escort the force to the nearest British post, provided that none of the supplies within the camp were destroyed, 'in recognition of your courage in defence of your camp'. He even offered to let the officers retain their weapons.

Australian officers sent a written reply, which read:

> If De La Rey wants our camp, why does he not come and take it? We will be pleased to meet him and his men, and promise them a great reception at the end of a toasting fork. Australians will never surrender. Australia forever!

The birth of our nation was still four months away but our fighting spirit was already characteristic. It was especially poignant as the 'Australians' fighting at Elands River were actually part-time militiamen from different colonies who had volunteered to go to the war.

When de la Rey sent a second offer of honourable surrender and safe passage, the British officer in command, Colonel Charles Hore, replied:

> Even if I wished to surrender to you—and I don't—I am commanding Australians who would cut my throat if I accepted your terms.

Meanwhile, a Boer messenger carrying a despatch was captured and it became known that the storage post at Elands River had not yet surrendered. Lord Kitchener's army was on the march (in a column that was 16 kilometres long) and detoured to Elands River. The siege was lifted early on 16 August 1900.

General Jan Smuts, who would later serve two terms as prime minister of South Africa, made the following comments about the defence of the Elands River post:

> There can only be one opinion about the fine determination and pluck of these stalwart Colonials, to many this terrific bombardment

must have been their first experience of serious warfare. Deserted by their friends and then, owing to unreasonable obstinacy, abandoned by their disappointed enemies, they simply sat tight until Kitchener's column . . . finally disinterred them from the carcass-covered Kopje.

Sir Arthur Conan-Doyle wrote in praise of the Australians:

They were sworn to die before the white flag would wave above them. And so fortune yielded, as fortune will when brave men set their teeth . . . when the ballad makers of Australia seek for a subject, let them turn to Elands River, for there was no finer fighting in the war.

Fifteen years later the Anzacs landed at Gallipoli and the story of the colonial Australian troops at Elands River faded from the nation's memory, but it was where the reputation of the 'Aussie digger' as a laconic and fearless soldier was born. A popular patriotic poem written about the siege by George Essex Evans concludes:

And we laughed, because we knew, in spite of hell-fire and delay,
On Australia's page forever
We had written Elands River—
We had written it forever and a day.

So, while Britain was the 'homeland' or the 'Old Country', and could do no wrong as far as most Australians were concerned, the Second South African War was also the birthplace of the legendary reputation of the Aussie soldier. Part of this reputation was based on the differences in attitudes towards discipline and 'fair play' between Australian soldiers and their British counterparts. Another difference that became apparent was the Australian soldier's ability to think for himself and act as the situation required, rather than follow traditional military protocols.

One Boer commando in the force attacking the garrison at Elands River later wrote:

For the first time in the war we were fighting men who used our own tactics against us. They were Australian volunteers and although small in number we could not take their position. They were the only troops who could scout into our lines at night and kill our sentries. Our men admitted that the Australians were more formidable and far more dangerous than any British troops.

The Boer War was the first major war in which British officers, most of them from India, were put in charge of colonial volunteers. The officers were used to commanding career soldiers in a professional army under strict barrack room rules and discipline. The colonial volunteers, who were actually better fighters than the British troops under the conditions of the war being fought, were disinclined to salute or obey officers they didn't respect, or to follow rules that seemed pointless.

The laconic bravery of the Australian volunteer soldiers, as well as their disregard for British military protocols, would become legendary at Gallipoli, where one British officer described the Australian fighting man as 'the bravest thing God ever made'. These characteristics were, however, already apparent in the Boer War.

There is anecdotal evidence of many incidents in which Australian colonial troops showed a disregard for British military practices. When a trooper of the 2nd New South Wales Mounted Rifles was convicted of stealing a case of officers' whisky, on the rather flimsy evidence that 'it was too dark to see him, but his voice was recognised', he was sentenced to a term of 'field imprisonment', which involved being 'crucified', tied arms outstretched to the wheel of a wagon all day.

His mates, who felt the punishment did not fit the alleged crime, simply cut him free on the first two days and informed the British officer in charge, Major Charles Lydiard, who had hinted that they could be shot for their actions, that they would certainly continue to do so if that form of punishment was persevered with.

There are also stories of colonial troops refusing to burn farms. On one such occasion this led to British rifles being aimed at Australian troops. Evidently, however, a compromise was reached and the Australians took up defensive positions while the British troops performed the burning.

Banjo Paterson, as a war correspondent in South Africa, came to realise that the differences between the British and Australian way of soldiering were incompatible. Australian soldiers, he believed, needed to be led by Australian officers and fight, albeit *for* Britain, under their own flag, not Britain's flag:

Our Own Flag

> They mustered us up with a royal din,
> In wearisome weeks of drought.
> Ere ever half of the crops were in,
> Or the half of the sheds cut out.
>
> 'Twas down with the saddle and spurs and whip
> The swagman dropped his swag.
> And we hurried us off to the outbound ship
> To fight for the English flag.
>
> The English flag, it is ours in sooth
> We stand by it wrong or right.
> But deep in our hearts is the honest truth
> We fought for the sake of a fight.
>
> And the English flag may flutter and wave
> Where the World-wide Oceans toss,
> But the flag the Australian dies to save
> Is the flag of the Southern Cross.
>
> If ever they want us to stand the brunt
> Of a hard-fought, grim campaign,
> We will carry our own flag up to the front
> When we go to the wars again.

The first time these differences in attitude towards soldiering led to Australians being court-martialled and sentenced to death was not the Bushveldt Carbineers' courts martial. It was the infamous incident that became known as the 'Wilmansrust Ambush'.

On 12 June 1901, 270 men of the 2nd Battalion 5th Victorian Mounted Rifles were detached from a column commanded by Major-General Stuart Beatson, an ex–Indian Army officer known for his dislike of 'volunteer troops'. They were sent with two Vickers-Maxim 'pom pom' artillery pieces to look for a small Boer commando force believed to be some 40 kilometres to the east. Major McKnight, a Victorian, was the senior officer, but the force was under the command of another British ex–Indian Army officer, Major Morris.

While encamped at Wilmansrust Farm the force was ambushed in a surprise attack by Boer commandos and the guns and 100 horses were stolen. Fourteen Victorians were killed and 42 wounded.

Morris, who was an artillery officer in command of mounted riflemen, had set the sentry posts and pickets wide apart, cavalry fashion. The main outpost to watch for Boers was 1½ kilometres from the camp. He had posted the picket stations in broad daylight, with the enemy in hiding watching his every move.

The Boers, guided by the farmer, easily sneaked between the sentries under cover of darkness and the ambush was a total success. The Victorians taken prisoner were simply marched several kilometres out onto the veldt and released.

Military historian Chris Coulthard-Clark's assessment of the event is:

> The action at Wilmansrust was the most serious reverse to befall any overseas colonial force sent to the conflict in South Africa, and unfortunately was taken as an indictment of the courage and soldierly qualities of Australian contingents generally. There was no denying that a deplorable lack of vigilance and attention to security had been displayed—although the responsibility for this rested squarely on an Imperial and not an Australian officer.
>
> *The Encyclopaedia of Australia's Battles*, 'Wilmansrust'

Several days after the ambush Major-General Beatson rode over to a group of Victorian troopers and reputedly told them that they were a 'fat arsed, potbellied, round shouldered lot of wasters' and added 'all Australians are the same'. The Victorian officer present, Major Harris, apparently replied that he was sorry to hear that and pulled out a notebook and said that he would take the words down.

Beatson apparently then said, 'Do by all means and you can add if you like that in my opinion they are a lot of white livered curs ... you can add dogs too.'

Harris reported to McKnight, who sent a report of the incident to the Victorian government and then asked permission from his superiors to go to Pretoria to ask for a full inquiry into the ambush.

This was denied, but the men were paraded and a memo from the man commanding the 5th Victorians, Major Umphelby, was read to them. It contained an apology from Beatson, who had pressured Umphelby into getting McKnight to back down. The Victorians were, however, sick of the treatment they received from British officers and wanted a direct apology.

In his report to the man commanding Victoria's military, Major-General Downes, McKnight said that the Victorians 'did their work loyally and well' and stated:

> I knew it was the intention of the men to lay down their arms unless they could get another command ... They said they could not serve with confidence under the present General ... The men felt that there was no regard shown for their lives and in some cases the punishments awarded were of a most humiliating character ... when it became a question as to the reputation of the Victorians and consequently of the state that sent me out to Africa, I was compelled to protest strongly ...
> I could see that the treatment of the officers and men from Victoria by the chief of staff, Major Waterfield, and afterwards by General Beatson, must eventually cause trouble ... had the regiment been handled with even an ordinary amount of tact ... no trouble would have arisen afterward between the men and their commander.

Indeed, it did cause trouble. Three men, troopers Steele, Parry and Richards, who were overheard saying that they did not trust Beatson and would not serve under him, were court-martialled and sentenced to death.

The new Australian Commonwealth government was not informed of this by the British, but men were writing letters home. The *Adelaide Advertiser* had already reported Beatson's insults and, by the time the court martial was reported—by means of 'a private letter placed at our disposal', on page 13 of the Melbourne *Age* on 28 September 1901 (complete with a photo of the court martial charge sheet)—the men were already in prison in Britain, having had their sentences commuted; Steele to ten years and the other two to one year's hard labour. The headline in *The Age* was:

A QUESTION OF MUTINY

VICTORIAN SENTENCED TO DEATH

COMMUTED TO TEN YEARS IMPRISONMENT

The Age reported on the result of Beatson's comments after the 'unfortunate affair at Wilmansrust' this way:

> The words he used, I have reason to believe, were 'you are white livered curs'. He afterwards made an apology through the agency of Major Umphelby. The men thought he ought to have apologised personally, and this consequently led to a lot of unsoldierlike talk and discontent.

The article then goes on, in a style 'more British than the British', to criticise those opposing the war in Britain as 'would-be philanthropists' and continues the jingoistic tone:

> About those pom-poms, they have been re-taken, or, at least, one has for a certainty, so they bark again on the right side. The 18th and 19th Hussars were the heroes on this auspicious occasion. Some of them have been recommended for the distinguished conduct medal almost the acme of a soldier's ambition, as it takes precedence after the Victoria Cross. The capture was very ably accomplished near Blood River.

Although the pro-British Melbourne *Age* did not seem inclined to call for an inquiry, there were certainly questions asked in the new federal parliament, with the result that Governor-General Lord Hopetoun was asked to seek the facts from Colonial Secretary Joseph Chamberlain, who replied in October, stating:

Prisoners were sent to this country, but on receipt of proceedings of courts martial, Judge Advocate-General declared that there were legal flaws in the convictions, the men having been tried under the wrong section of the Army Act. Instructions have been issued for their immediate release, and joining provisional battalions shortly.

It was Lord Kitchener who had commuted the sentences to imprisonment, which removed the men to Britain, before a convenient excuse was found to free them. It is obvious that the British wished to avoid an inquiry into the Wilmansrust Ambush at all costs, in order to avoid the embarrassment of exposing British officers to charges of poor leadership and inappropriate tactics. Major Morris was censured but Kitchener decided to take no further action, telling the secretary for war, St John Brodrick, that the bitter lesson Morris had learned about setting pickets properly in South Africa was 'punishment enough'.

The Victorians continued to be blamed for the disaster and the loss of the guns. In one official British record of the war there is even an 'artist's impression' drawing of the ambush with the caption 'The Australians fell like rabbits'.

So, in spite of Australia being 'more British than Britain' in 1901, these incidents, and others mentioned in letters home and reported anecdotally, along with the courts martial of Morant and three Australian officers and the execution by firing squad of lieutenants Handcock and Morant, have fuelled the fires of republicanism in Australia for more than a century and still serve today as a rallying point for anti-British sentiment in Australia.

THE 'WHITE MAN'S WAR'

This is a story of murder and mayhem, plots and politics, spies and complexities, treachery and cover-ups. The characters involved rise from the pages of history as 'larger than life', colonial caricatures—fearless daredevils, wild colonial boys, cloak and dagger mystery men, comical moustachioed 'Colonel Blimps'. In reality some were also mass murderers, liars and thieves who cold-bloodedly killed bed-ridden civilians, prisoners unable to walk, children, and even their own regimental comrades.

Everyone who researches the Morant case inevitably ends up with a theory, and I am no exception. I am of the opinion that members of British Army Intelligence constructed their case with the specific aim of ridding the army and the British Empire of one man, who was not even a member of the Bushveldt Carbineers, although he was, in effect, the commanding officer of the Bushveldt Carbineer troopers at Fort Edward.

That man was Captain Arthur 'Bulala' Taylor who, having resigned his commission when arrested, was tried by a British military court under martial law—rather than a court martial. I believe that the four Bush-veldt Carbineer officers found guilty were the 'small fry' in the case being built against Taylor and, when the case against him failed to produce the desired result, they became 'collateral damage' and two were executed in an effort to show that the British were fighting a fair and civilised war in the Transvaal—which they undoubtedly and patently were not.

Why did certain members of British Intelligence want to 'get' Captain Taylor?

Well, strange as it may seem, there was an unwritten gentleman's agreement between the Boers and the British that the war should be fought as a 'white man's war' to determine which white authority had real power in South Africa.

Both sides were terrified of the results of mobilising and arming African tribes and involving them in the conflict. In spite of 250 years of European occupation, in South Africa the white population was still vastly outnumbered by the original indigenous population and there were many long-standing historical grudges to be settled. The memories of conflicts such as the Zulu and Ndebele wars were still fresh in the minds of white South Africans. The Second South African War was fought over territory that traditionally (and most modern minds would think morally) belonged to various African tribes. Eighty per cent of the population living in the area being fought over was indigenous.

It was commonly believed by both sides that any war involving native tribes would be more brutal than a 'white man's war', that white women and children would be shown no mercy and that such a war would increase the future possibility of whites losing control of the tribal lands they had previously taken.

Both sides recognised that whoever won by using such methods would then have to deal with the consequences of the threat to white dominance that it would entail, not to mention any tribal wars that would result. When the war began, British officials instructed all magistrates in the Natal colony to appeal to Zulu chiefs to remain neutral, and, in the Transvaal, President Kruger sent emissaries asking local tribes to stay out of it. Both sides denied using native troops to fight and both sides accused the other of doing so.

On the Boer side, natives were used as wagon drivers or servants to perform menial tasks and support roles in camps and to look after the horses. In battle, native servants carried ammunition and spare rifles and might even load rifles for their masters, but it was against the law, in the Transvaal, for natives to carry arms. Natives could be conscripted to build forts and perform non-combatant duties, for which they were not paid. Those refusing to work could be given 25 lashes and gaoled.

Although Kitchener probably covertly approved using native tribes to attack Boer farms, in the same way that he gave unwritten orders to 'take no prisoners', he denied doing either. When he was under enormous pressure from the British parliament to end the conflict and cease annihilating the Boer population and burning their farms, he finally admitted, a month before the war ended, that some 10,000 natives had been issued with weapons by the British army. This was not the same thing as 'raising the natives', yet there is plenty of evidence to prove that that was also happening:

> It was stated at times during the war by those in authority that the natives were not permitted to take any part in the fighting, but such was not the case. During the time I was in the Spelonken district with the Carbineers the natives were twice raised, and it has been openly stated that, with the connivance of others, when Colonel Grenfell went through the district he had thousands of these savages, who were fed and paid, attached to his column, and they committed the most hideous atrocities which no one has yet been made to account for.
>
> Lieutenant George Witton, *Scapegoats of the Empire*, 1907

The natives were raised the night Harry Morant's best friend, Captain Percy Hunt, was killed attacking a Boer stronghold on 5 August 1901. When the news reached Fort Edward on the morning of 7 August, Morant was emotionally distraught and unable to address the men. Captain Taylor took charge of the situation, instructed the patrol to show 'no quarter', and provided Morant with a local guide and intelligence agents from his staff to accompany the patrol.

The natives were again raised several nights later. George Witton later wrote: 'By nightfall we had covered more than 40 miles, and then put up at a native kraal to give the horses a feed and wait until the moon rose. Here one of the intelligence agents left us to gather up an army of natives.'

When the patrol found the Boer encampment, Morant impetuously attacked before his troops had established proper positions and the Boers mounted and escaped, except for one wounded man who could not walk and was executed by firing squad the next day on

Morant's orders. After the execution, according to Witton: 'The intelligence agent, who had left us to raise the natives, now returned with several hundred savages, but as their services were not now required, they were fed, and, when they had held a war dance, were dispersed.'

It's obvious that Kitchener hoped his brutal tactics—burning farms, deporting or hanging captured Boer soldiers, and sending women and children to concentration camps—would succeed before the outcry at home forced him to stop. Indeed, they were successful, and that success was helped immensely by two other tactics to which he gave tacit consent but always denied approving: 'taking no prisoners' and 'raising the natives'.

'Arming of blacks' by the British was one of the reasons given by the Boers for their decision to discontinue the war in May 1902. When all was lost they would rather negotiate a peace with a white enemy than a black one that they had treated as slaves for more than two hundred years.

There were tribes eager to enter the war with the specific aim of reclaiming land confiscated by the Boers and certain elements within British Intelligence, very close to Kitchener, were actively aiding and abetting that possibility: none more so than Captain Arthur Taylor.

THE REGIMENT

The Bushveldt Carbineers was a unit formed by Major Robert Poore in February 1901, at the request of Lord Kitchener, in response to a number of mobile Boer commando units making hit-and-run raids on British troops, railways and infrastructure in the northern Transvaal. These Boers were 'bitter-enders' who could camp out and move regularly or even melt back into the general Afrikaaner population in Boer farms and towns.

A tough mounted mobile force was required to find and destroy these Boer commando units, rather than sit in blockhouses waiting for them to strike. The regiment was partly funded by loyal supporters of the British living in the area who wished to see an end to the conflict.

Poore was the provost marshall in the Transvaal, responsible for discipline in the field. He gave the task of forming the unit to Major Robert Lenehan. The recruiting base was Durban and 660 men served during the unit's eighteen-month history—43 per cent were Australian, 31 per cent English, and the rest were mostly South Africans, New Zealanders and Canadians. Although the unit's authorised strength was 500, its actual fighting strength was never more than about 350.

In many ways the history of the Bushveldt Carbineers serves as a microcosm from the last phase of the Second South African War and exposes to scrutiny Kitchener's policy of 'clearing out the Boers' and answering the guerrilla-style war being waged by Boer farmers with tactics like 'scorched earth', concentration camps, murder and deportation.

Many of the men who joined the Bushveldt Carbineers were colonial troopers released from their units after the British victory over the Boers in the second phase of the war. Others were locals who had pledged loyalty to Britain after the annexation of the Transvaal. Most were attracted by the prospect of further action, and by the high rate of pay of 5 shillings a day. It was a tough unit with a tough leader, Major Robert William Lenehan.

Lenehan was given command of the Bushveldt Carbineers, with the rank of major. Lieutenant Peter Handcock was commissioned and joined when the regiment was formed. Lieutenant Harry Morant, who had known Lenehan in Sydney, followed his best friend Captain Percy Hunt, and joined in May. Lieutenant George Witton joined in June.

These four men—three Australians, Lenehan, Handcock and Witton; and Morant (who was British but is regarded as an Australian by many)—would later be the only ones, of the eight officers charged and six court-martialled, to be found guilty of war crimes in the Spelonken district during 1901.

The regiment was part of Lieutenant Colonel Herbert Plumer's column of 1300 men, which left Pretoria in March 1901 and advanced to capture Pietersburg, 240 kilometres to the north. The Bushveldt Carbineers' first job was to ensure the British supply trains were safe from the Boers' attempts to blow up all trains on the Pietersburg–Pretoria line. This they did by placing Boer prisoners in the second carriage of a train and telling them that if they did not reveal the location of the explosive mines on the line they would be blown up with the train. The Carbineers ran the train until the first wagon was blown up, after which the Boers revealed the positions of all the mines.

Pietersburg was taken on 14 April and the regiment became part of the Pietersburg garrison. They established an outpost in the wild northern frontier Spelonken district of the Transvaal where 'A' Squadron, under Captain James Robertson, was stationed at Fort Edward, north of Pietersburg, 2 kilometres away from Captain Taylor's headquarters at Sweetwaters Farm and Hotel. This squadron was specifically given the task of 'assisting Captain Taylor' to rid the area of roving Boer commando units.

Sweetwaters had been the site of a Boer commando camp but, when the Bushveldt Carbineers moved into the district, the Boers had withdrawn from the area so as not to cause any problems for the farm and hotel owners Charlie and Olivia Bristow.

'B' Squadron of the Bushveldt Carbineers, under Lieutenant Harry Morant, was established at Strypoort, further south on the other side of Pietersburg, in an area that was rather easier for the British to control.

DRAMATIS PERSONAE

To understand anything about the history of the Bushveldt Carbineers and the subsequent courts martial, it is necessary to look at the cast of characters who played some major role in the drama.

As with any event in history, understanding the social and political context in which it occurred is essential to making any sense of it in retrospect. Likewise, some understanding of the backgrounds and motivations of the principal players is an essential element to any accurate understanding of what eventuated.

Here are the important *dramatis personae* who need some introduction in this case.

Edwin Henry Murrant
(alias Lieutenant Harry Harbord Morant, 'The Breaker')

The man best known as 'Breaker Morant' claimed that he was born in Devon and was the illegitimate son of Admiral Morant, and that he was sent to Australia in disgrace as a 'remittance man' to be kept out of the way of the family after some gambling debts were unpaid.

However, both *The Northern Miner* and *The Bulletin* newspapers identified him as Edwin Henry Murrant, who had arrived at Townsville in Queensland on the SS *Waroonga* on 5 June 1883.

Murrant was, in fact, born in Bridgewater, Somerset, on 9 December 1864 and was registered as the son and second child of Edwin and Catherine Murrant, master and matron of the Union Workhouse at

Bridgewater. Edwin senior had died of rheumatic fever four months earlier, in August 1864, and, after his death, his wife Catherine continued her employment as matron until her dismissal in 1882.

This was rather unusual, as it was customary for the wife of the master of the workhouse to have the position of matron. The Board of Guardians of the Bridgewater Union Workhouse, however, allowed Catherine to retain her position, on a miserable annual salary of £40, which was less than half of what she and her husband had received previously.

Apparently all was well until the appointment of James Winterson as the new master of the workhouse in 1878. It appears that he wanted his wife to have the position of matron and conducted a vendetta of accusations against Catherine. He accused her of having her children, Annie and Edwin, staying at the workhouse and she was reprimanded and wrote a letter of apology. Catherine was also reprimanded for drunkenness, which was a sackable offence, and the situation came to a head when she was reportedly 'disrespectful, violent and defiant' at a meeting with the Board of Guardians.

As a result of this 'feud', both Catherine and James Winterson were dismissed in 1882. She moved to Devon and found a position as matron in the County Asylum, and then became housekeeper at a grand house in Torquay, where she resided, with her unmarried daughter, Annie, who was two years older than Edwin. Catherine died in 1899 about the time that her son enlisted in the South Australian Mounted Rifles in Renmark, South Australia.

Now we come to the point where the story of Edwin Murrant/ Harry Morant enters the realm of the unknown and unknowable.

While their mother is existing on £40 per annum at the Bridgewater Workhouse, Annie and Edwin somehow both manage to get an excellent education. Annie becomes a professional musician, music tutor and organist, and can honestly describe herself in the 1881 census as 'professor of music'.

According to stories told by Murrant, he spent much of his childhood with an 'uncle', to whom he was evidently not related. Major George Whyte-Melville, a famous Scottish author, golfer and renowned horseman with properties in Gloucestershire and Fifeshire in Scotland, took Edwin under his wing. Whyte-Melville is remembered for writing popular historical novels and entertaining novels about fox hunting. He spent much of his time riding to hounds with various hunts around the south of England and served as a cavalry officer in the Crimean War.

Under the guidance of Whyte-Melville, Edwin was taught to ride and prepare and train horses for hunting and developed a love of literature. Sometime around 1876 Edwin was sent as a boarder to Silesia College at Barnet on the outskirts of London, where he received an education reserved for only the privileged classes and was bright enough to become a tutor after completing his education there at the age of fifteen or sixteen.

During school holidays his mother had to ask permission of the Board of Guardians for him to stay with her—at the Bridgewater Workhouse!

What on earth is going on? The truth is, no one knows.

The obvious assumption is that Edwin was the illegitimate son of either Whyte-Melville or his friend Digby Morant, with whom he served in the Crimean War. Edwin Murrant/Harry Morant always claimed that he was the illegitimate son of Admiral Sir George Digby Morant, and it is logistically possible that his mother and the young unmarried naval lieutenant had some sort of a liaison around Easter 1864.

What makes that possibility seem far from credible is the fact that Catherine was an apparently respectable, poorly paid, married woman from the lower middle class, with a young baby daughter, working in a workhouse, while George Morant was a naval officer from a privileged Irish family.

However, these things did happen. Whyte-Melville himself had fought a very public paternity suit in 1849, two years after he married, and the case was only dismissed when it was found that another man had been paying the child's and mother's expenses. Such things were possible in 1864, no matter how improbable they might be. Family histories are full of such secrets but it is hard to build a credible scenario of connections in this case. If, however, the *possibility* is more than an unlikely *probability* and is the truth, then the strange similarity of the names Murrant and Morant must be considered a mere coincidence.

Admiral Sir George Digby Morant denied to his dying day that Edwin Murrant was in any way connected to his family. When an effort was made, in line with the executed lieutenant's last wishes, to return his belongings to the admiral's family, they refused to accept them.

Those who believe that George Digby Morant was, or could have been, the father of Edwin Murrant argue that he *could have* refused to acknowledge his son later in life because of the shame and disgrace that sent Edwin to Australia (gambling debts and/or sexual misconduct). Others suggest it was perhaps his shameful conduct in South Africa and the ignominy of his execution. Of course, it could also have been Digby's feeling of shame at his own behaviour and the desire to protect his own reputation. It could also have been because he was *not* his father!

During his six or seven years at Silesia College, there is anecdotal evidence from fellow students, and pupils tutored by Murrant, that he spent much of his time at local racetracks, both at Barnet and Finchley, and developed the habit of not paying his debts. There is also anecdotal evidence of some sexual misdemeanour with a girl who was a ward in Chancery; that is, an orphan who would claim her inheritance once she came of age.

Those who wish to portray Murrant as a cad and a bounder claim that he was running from responsibility for this ungentlemanly crime and his gambling debts when he left for Australia aged nineteen. Those who prefer the more romantic version claim that he left England in order to protect the girl's reputation, and never recovered from his heart being broken.

Soon after he arrived in Townsville, Murrant found work with a travelling rodeo and circus and made his way to Charters Towers, where records show that Edwin Henry Murrant, son of Edwin Murrant, and his wife, Catherine, née O'Reilly, married Daisy May O'Dwyer on 13 March 1884 at the residence of James Hopgood Veal in Plant Street. Daisy May O'Dwyer would later become known as the famous anthropologist and champion of the Aboriginal people Daisy Bates.

The marriage did not last very long. Evidently our hero established a pattern of not paying his debts quite early in his life in Australia and the bill for the marriage celebrations was never paid. The couple separated within months after Murrant was arrested on a charge of stealing pigs and a saddle. He was acquitted and went to work further west at Winton; later he began overlanding cattle south, through the Channel Country.

Daisy moved south, was employed as a governess at Berry, New South Wales, and in February 1885 at Nowra married cattleman Jack Bates. When he went off droving she travelled to Sydney where, on 10 June 1885, she married again, to Ernest Baglehole. There is no record of her ever divorcing any of them.

Murrant, who from this point in his life called himself Harry Morant, developed a legendary and romantic reputation as a hard-drinking horse-breaker, bush poet and ladies' man. A fearless and expert horseman, he was one of the few who managed to ride the notorious buckjumper Dargan's Grey, and once jumped his horse Cavalier over a six-foot fence to win a bet. He contributed bush ballads to *The Bulletin* and used the pen name 'The Breaker'.

He also gained a reputation as a reckless show-off and woman-ising drunkard who rarely paid his bills. He was friendly with other poets like Banjo Paterson and Will Ogilvie, who liked him and helped him, but acknowledged he was not to be trusted with money, or the truth.

Paterson described Morant as attention-seeking and 'plucky to the point of recklessness' and said, 'He suffered from a theatrical complex which made him pretend to be badly hurt when there was, really, not much up with him.'

In a radio talk late in his life, Banjo told an anecdote about his fellow versifier, who was visiting Sydney at the time of the annual Rosehill amateur steeplechase, which Paterson described as 'a sort of Custer's last stand':

Arriving in Sydney at the time of the amateur steeplechase, he set out to look for a mount. Mr Pottie, of the veterinary family, had a mare that could both gallop and jump, but she was such an unmanageable brute that none of the local amateurs (and I was one of them) cared to take the mount. Morant jumped at the chance, but as soon as they started the mare cleared out with him and fell into a drain, rolling her rider out as flat as a flounder.

He was carried in, supposed to be unconscious, and I was taken up to hear his last wishes. The doctors could get nothing out of him, but after listening to his wanderings for a while I said, very loudly and clearly, 'What'll you have Morant?' and he said, equally clearly,

'Brandy and soda.'

Paterson also said in the *Sydney Mail*: 'Morant was always popular for his dash and courage ... Money he never valued at its true worth; he was a spendthrift and an idler, quick to borrow and slow to pay.' 'The Banjo' summed up the life of 'The Breaker' like this:

Those who knew him best say that he would sooner have given a sick Boer the coat off his back than shot him for any money ... As it turned out he got into exactly the worst company that a man of his temperament could have met—it was always so with him. What is it that such men lack—just a touch of determination or caution maybe—to turn their lives from failures to successes?

Sydney Mail, 12 April 1902

Scottish poet Will Ogilvie, who spent twelve years of his life in the Australian bush, knew Morant well and liked him. He predicted, five years before Morant's execution, that, whenever he died, there would be obligations left neglected:

He will leave when his ticket is tended
A bundle of debts, I'm afraid –
Accounts that were many times rendered
And bills that will never be paid.

'When The Breaker Is Booked For The South', *The Bulletin*,
vol. 17 no. 883, 16 January 1897

When the Second South African War broke out in 1899 Edwin Murrant enlisted, on 17 October 1899 in Renmark, in the 2nd Contingent, South Australian Mounted Rifles, as Harry Harbord Morant, and was almost immediately made lance-corporal. By the time the contingent arrived in South Africa, he was a sergeant.

His skill as a horseman, and his ability to 'acquire horses and mules' by dubious methods, as well as his charm and ability to pass as an educated gentleman, led to him becoming a despatch rider for General French, and he also worked as an aide and guide for Bennet Burleigh, a famous British war correspondent. Also, at some point, he met Captain Percy Hunt. Morant had enlisted for one year, and had served in South Africa for nine months when that assignment ended. At the completion of his one-year enlistment, his work was highly commended and he was offered a commission.

Morant, however, was not committed to the war and decided to take the opportunity to return 'home' to England, and spent five months there. He claimed he sailed home with Captain Percy Hunt of the 10th Hussars, but there is documentary evidence to prove this was a lie. He certainly stayed at the Mount Nelson Hotel at Cape Town in November 1900, claiming to be a correspondent for a British newspaper and the son of Admiral Morant. We know this because, as was his custom, he never paid the bill and there is a letter from the hotel addressed to Admiral Sir George Morant: 'We shall esteem it a favour if you will let us know the course we had better adopt. We are averse to taking the matter to court till we had heard from you.'

During his time back 'home' Morant linked up with Hunt and the two men became best friends, rode to hounds and were engaged to two sisters. Hunt was still 'signed on' and returned to South Africa in March 1901. Morant followed and the two were commissioned into the Bushveldt Carbineers.

At first Morant was in command at Strypoort to the south of Pietersburg but, after discipline 'troubles' at Ford Edward in July and the clean-out of the personnel, only Handcock remaining at the fort, some 60 troopers under the command of Captain Hunt and Lieutenant Morant were sent to replace the troublesome ill-disciplined crew that had been withdrawn.

After the death of his friend Percy Hunt, Morant was left in charge and, perhaps in a spirit of revenge, or under the influence of Captain Taylor, committed what were later to be deemed war crimes.

In spite of a successful operation, in which he captured the leader of one of the last two commando groups operating in the area along with his troops and supporters, Morant was arrested in October 1901, court-martialled and found guilty in January 1902. He was executed by firing squad on 27 February 1902.

Captain Arthur 'Bulala' Taylor

The Bushveldt Carbineers Regiment, by strict army regulations, was answerable to Area Commandant Colonel F.H. Hall at Pietersburg. The squadron at Fort Edward, however, was under the influence of Arthur Taylor, a captain in the Intelligence Department of the British Army at Spelonken, 115 kilometres to the north, who had led a small team of six agents into the area to gather information about the Boers from local tribes.

Taylor had worked as a scout and mercenary for Cecil Rhodes's British South Africa Company in their invasion and conquest of Matabeleland and the creation of Rhodesia. He was a veteran of the Matabele (Ndebele) War and the later rebellion (Second Matabele War), during which he commanded a unit of mounted scouts with Lieutenant-Colonel Plumer's army.

Recalled as an agent in 1900, he was, by his own account, 'sent to the Transvaal to get information on Boer movements', and also to scout Boer positions in the Makato Mountains and find and destroy the Boer communications station at Fort Botha, which he did. Taylor stated that these orders came second-hand from Kitchener. While engaged in this mission Taylor had the chief of the Mamadi tribe shot dead on suspicion of collaborating with the Boers.

Fort Botha turned out to be a communications station in the mountains manned by two men. Having smashed up the equipment, Taylor 'questioned the two Boers' and discovered evidence of Boer activity in the township of Louis Trichardt. He subsequently led a force of 600 men, including 'native irregular troops', to sack the town. The troops were allowed to loot the houses and the town was burned to the ground. Ninety men were taken prisoner and the rest of the population was marched to the concentration camp at Pietersburg.

Taylor was then appointed acting native commissioner by Kitchener and told to 'liaise with' the Bushveldt Carbineers. He set up headquarters at Sweetwaters Farm, 1½ kilometres from Fort Edward, and was acknowledged as their commanding officer by Captain James Robertson, leader of 'A' Squadron at Fort Edward.

In its version of the story of the Bushveldt Carbineers, the official website for the Boer War Memorial in Canberra mentions 'Captain Taylor' four times, as if he was an officer in the regiment. Taylor was never a member of the Bushveldt Carbineers, but he was the man who was most responsible for the regiment's shameful reputation.

Born into a middle-class Protestant family in Dublin in 1861, Taylor went to sea as a young man and arrived in Africa in 1886.

Taylor has been variously described by historians as a 'sadistic, ruthless mass murderer', 'war profiteer', 'cattle thief' and 'war criminal'. He was notorious for his atrocities against the Matabele (Ndebele) people, who gave him the name '*Bulala*' ('Killer').

In his role as acting district native commissioner, Taylor waged a war of extermination against the Tsonga people, who had a close association with the local Boers. He also encouraged the local Venda and Sotho tribesmen to kill Boer farmers and help themselves to the land and whatever else they wanted, as 'the Boers would not be returning after the war'. Tribesmen from these groups were allowed to follow British soldiers into action and loot farms and massacre local Afrikaaners after the troops departed. On at least two occasions the Bushveldt Carbineers 'raised the natives', as this action was called, to help them attack farms.

Under Taylor's influence, discipline in the Bushveldt Carbineers was a constant problem and the 'rules of engagement' were vague and arbitrary at best—and criminal at worst.

In May 1901, when Captain Frederick de Bertodano, an experienced Australian-born intelligence officer, sought out Major Lenehan at Pietersburg, he was shocked to find Taylor sitting at Lenehan's desk filling in for the major, who was away from his headquarters. At that time, de Bertodano was acting as district commissioner in the Orange River Colony, which was the Boer Orange Free State, south of the Transvaal, that had been annexed by Britain although it was not yet wholly occupied by British troops.

Back in Pretoria, de Bertodano informed Colonel David Henderson, Director of Military Intelligence, that Taylor's reputation 'stank to Heaven' and warned him that 'trouble was bound to ensue'. De Bertodano suggested that Taylor's appointment as acting district native commissioner be reversed and was told it was too late. He was then given the task of 'keeping an eye on *Bulala* Taylor'.

De Bertodano described Taylor as:

> ... an Irishman who had spent years among the natives and was known as a sadist. He frequently stirred up trouble in native Kraals and then shot some native 'in self defence', as he always stated. He was notorious and was distrusted by most white men he came into contact with.

Two incidents that show Taylor's *modus operandi* were later used in evidence against him. On 4 May 1901 he was part of a patrol that arrived at the Perdeplaas Farm to take the wife and children of Boer commando Coenraad Jacobus van den Berg to the concentration camp at Pietersburg. Unknown to the British, van den Berg had returned home and was sick with malaria. When Taylor's men started looting the farm the sick man, who had left the house and was hiding nearby, shot and wounded one of the troopers. Taylor, believing he was surrounded by Boer commandos, called a truce. Mrs van den Berg promised to care for the wounded man and, before withdrawing, Taylor promised no harm would come to her family and a patrol would be sent for the man.

This was agreed, but the wounded man died and was buried by the van den Bergs.

Six days later Taylor returned and ordered Mrs van den Berg to help her sick husband from his bed to the yard, where, in front of his family, van den Berg was shot by fifteen troopers. Mrs van den Berg and her children were then immediately marched to the concentration camp. After the war Mrs van den Berg returned to the ruined farm, where her first task was to pick up the bones of her husband, which had been scattered around the yard by wild animals.

On another occasion, in pursuit of retreating Boer commandos, Taylor entered a native kraal and asked the head man which way the Boers had gone. When the man did not reply, Taylor simply took out his revolver and shot him in the head. Later, in court, Taylor was found not guilty of this action, claiming that he attempted to shoot over the man's head but missed.

There was a reorganisation of the Department of Native Affairs in September 1901. A new commissioner, Sir Godfrey Lagden, was appointed and the man who would become the permanent native commissioner in the northern Transvaal, Francis Enraght-Mooney, started to understand the manner in which Taylor had been operating. Anticipating his removal as soon as Kitchener approved it, in the lead-up to the Court of Inquiry, Colonel Hall and Colonel Henderson, Head of Intelligence in Pretoria, told Taylor about the changes and said that everything was fine. Enraght-Mooney wrote to Lagden in the first week of September and Henderson and Hall were able to agree with his suspicions. On 24 September, Kitchener finally gave in to the inevitable and Taylor was recalled to Pretoria and Enraght-Mooney proceeded to Sweetwaters and, on 21 October, had access to Taylor's files.

Taylor was allowed to resign his commission and, after a period of three months had elapsed, he was tried as a civilian under martial law, rather than court-martialled under the *Army Act*.

After the trials and his acquittal, Taylor returned to his farm near Plumtree, in southern Rhodesia. He was recalled to active service during World War I and served in France during 1917 and 1918 and was wounded in the leg.

Arthur Taylor died from pneumonia in Bulawayo Memorial Hospital on 24 October 1941 and is buried in Bulawayo General Cemetery. He was described as one of Rhodesia's 'pioneers' in his obituary in the *Rhodesian Herald*.

In 1887 he had married Phoebe Wolfenden, a widow of mixed British and Bechuana descent. They had eight children, who reportedly remembered him as a loving and caring father.

Major Robert William Lenehan

'Bob' Lenehan was born in 1865 at Petersham, Sydney, educated at St Ignatius College, Riverview, studied law, married Harriett Hodge in 1889 in the St Ignatius Chapel and was practising as a solicitor in 1890—the same year that he was commissioned as a second lieutenant in the 1st Infantry Regiment. Promoted to captain in 1896 in the New South Wales Field Artillery, he was promoted again to major in December 1898 to command 'C' Battery of the New South Wales Artillery. In 1900 he switched from artillery and dropped a rank to serve as a captain with the 1st New South Wales Mounted Infantry and embarked for South Africa in January 1900.

For the next year Lenehan was constantly engaged in the action. From February to May 1900 he served in the Orange Free State and then in the Transvaal until June. He was present at the relief of the Elands River staging post in August and, from September 1900 to February 1901, was again part of operations in the Orange Free State. His service entitled him to the Queen's South Africa Medal with six clasps.

Bob Lenehan proved to be an efficient and energetic officer and a good leader. In February 1901 he was appointed to command the Bushveldt Carbineers, with the rank of major.

George Witton said that Lenehan was commander 'in rank and name only' and that: 'The major rarely visited the outposts, which were practically under the direct control of the officers in charge; he was a good-natured man and much attached to his officers.'

Lenehan was arrested in October and finally told he would be court-martialled in January. He then sent three desperate telegrams to an old legal acquaintance, Major Thomas, who was about to depart for home having resigned in disgust when a contingent he had raised in Australia and brought to South Africa were not allowed to fight together as an Australian unit under Australian officers. Thomas then travelled to Pietersburg and defended Lenehan and the other Carbineer officers.

Lenehan appeared before the court martial on charges of failing to report two incidents: the shooting of two men and a boy, and the shooting of Trooper van Buuren. He was found guilty of 'When on active service by culpable neglect failing to make a report which it was his duty to make' in the case of the shooting of van Buuren. He was found not guilty of the other charge and was 'reprimanded', which was the lightest possible sentence, imprisoned at Cape Town and deported on the SS *Aberdeen*.

It was only after the ship docked in Melbourne on 25 March 1902 that Prime Minister Edmund Barton and the parliament learned that an Australian officer, Peter Handcock, had been executed and another, George Witton, had a death sentence commuted to penal servitude for life.

At first Lenehan was not transferred from the New South Wales Colonial Military list to the Australian Military Forces—but was placed on the 'retired list'. He continued to seek justice, insisting that he verbally reported both incidents to Colonel Hall, who was not called as a witness as he was in India.

After Labor won government in 1904, Prime Minister Chris Watson took up the case, requested that the British War Office provide a copy of the court martial proceedings and asked if there was any further evidence against Lenehan. When the War Office replied that there was not, Lenehan was placed on the active military list, backdated in seniority to 1 July 1903, and commanded No. 1 Battery, Australian Field Artillery until appointed to command the 4th Field Artillery Brigade with the rank of lieutenant-colonel.

During World War I he was on full-time duty commanding the military camp at Menangle until late in 1917, when he was named as co-respondent in a very public divorce case. He was relieved of his position at Menangle Camp and later placed on the retired list in August 1918 and died in Sydney in 1922 of cirrhosis of the liver.

Lieutenant Peter Handcock

Veterinary Lieutenant Peter Handcock was born at the village of Peel, 15 kilometres north of Bathurst, New South Wales, in 1868. He was the third of eight surviving children of an Irish mother and an English father, a farmer who died when Peter was six years old. He was apprenticed to a blacksmith when he was twelve years old and described himself as a labourer from Dubbo when, aged twenty, he married Bridget Martin at the Catholic Cathedral in Bathurst. He later worked as a blacksmith on the railways.

After saying farewell to his wife and three children, Handcock enlisted for the Second South African War as a 'shoesmith' (farrier) in the second contingent of the 1st New South Wales Mounted Rifles. He arrived in Cape Town in February 1900, and was promoted to farrier-sergeant and also served for some time in the Railway Services Police Force. One year after arriving in South Africa, he obtained a lieutenant's commission as Veterinary and Transport Officer in the Bushveldt Carbineers.

At the court martial, Handcock was accused of killing Boer prisoners, a fellow Bushveldt Carbineers' trooper and a Lutheran missionary. He was found guilty of the first two charges and was sentenced to death. In his defence, it is patently true that he was carrying out orders given by Morant and Taylor.

The often-forgotten Australian in the story is intelligence officer Captain Frederick de Bertodano, who encouraged British Intelligence to build the case against Taylor. He referred to Handcock as a 'poor fool', a man who blindly followed orders and did the dirty work for Taylor in order to cover up any evidence of theft and profiteering.

In his own defence at the trial, Handcock claimed: 'I have had a very poor education. I never cared much about being an officer; all I know is about horses, though I like to fight. I did what I was told to do, and I cannot say any more.'

In what almost amounts to a confession, Handcock wrote to his sister: 'If I overstepped my duty I can only ask my People and Country for forgiveness.'

In 1910 Lord Kitchener visited Australia. He was asked to travel to Bathurst to unveil the magnificent memorial to those who lost their lives in the Boer War. Peter Handcock's name was not on the monument, which gave rise to a story that Kitchener had it removed. There is one third-hand anecdotal account of this possibly happening, based on a report that the ceremony was alleged to have been delayed and Kitchener left without attending the reception after the ceremony, but otherwise there is no evidence to support this story. Handcock's name was added in 1964 and a further 39 names have been added since. Verification of the names to go on the monument was the responsibility of the local council, and at least one of the names was that of a man who had never left Australia. There is no sign of any damage from the removal of a name.

In Handcock's defence it can be said that, although he cold-bloodedly killed one man, probably two, neither of whom were enemy combatants, he was undoubtedly following orders and not making personal decisions to kill. Handcock was executed by firing squad on 27 February 1902.

Lieutenant George Ramsdale Witton
George Witton was born into a farming family on a dairy farm near Warrnambool in 1874 and was 24 when he joined the 4th Contingent

of the Victorian Imperial Bushmen as a corporal and sailed for South Africa on 1 May 1900. He had served in a volunteer artillery unit that had a role in manning the guns at Fort Queenscliff, protecting Port Phillip Bay, and was part of the permanent artillery unit there when the war started.

He had risen to the rank of sergeant-major while serving in South Africa with the Victorian Imperial Bushmen and, when the unit was being disbanded and sent home in May 1901, Witton was offered a commission as a lieutenant in the Bushveldt Carbineers by Major Lenehan (who was having trouble finding enough men to keep the Bushveldt Carbineers' ranks operational) on the condition that he recruited the 30 men necessary for an artillery unit.

The Bushveldt Carbineers never operated at full strength, and after the reorganisation at Fort Edward following the shooting of six Boers attempting to surrender and a Carbineer trooper suspected of Boer sympathies in July 1901, a group of near-mutinous troopers were allowed to leave the regiment without penalty.

Just after this, Witton arrived at regimental headquarters in Pietersburg to be told by Lenehan that the guns he was hoping to take charge of had not arrived. He reluctantly acted briefly as quarter-master before being ordered to replace his friend Lieutenant Baudinet, who had injured a leg playing polo, as the officer in charge of a group of nineteen reinforcements being sent to assist the newly reorganised Squadron 'A' unit at Fort Edward. Baudinet was possibly the reason Witton joined the Carbineers; he had acted as best man at Baudinet's wedding in Cape Town.

By the time Witton arrived at Fort Edward, the officer in charge, Captain Percy Hunt, had been killed and Morant had taken over the command.

None of the 'troubles' at Fort Edward were of Witton's making. He denied shooting any prisoners except in self-defence when one man grabbed his rifle and attempted to kill him with it. He claimed he tried to convince Morant not to execute a wounded prisoner and 'walked away' while the execution went ahead.

Nevertheless, he was the third officer sentenced to death at the courts martial. Having had his sentence commuted to life imprisonment by Kitchener, he spent three years in British prisons, where he suffered typhoid and arsenic poisoning from working at the prison furnaces before being released after constant agitation from the Australian parliament and others. He was never pardoned.

Witton returned to Australia and was a dairy farmer in Victoria until his marriage to Mary Humphrey in 1913. He then took up farming near Biggenden, about 100 kilometres west of Maryborough in Queensland, where he became a justice of the peace and director of the Biggenden cheese factory.

In 1907 he wrote a book giving his version of the events in the Spelonken district in 1901 and the trials and his time in prison. The book was called *Scapegoats of the Empire*, and it was the standard source of information for historians researching the affair for many years.

When Andrew Fisher famously pledged, at the start of World War I, that Australia would defend Britain to our 'last man and last shilling', Witton commented sarcastically that he would be 'that last man'.

After Mary died in 1931, he remarried and moved back to Victoria, living first in Gippsland and later in the eastern suburbs of Melbourne at Canterbury. When he died on 14 August 1942, after having a heart attack while cranking his car, he was described as a retired real estate agent.

Witton was survived by his second wife, Carolyn, and there were no children by either marriage. Brisbane City Council records show his ashes were interred in the grave of his first wife, Mary, in Lutwyche Cemetery in Brisbane on 1 October 1942.

Lutwyche Cemetery is, ironically, situated on Kitchener Road.

Frederick Ramon de Bertodano Lopez, 8th Marquis Del Moral

Frederick de Bertodano Lopez was born in 1871 at Lismore, New South Wales. He was the grandson of a Spanish nobleman, Ramon Roman de Bertodano y Lopez, who, in 1837, married Henrietta, daughter of James Pattison, the governor of the Bank of England. The gold chain on their family crest commemorated their ancestors who fought the Moors in 1212.

Frederick's father, Ramon Edward de Bertodano Lopez, was born in Stoke, Surrey, in 1848. He married Mary Jane Brand Wilson in Grafton in 1870 and became a well-known colonial racehorse breeder in northern New South Wales. Frederick was the eldest of their four children, and later inherited the rather useless family title.

Educated at Armidale Grammar School and Sydney University, Frederick passed his law exams, left for England and trained as a lawyer. He travelled to Rhodesia and took part in the fighting against the Matabele (Ndebele) in 1896 and was a solicitor in Bulawayo. Back in England he joined the Manchester Regiment as second lieutenant in 1899, was promoted to captain in January 1900 and seconded to South Africa.

He served as district commissioner in the newly annexed Orange Free State, and when there was an inquiry into his activities dealing with cattle as district commissioner, he indignantly defended himself by threatening to 'spill the beans' about the far worse activities and war crimes being committed in the Spelonken district. As a result of this he was exonerated and seconded to the Intelligence Unit in Pretoria.

De Bertodano established a network of intelligence gathering and was probably using the Lutheran missionary Daniel Heese and some of his trusted native workers to gather information about the illegal activities of Taylor and the Bushveldt Carbineers. Heese was driving a mule buggy that de Bertodano had lent him when he and his servant were shot dead, allegedly by Handcock, on orders from Taylor and Morant.

Whether de Bertodano was aware that a case against Taylor was being built at a higher level, without Kitchener's knowledge, is uncertain. The political inner workings of the Intelligence Headquarters at Pretoria were dark and mysterious and there were plans afoot to 'get rid of' Taylor before Heese's murder. It was the event, however, that most historians think finally got Kitchener to agree to the courts martial.

De Bertodano was not called to give evidence at the courts martial. After the war he returned to London and, in 1908, married Lady Ida Elizabeth Dalzell, the daughter of Robert Dalzell, 11th Earl of Carnwath. Between the Boer War and World War I, Frederick de Bertodano was London director of the Fiat Motor Company and the couple lived at Fulham, employed six servants and eventually had six children. On the outbreak of war in 1914, Frederick was commissioned as a major in the Nottinghamshire Yeomanry and later served as a general staff officer from December 1915 until the armistice and was Mentioned in Despatches.

His wife Ida died in 1924 and, having inherited the family title on his father's death in 1932, he married again, in 1934, to Gytha Mary Dorothy Stourton, daughter of Herbert Stourton OBE. They had one child, a son, Alfonso Michael George de Bertodano, who outlived his stepbrothers to become the 9th Marquis Del Moral in 1955.

Two family trees record Frederick's death as occurring in Zimbabwe in 1955, but he is buried at St John's churchyard in Hampstead.

Lord Kitchener

Horatio Herbert Kitchener was born in County Kerry, Ireland, the son of a British army officer who had purchased land there when he gave up his commission. When Kitchener was a child, the family moved to Switzerland and he was educated in Montreux and later at the Royal Military Academy at Woolwich in London.

He spoke perfect French and was an excellent linguist—fluent in Arabic and Turkish, as well as quite a few Bedouin dialects. At 6 feet 2 inches he was the archetypal moustachioed British army officer. When Kitchener was nineteen he joined the French Army and served in the Franco–Prussian war as an ambulance officer, in violation of the British neutrality during that conflict.

At age 24 he joined a British military expedition that spent four years surveying and mapping the Holy Lands and Jordan. He was British vice-consul in Turkey until he was promoted to captain, then he was sent to Egypt, a British protectorate under nominal Turkish rule, to help rebuild the Egyptian Army.

Kitchener became a national hero when he led an army into the Sudan, and at the Battle of Omdurman in 1898 he avenged the death of General Charles Gordon at Khartoum thirteen years earlier.

Gordon had been killed and beheaded when the Sudanese capital of Khartoum fell to the army of the Sudanese Sufi sheikh Muhammed Ahmad, who claimed to be the messianic 'Mahdi' of Islamic legend. The year-long siege ended in 1885, with the massacre of 10,000 British troops and civilians.

Muhammad Ahmad died shortly after his victory at Khartoum, but the 'Mahdist' state he had established continued under his successor, Abdallahi Ibn Muhammad, until the Battle of Omdurman in 1898.

Kitchener, whose army was hugely outnumbered, laid siege to the Mahdist capital of Omdurman, with the River Nile to his rear, and gunboats and artillery pounded the city. When the Mahdist army (known as 'Ansars' but labelled 'dervishes' by the British) poured out to attack, they were crushed by the smaller British force.

Kitchener lost 500 men, while the Ansar losses were 11,000 dead and 17,000 wounded.

Kitchener's troops then massacred the wounded and Kitchener ordered the tomb of the Mahdi to be blown up and his bones thrown into the Nile.

Winston Churchill, who fought in the battle as a cavalry officer, later wrote that the victory was 'disgraced by the inhuman slaughter of the wounded'. Later that year Kitchener was made 'Baron Kitchener of Khartoum' by Queen Victoria, negotiated the French withdrawal from the Sudan without bloodshed and became the governor-general of the Sudan.

Kitchener was described by British war correspondent George Washington Steevens, in his book *With Kitchener to Khartum*, as 'more like a machine than a man'. He was, however, a very effective governor-general. He set about making the country an efficient and well-governed part of the British Empire. He established the Gordon Memorial College, which was open to children of all backgrounds and religions and later became Khartoum University. He established freedom of religion and recognised Islamic holidays. He even attempted to stop Christian missionary groups trying to convert Muslims to Christianity.

When the Second South African War was not going well at the end of 1899, Field-Marshall Lord Roberts took over from General Redvers Buller and Kitchener was made chief of staff to Roberts. When Roberts returned home in December 1900, after the annexation of the Orange Free State and the Transvaal, Kitchener took over and continued Roberts' policies of burning farms, putting women and children into concentration camps, and sending captured Boers to prisons in St Helena and other parts of the British Empire.

Kitchener was under extreme pressure to end the war but was prevented from any compromise solution by the arch conservative governor of the Cape Colony, Sir Alfred Milner, who wanted to destroy the Boer language and culture and make the new territories totally 'British'. At the same time Kitchener was being criticised at home for using 'inhumane' tactics in the Transvaal.

Having aided and encouraged Captain Arthur Taylor's tactics in the Transvaal in an effort to hasten the end of the war, Kitchener finally gave in to the pressure from within his own Intelligence Unit at Pretoria and agreed to let Taylor be arrested.

Taylor was allowed to resign his commission, which meant that he could only be tried under military law for a period of three months. Oddly, those arrested were kept in solitary confinement and the trial was delayed for exactly three months.

When only two ex-Carbineers, Captain James Robertson and Lieutenant Picton, agreed to testify against Taylor, and he was found not guilty, Kitchener, under pressure to show some evidence that the British were fighting honourably, signed the death warrants for Morant and Handcock.

Negotiations for a peace treaty had begun in December 1901. Kitchener argued for a generous compromise peace treaty that would recognise certain rights for the Afrikaaners and promise future self-government. The Treaty of Vereeniging, which included many of his proposals, was signed in May 1902.

Kitchener, as field marshall, was commander of the British Forces in India until 1911, when he returned to Egypt as consul-general. In 1914 he was created Earl of Khartoum and Broom, and was the secretary of state for war when World War I began.

On 5 June 1916, he was aboard the cruiser HMS *Hampshire*, on his way to negotiate with the Czar of Russia, when the vessel hit a German mine just off the Orkney coast in a force-nine gale and sank. There were only twelve survivors; Kitchener and his entourage were among the 737 who drowned.

A ruthless and efficient soldier and administrator, Kitchener was described by a fellow officer as 'morbidly afraid of showing any feeling or enthusiasm', and someone who 'preferred to be misunderstood rather than be suspected of human feeling'. Kitchener said of himself, at age 34, 'I have become such a solitary bird that I often think I were happier alone.' (In Mark Urban, *Generals: Ten British Commanders Who Shaped the World*, 2005.)

He never had a close relationship with a woman and was possibly either latently or actively homosexual. His friend and aide-de-camp, Captain Oswald Fitzgerald, described as his 'constant and inseparable companion', was also drowned when HMS *Hampshire* went down.

Major John Francis Thomas

Born on 25 July 1861 into a respectable middle-class family in the Sydney suburb of St Marys, Thomas attended The King's School in Sydney and Sydney University before becoming an articled clerk in a Sydney law firm and qualifying to practise as a solicitor in 1887. After an unsuccessful attempt to build a practice in the tough northern New South Wales tin-mining town of Emmaville, he moved, in 1890, to the nearby town of Tenterfield, in New South Wales but close to the Queensland border, where he established a very successful law practice and, in 1898, became the owner and editor of the *Tenterfield Star* newspaper.

Thomas was a staunch supporter of Federation and also active in the colonial militia, becoming a captain in the Tenterfield Rifles. When the Second South African War began, he helped to raise a unit of men from nearby towns in the colonies of Queensland and New South Wales that became part of the 1st New South Wales Mounted Rifles. They sailed for South Africa just three weeks after war was declared.

Thomas himself departed Sydney as a captain with 'A' Squadron of the New South Wales Citizens' Bushmen, on 28 February 1900. Six months later he was among the 105 New South Welshmen present at the legendary defence of the outpost at Elands River. Bob Lenehan was a member of the relieving force at Elands River. The two men had known one another through legal circles in Sydney; Lenehan had been a practising lawyer when Thomas was doing his articles.

In January 1901 Thomas was in charge of a convoy of supply wagons with an escort of twenty New South Wales Bushmen and 53 members of the West Riding Infantry, who had just been discharged from hospital. They were attacked by 300 Boers and, after the West Riding troops ran out of ammunition, they surrendered and the supplies were lost.

Thomas and the New South Wales men were blamed for the loss, although Kitchener later exonerated the Australians of any blame, and Thomas was promoted to major.

He was then allowed to return home to raise another contingent, which he did. This time, however, he was determined to make one important condition when raising another unit of Australians. He stipulated to the military in South Africa that the men who volunteered to fight should fight as Australians under Australian officers.

On arrival in South Africa, however, the officers were told they were not needed and the men were assigned to imperial units. Many of the Australian recruits were commandeered to fight with Major John Stewart-Murray as part of a Scottish regiment and others were enlisted into the Canadian Scouts, whose reputation for brutality would become as bad as that of the Bushveldt Carbineers.

Thomas was offered a commission in this unit, but refused to accept unless the unit was renamed the 'Canadian and Australian Scouts'. When this was refused he was offered a free passage home. Totally disillusioned, he accepted the offer and was about to depart when he received Bob Lenehan's desperate telegrams asking for help.

Thomas had only a day to acquaint himself with the case and, with no experience as a criminal lawyer, conducted a spirited defence of the charges. After the decisions were handed down he continued to argue for clemency, and even a pardon based on the heroic defence of the Pietersburg garrison by Morant and Handcock during the trial.

He was the one to claim the bodies of Morant and Handcock and see to their burial. He arranged the burial service, which omitted much of the traditional liturgy and mentioned that they were buried in 'unconsecrated ground'. There is a photo of him at the grave site.

He was active in petitioning for Witton's release and assisted Witton in the preparation of his book *Scapegoats of the Empire*. He resigned his commission and never used the title 'major' after returning home. He considered writing his own account of the trial but instead assisted Witton to write his account.

Thomas sold the *Tenterfield Star* in 1915 and his legal practice in 1919. In 1925, having returned to practising law, he was sued by a client, declared bankrupt and gaoled in Long Bay Prison for refusing, on principal, to pay damages. Bankruptcy and refusal to release monies from a deceased estate led to him being debarred from practising law and the Supreme Court upheld the decision in 1928.

He spent the last seventeen years of his life running a small accountancy practice in Tenterfield and died, aged 81, on his small farm holding at Boonoo Boonoo, 17 kilometres from the town.

UNDER RULE 303: THE SHORT AND SHAMEFUL HISTORY OF THE BUSHVELDT CARBINEERS

So, what exactly did happen in the Spelonken during those 283 days, between 21 February 1901, when the Bushveldt Carbineers Regiment was formed, and 1 December 1901, when the regiment ceased to exist?

As Frederick de Bertodano had predicted, trouble began when Captain Taylor received word, on 2 July 1901, that a group of six Boers accompanied by two covered wagons and a large herd of cattle were coming into the fort either to surrender or seek a truce for medical treatment. Taylor told Captain Robertson the fort was possibly going to be attacked and ordered Sergeant-Major Morrison to intercept the group, ignore any white flags, take no prisoners and 'make it look like a fight'. Morrison apparently turned to Robertson and asked if he should obey Taylor's orders and Robertson replied, 'Certainly, he is commanding officer here.' Morrison then sent Sergeant Oldham, Corporal Primrose and five other troopers from Sweetwaters Farm to meet the group.

The party consisted of two ox-wagons, driven by two boys aged twelve and eighteen, carrying 65-year-old farmer Jan Geyser and three other men who had been members of the local Boer commando unit. All were suffering from malaria and seeking treatment. They had a large herd of valuable cattle with them and a wooden cash box containing a large sum in paper money and gold bars, possibly being taken to safety away from the farm raids and burnings then sweeping the district.

What happened next was later reported by witnesses at the Court of Inquiry. The patrol fired on the wagons and a white flag was raised. Believing that women and children might be present, Sergeant Oldham called 'cease fire', disarmed the Boers and then followed Taylor's orders by having each member of his patrol execute one of the group. Jan Geyser was found lying sick in one of the wagons and Trooper Eden 'climbed into the wagon and shot him where he lay on his bed'.

Corporal Primrose returned to Sweetwaters to report and most of 'A' Squadron then rode to the scene where, according to later witness testimony, five unarmed Boers were lying in the road 'shot in the head save one who was shot in the neck'. Another was 'lying dead in the wagon under his blankets never having got out of bed ... shot in the head'. Trooper Robert Cochrane testified that the oxen and cattle were 'stolen by Captain Taylor, secretly driven to Rhodesia, and sold at Bulawayo'. Lieutenant Handcock took possession of the cash box and the bodies were buried in a mass grave at the site.

After the war, Jan Geyser's daughter wrote a letter describing the number of cattle involved and the contents of the wagons. Nothing was ever returned to the Geyser family. Captain Robertson reported to Major Lenehan that six 'train-wreckers and murderers' had been shot. This became known as the 'Six Boers Affair'.

Later that day, back at Fort Edward, Trooper van Buuren, an Afrikaaner member of the Bushveldt Carbineers, was seen talking to some women from the families of the victims, who were being held for transport to the concentration camp at Pietersburg. Local men who signed up with the British were known as 'joiners' and Taylor often made use of them in his 'intelligence' work. He was, however, worried about van Buuren and ordered Handcock to 'attend to the matter'.

Two days later Handcock took a patrol of four men, including van Buuren, scouting for Boer commandos. At the Court of Inquiry later that year, Trooper Churton testified that he saw Handcock ride up behind van Buuren and shoot him three times in the back. Handcock then said to Churton, 'Keep a sharp lookout. We just lost a man back there.' Handcock wrote a report that Captain Robertson amended as he 'deemed it unsuitable'. Robertson reported to Lenehan at Pietersburg that van Buuren was 'shot in contact with some Boers'.

Major Lenehan and Colonel Hall were aware of the 'poor discipline, unconfirmed murders, drunkenness, and general lawlessness' at Fort Edward, and when it was reported that a local woman had accused a British officer of rape, an investigation revealed that the alleged rapist was Captain James Robertson; he was given a choice of being court-martialled or resigning his commission, and chose the latter option.

Lenehan then withdrew the whole detachment from Fort Edward with the exception of Handcock, who, as the station's veterinary officer, was responsible for the horses. Some of the men withdrawn were ordered to remain at Pietersburg, awaiting an inquiry into their behaviour at Fort Edward. Some disobeyed this order and made threats about reporting on the activities of their officers at the fort. These men were allowed to leave by Colonel Hall without penalty and discharged from the regiment.

Lenehan then appointed Captain Percy Hunt, formerly of the 10th Hussars and a good friend of Harry Morant, to 'straighten out' the station. Lieutenant Morant and 60 men were also sent to Fort Edward with Hunt.

Lieutenant Witton's assessment of the situation, as it existed before he and Morant arrived at Fort Edward, was that Robertson:

> . . . was altogether unfit to command such a body of men, and allowed his detachment to drift into a state of insubordination verging on mutiny. The men did almost as they liked, and horses and other captured stock were being divided amongst themselves, while stills on neighbouring farms were freely made use of.

Any consideration of what later became generally known as the 'Breaker Morant Affair' should take into account the fact that all of the events described above occurred before Morant was ever stationed at Fort Edward.

Over the next month, eighteen Boers were captured and 500 cattle and fifteen wagons were confiscated. Taylor was still playing an active role in directing activities at Fort Edward and problems continued under Hunt's command, although he made an effort to improve discipline. He had the confiscated cattle disposed of correctly through military channels, he had Morant and Handcock locate and destroy stills the men were using to make spirits, and he had a group of troopers arrested for stealing rum and threatening to shoot Lieutenant Picton for reporting the theft to Hunt. When the men involved absconded, Lenehan had them caught and charged, but they made accusations of misconduct against the officers at Fort Edward and Colonel Hall ordered them to be discharged from service without a full inquiry.

Hunt at this time also admonished Morant for 'bringing in prisoners' on several occasions and told him that Kitchener's orders were to 'take no prisoners' and that any Boer prisoners found wearing items of British uniform could be executed by firing squad without being brought in for trial.

A new detachment of twenty men under Lieutenant Witton arrived at Spelonken on 4 August, while Hunt was on a mission to locate local commando leader Veldcornet Barend Viljoen.

Witton never met his commanding officer, as Percy Hunt was killed attempting a surprise attack with seventeen troopers on a farm at Duivelskloof, where a group of some 36 Boer commandos were believed to be gathered. The Reverend Reuter, a local missionary, had reported to Hunt that Viljoen's commandos had been 'harassing local non-combatant farmers' and had made threats against the mission station. When a Bushveldt Carbineer patrol was ambushed near the Medingen Mission Station, Hunt led a patrol from Fort Edward on 2 August, accompanied by Tony Schiel, a defector from the Boer commandos working as an intelligence scout for Captain Taylor, with the intention of ambushing the Viljoen commando force. In effect Schiel's task was to 'raise the natives' to attack Boer farms and he commanded some 400 'irregular' troops, Modjadji warriors from the local Lobedu people.

Hunt was warned not to attack the farm at night without Schiel's support and normal reconnaissance. Against this advice he did so and found the Boers had more numbers than expected and were able to drive off their attackers, killing Hunt and another trooper in the process. At least two Boers, including Viljoen, were also killed.

When news of the failed attack reached Morant, he assumed command but was visibly distressed to the point of being unable to address the men. Morant always claimed that he and Hunt were best

friends, were engaged to two sisters back in Devon and had joined
the Bushveldt Carbineers in order to fight as brothers in arms. He
led the mounted group to Sweetwaters, 2 kilometres away, where
Taylor addressed them, emphasising that no quarter should be given
in avenging their captain's death.

Morant's group met up with the survivors of Hunt's patrol an hour
after they had buried Hunt. Morant visited the grave before pursuing
the Boers and finally located them camped in a native kraal. Morant,
apparently grief stricken and angered by reports that Hunt's body had
been mutilated at Duivelskloof, attacked hastily and lost the element
of surprise. All the Boers fled except one named Visser, who had been
wounded in the foot and could not walk.

Visser had in his possession an old British Army coat and trousers,
which Morant claimed were Hunt's. In spite of pleas and protests from
Lieutenant Witton, Morant had Visser shot by firing squad the next
day. As he was too wounded to stand, he was shot while seated on the
ground. After all the men in the firing squad fired, he was still alive
and Lieutenant Picton shot him in the head at close range.

The trousers were later found to not be Hunt's and the mutilation,
which was said to be also apparent on the bodies of the dead Boers at
Duivelskloof, was thought by many to be the result of rituals performed
by local Lobedu witchdoctors. This must have been done after both
sides had retired. However, it was also reported, by those who buried
Hunt, that his neck had been broken and his face damaged.

On 22 August, a report reached Fort Edward that eight prisoners
were being brought in by a patrol. A detailed account of the events that
followed was later written by Lieutenant Witton:

> A patrol subsequently set out, consisting of Lieutenants Morant,
> Handcock, and myself, Sergeant-Major Hammett . . . and two troopers.
> We first called at the office of Captain Taylor. Morant dismounted and
> had a private interview with that officer; I was not informed as to the
> nature of it . . .
>
> We went on, and Morant said that it was his intention to have
> the prisoners shot. Both myself and Sergeant-Major Hammett asked
> Morant if he was sure he was doing right. He replied that he was quite
> justified in shooting the Boers; he had his orders, and he would rely

upon us to obey him. I also afterwards remonstrated with him for having the prisoners brought in and shot so close to the fort, but he said it was a matter of indifference where they were shot.

We met the patrol with the prisoners about ten kilometres out. Morant at once took charge, and instructed the escort to go on ahead as advance guard . . . I rode on in front of the waggon, and I did not see any civilian speak to the prisoners as we were passing the mission hospital. When we had trekked on about five kilometres Morant stopped the waggon, called the men off the road, and questioned them. Upon his asking, 'Have you any more information to give?' they were shot. One of them, a big, powerful Dutchman, made a rush at me and seized the end of my rifle, with the intention of taking it and shooting me, but I simplified matters by pulling the trigger and shooting him. I never had any qualms of conscience for having done so . . . By just escaping death in this tragedy I was afterwards sentenced to suffer death.

While Morant and some troopers buried the Boers, Witton returned to the fort with the wagons, the dead men's belongings and the oxen, and handed everything to Taylor. Not long after Morant returned, a German missionary, Reverend Daniel Heese, who had been talking to the prisoners when the convoy stopped at the Swiss mission hospital, was seen passing the fort in his buggy, on his way to Pietersburg.

At the Swiss mission hospital, Heese had spoken to the Boer prisoners, some of whom said that they were afraid they would be shot. He was threatened with arrest by Morant and ordered to report to Taylor at Sweetwaters. Heese told Taylor that he would report what he knew to a British officer at Pietersburg. Taylor suggested he tie a white flag to his mule buggy and Heese left. Morant then saw him passing the fort and rode out and spoke to him. When he returned to the fort, he told Witton that he'd advised the man to wait until he could be escorted on the dangerous road, but the missionary had a permit to travel signed by Taylor. Morant then went to Sweetwaters and talked with Taylor. According to Witton, Morant came back and talked to Lieutenant Handcock, who 'had his breakfast, and . . . went away again'.

Almost a week later the missionary's body, and that of his native servant, Silas, were found some distance off the road, 25 kilometres from the fort. Heese had been shot through the chest. Morant said he had warned him not to travel alone and the Boers must have shot him. It has always been assumed, however, that Morant and Taylor discussed the matter and sent Handcock to shoot Heese to prevent him reaching Pietersburg and informing the British authorities of the Carbineers' activities.

The 'British officer at Pietersburg' to whom Heese referred was probably Frederick de Bertodano, who had lent him the mule buggy to take a sick friend to the Swiss mission. It is also quite likely that Silas, and other native boys, were gathering information for de Bertodano from native servants working at Fort Edward.

Major Lenehan arrived at Fort Edward on 7 September 1901, the same day Roelf van Staden and his sons Roelf and Christiaan were coming in to surrender and get medical treatment for fourteen-year-old Christiaan, who was suffering from fever. Morant, Handcock and two others met them and shot them near Sweetwaters Farm. It was alleged that the three were made to dig their own graves before being shot. It was also later alleged that Lenehan was aware of this incident and failed to report it to Colonel Hall.

While staying at Fort Edward, Lenehan gave permission for a patrol of 30 men led by Morant and Witton to attempt to capture Tom Kelly, a local Boer guerrilla leader who had fled the district when the Carbineers arrived in May and was now rumoured to be returning with artillery. Lenehan insisted, however, that Kelly be brought in alive, and he was, on 22 September. Morant had patiently conducted an excellent and successful operation.

Witton, who was full of praise for Morant's tactics, leadership and *sang froid*, told the following anecdote about the long wait for dawn as they lay in ambush, surrounding Kelly's camp: 'The night was intensely cold, but we lay there within 50 metres of them until the first streak of dawn. During the night a dog scented us and started to bark; a Boer got up and gave it a kick to quieten it, at which Morant remarked, "A man never knows his luck in South Africa."'

Morant was congratulated by Colonel Hall and, as it seemed the Bushveldt Carbineers now had the district under control, he was granted fourteen days leave, which he spent in Pretoria making arrangements for Percy Hunt's belongings to be sent home and sorting out his dead friend's finances and affairs.

When he returned to Pietersburg from leave, however, Morant was arrested and placed in solitary confinement, Fort Edward was abandoned and the detachment ordered back to Pietersburg where Lenehan, Handcock and Witton were all placed under arrest on 23 October. After a Court of Inquiry in November, they were informed of the charges against them and, in December, they were told they would be tried by court martial. Colonel Hall was transferred to India and the Bushveldt Carbineers were reformed as the New Pietersburg Light Horse, the name they kept until the disbanding of the regiment in June 1902 with the end of the war.

The men were held in solitary confinement for three months and refused permission to advise the Australian government of their position.

On 15 January 1902, the men were shown the charges against them and Major James Thomas was appointed to defend them. Thomas had commanded 'A' Squadron New South Wales Citizens Bushmen at the siege of Elands River post; he had no experience in criminal or military courts.

Four Australian officers, Major Lenehan and lieutenants Handcock, Witton and Hannam, and three British officers, Captain Taylor and lieutenants Morant and Picton, had charges made against them, as did Sergeant-Major Morrison. Put in simple terms, the following six charges were made:

1. On 2 July six Boers captured and shot. (Robertson, Taylor and Sergeant-Major Morrison charged with 'murder while on active service'.)
2. On 4 July Trooper van Buuren was shot. (Handcock charged with murder. Lenehan charged with 'culpable neglect failing to make a report which it was his duty to make'.)
3. A prisoner named Visser was captured, court-martialled and shot. (Morant, Handcock, Witton and Picton were charged with 'the offense of murder'.)
4. On 3 August, eight Boers surrendered and were shot. (Morant, Handcock and Witton charged with 'the offense of murder'.)

Reverend Heese shot. (Morant and Handcock charged with 'the offense of murder'.)

5. On 5 September, Lieutenant Hannam ordered his men to shoot into three wagons and 250 rounds were fired, two little boys were killed and one little girl wounded. (No charges were filed.)

6. On 7 September, Morant had two Boers and a boy aged fourteen taken prisoner and shot. (Lenehan charged with 'culpable neglect failing to make a report which it was his duty to make'. Morant and Handcock charged with 'the offense of murder'.)

The evidence had been gathered over several months, much of it by British Intelligence officers, among them de Bertodano. They were attempting to build a case against Taylor and had informed Kitchener of the death of Heese. The killing of Boers was one thing, but murdering a German Lutheran missionary was another matter and was bound to bring official protests from Germany, which it did.

Many researchers believe that it was the death of Heese that triggered the inquiry and the courts martial, and that Kitchener, who had appointed Taylor and covertly approved his 'methods', was then reluctantly convinced that Taylor had become a liability and approved the building of a case against Taylor and the officers of the Bushveldt Carbineers, which intelligence officers had already been doing for some time without Kitchener's knowledge.

There was a letter, signed by fifteen Bushveldt Carbineer troopers and given to Colonel Hall, that was written by a mysterious character named Robert Cochrane, an English-born trooper who had been a mining engineer and justice of the peace in Western Australia and was also a journalist. Written in very formal language, the letter called for 'a full and exhaustive inquiry' into 'the following disgraceful incidents which have occurred in the Spelonken district'. It then listed in detail the six incidents that later became the formal charges.

Cochrane wrote:

Sir, many of us are Australians who have fought throughout nearly the whole war ... We cannot return home with the stigma of these crimes attached to our names therefore we humbly pray that a full and exhaustive inquiry may be made by impartial Imperial officers in order that the truth may be elicited and justice done.

There are three 'odd' things about the letter, apart from its formal language and thoroughness of detail. Firstly, only two of the fifteen troopers who signed it were Australian; secondly, Cochrane had never served at Fort Edward; and, lastly, only one of the men who signed it was called to give evidence against Morant, Handcock and Witton. Two others gave evidence against Taylor.

It would seem that British Intelligence, in collusion with Cochrane, sought out witnesses, built a case against Taylor and the other men, and arranged for the letter to be written. Lenehan's visit to Fort Edward in September was also part of this plan; he was there to gather information about the shooting of the Boer prisoners and Heese.

After the arrests, and the disbandment of the Bushveldt Carbineers, Boer commando activities quickly increased in the Spelonken. Veldtcornet Christiaan Frederik Beyers returned and occupied Fort Edward and Taylor's old headquarters at Sweetwaters. The reconstituted Carbineers regiment, known as the New Pietersburg Light Horse, proved ineffective at suppressing the renewed Boer commando activity.

Beyers' men attacked the blockhouses at the prison compound at Pietersburg and freed some 150 Boer prisoners on the night of 22 January 1902. As was expected, the reinforced guerrilla army, now numbering around 300 men, attacked the garrison the following night in an attempt to steal the badly needed British horses and valuable supplies of food and military equipment.

The loss of the Pietersburg garrison would have been a crushing blow to the British and, had it been successful, could have restarted all-out war in the northern Transvaal. With this possibility imminent on the night of 23 January, the prisoners were released from their cells, armed and ordered to help defend the garrison.

The blockhouses, which formed the defence posts for the garrison, were overcrowded with men attempting to shoot through the apertures provided, so Morant and Handcock climbed out onto the roof and proceeded to shoot the attackers with scant regard for their own safety. Morant was credited with shooting one of Beyers' commanders,

Marthinus Pretorius, and the heroic actions of the two prisoners inspired a spirited defence that forced Beyers to withdraw.

Major Thomas later requested clemency or pardon for Morant and Handcock on the time-honoured precedent of a British military custom established by none other than the Duke of Wellington. There was no harsher disciplinarian of troops than the famous 'Iron Duke', the hero of Waterloo and later British prime minister. Although he was known to refer to his troops as 'scum' and treat men as expendable, he also believed in a system of honour and fair play and stated the dictum that: 'The performance of a duty of honour and trust after knowledge of a military offence ought to convey a pardon.'

On that basis alone, the actions of Morant and Handcock on the night of 23 January 1902 should have secured clemency at least, a pardon in any case, and probably a medal for bravery.

THE TRIALS

Many Australians believe that Handcock and Morant were truly *Scapegoats of the Empire*, which happens to be the title of the book written about the case in 1907 by the third man sentenced to death, Lieutenant George Witton. The execution of Handcock and Morant, which was carried out with unseemly haste and without any attempt to inform Australian authorities of the decision, has been regarded by many as yet another example of British perfidy and criminal disregard for Australian soldiers, who were treated as mere 'expendable colonials'.

The question of the measure of British unfairness, or even treachery, hinges upon the fact that the accused stated time and again in their own defence that they were certain they had been ordered to behave and fight in a particular way but were being tried and judged by a completely different set of military rules.

The *moral* debate over the case centres around the dilemma as to whether it is just and reasonable to select and punish a few individual soldiers for what were obviously criminal acts, while ignoring the fact that hundreds of other troops were doing similar things and not being required to answer for their actions. Put simply, did the accused men make criminal decisions of their own volition? Or were they following 'orders' that were not in the British military handbook and, if so, how far up the chain of command did those orders originate?

Taylor had been arrested at the end of September. The other accused were arrested at Pietersburg on 23 October and held in separate parts of the prison until the preliminary hearing, the Court of Inquiry, two weeks later, on 6 November. They were then held in solitary confinement until the end of December when the court reconvened and they were told they were to be court-martialled.

Lenehan was able to secure the legal services of Major Thomas, who was just about to sail for home when the telegram reached him. The two men had known each other in Sydney and Lenehan was aware that Thomas was a trained solicitor. When he arrived in Pietersburg, Thomas became aware that neither Handcock, Morant, Picton nor Witton had any legal representation and agreed to represent all of them.

The trials began on 16 January 1902.

As previously related, while the trial was underway, Boer commandos led by Christiaan Frederik Beyers launched an attack on the Pietersburg garrison.

The prisoners were released from their cells and armed, and Morant and Handcock turned the tide of the attack and the Boers withdrew. Major Thomas later filed for clemency, but the court dismissed his request.

Upon being cross-examined, witnesses stated that Captain Hunt had given them orders not to take prisoners, and they had been reprimanded for bringing them in.

Morant stated that under Captain Hunt, he had been 'clearing the northern district of Boers'. He said he believed Captain Hunt acted on orders from Pretoria to clear the Spelonken district and take no prisoners. He stated that Captain Hunt told him that Colonel Ian Hamilton, military secretary, had given him the orders at Lord Kitchener's private house just before his departure to take charge at Fort Edward.

Morant also stated in his defence that it was known that other units, notably the Canadian Scouts, Strathcona's Horse and other brigades of Kitchener's, had acted in exactly the same manner. Morant stated that he had 'never questioned the validity of the orders, he was certain they were correct'.

When questioned as to whether his open-air court martial and summary execution of Visser had been constituted under the King's regulations, Morant famously replied:

No; it was not quite so handsome. As to rules and sections, we had no
Red Book, and knew nothing about them. We were out fighting the
Boers, not sitting comfortably behind barb-wire entanglements; we
got them and shot them under Rule 303.

The verdicts and outcomes varied considerably.

Lieutenant Hannam was not even brought to trial on the fifth
charge as there was some evidence that he was unaware children were
present in the wagons and some of those on the wagons had run when
called on to surrender. Lieutenant Picton was simply cashiered from
the army. Sergeant-Major Morrison was not convicted.

Captain Taylor, who had resigned his commission when arrested,
stood accused of 'ordering the massacre of six unarmed men and
boys on 2 July 1901 and the theft of their money and livestock, and
the murder of an unarmed native'. All charges against him were
dismissed.

Captain Robertson, having been forced to resign his commission in
July, turned prosecution witness and no charges were ever laid against
him. He gave evidence against Taylor, as did Lieutenant Picton.

Morant, Handcock and Witton were petitioned by the prosecution to do the same, and testify against Taylor, but all three refused
and stuck fast, insisting that they had been ordered to take no prisoners and had been told that Boer prisoners wearing items of British
uniform could be shot after a summary court martial in the field. They
believed that those orders came from Kitchener via Colonel Hamilton
via Captain Hunt to them. Morant was acquitted of murdering Heese,
but Morant, Handcock and Witton were found guilty of the murder of
the eight Boers and all other charges.

I believe that in refusing to testify for the prosecution against
Taylor, Morant, Handcock and Witton metaphorically 'signed their
own death warrants'.

All three were sentenced to death and Witton's sentence was
commuted to penal servitude for life. He was imprisoned in Britain
and there was strong pressure from Australia for his release, including
legal advice from Sir Isaac Isaacs, who would later become Australia's
governor-general. Witton was released in August 1904, but not
pardoned.

On 27 February 1902 Morant and Handcock were shot by a firing squad of Cameron Highlanders.

There is certainly a case to be made that Morant and Handcock were victims of Kitchener's attempts to back down and soften the savagery of the campaign he had covertly approved against Boer civilians. The attempt to show that British justice existed, even in war, was a gesture meant to appease both the Boers and the Germans. It was also a token response to the voices of criticism at home in Britain.

British welfare campaigner Emily Hobhouse published a report on the concentration camps in June 1901 that led Lloyd George to accuse the government of 'a policy of extermination against the Boer population'. Liberal opposition party leader Henry Campbell-Bannerman asked in parliament, 'When is a war not a war?' and gave the rhetorical answer, 'When it is carried on by methods of barbarism in South Africa.'

Labour peer Thomas Pakenham described Kitchener's 'scorched earth' tactic as 'organised like a sporting shoot, with success defined in a weekly "bag" of killed, captured and wounded, and to sweep the country bare of everything that could give sustenance to the guerrillas, including women and children'.

In Kitchener's defence he was merely taking the measures put in place by Lord Roberts to another level and was constantly being criticised in South Africa, by the governor of the Cape Colony and others, for not doing more to annihilate the Boers!

It was the clearance of civilians that dominated the last phase of the war. Thirty thousand Boer farms were destroyed by the British, and Afrikaaner men were hanged outside their houses. The plan included the systematic destruction of crops, the slaughtering or removal of livestock, and the burning down of homesteads and farms to prevent the Boers from returning to the fight.

The concentration camp system saw whole regions depopulated: 45 'tent city' concentration camps were built for Boer internees and there were another 64 for black Africans. Of the 28,000 Boers taken as prisoners of war, 25,630 were sent overseas, so the vast majority of Boers remaining in the local camps were women and children. Women whose husbands had not surrendered were given less rations than those whose husbands had been killed or transported to POW camps in Bermuda, Canada, St Helena and other parts of the empire so they could not rejoin the fight.

The official combatant death toll from the Second South African War is an odd statistic. Official British army losses were around 22,000 men and Boer army losses around 4000. However, it is estimated that between 26,000 and 28,000 people (one-quarter of all internees, almost all women and children) died in concentration camps of disease and starvation.

Banjo Paterson, as a war correspondent, was appalled at the acts of brutality carried out by British troops against Boer civilians:

> Come, let us join in the bloodthirsty shriek,
> Hooray for Lord Kitchener's 'bag'!
> Tho' fireman's torch and hangman's cord—
> They are hung on the English Flag!
> In the front of our brave old army! Whoop!
> The farmhouse blazes bright.
> And their women weep and their children die—
> How dare they presume to fight!
> And none of them dress in a uniform,
> The same as by rights they ought.
> They're fighting in rags and in naked feet,
> Like Wallace's Scotchmen fought!
> They clothe themselves from our captured troops—
> And they're catching them every week;
> But they don't hang them, that shame is ours,
> But we cover the shame with a shriek!

Morant and Handcock, as volunteers, were, perhaps, not *au fait* with the subtleties of regular army 'methods'. Hunt made several attempts to make Morant understand that 'no prisoners' meant 'shoot them before they surrender'. Morant was admonished for bringing in prisoners and then made the mistake of *taking* prisoners and *then* killing them.

Kitchener needed to make some effort to appease the Boers, Germany and those who opposed his 'all-out war' policy at home, and sentencing three 'war criminals' from the wild frontier territory to death, and executing two of them, was one way to do it. Although he

abandoned 'Bulala' Taylor after the death of Heese, Kitchener had a lot
to lose if 'his man' Taylor was found guilty and he possibly had the trial
delayed three months so Taylor could be tried as an 'ex-army' civilian.
Three other scapegoats, two of them colonials, did not pose any real
problem to Kitchener.

Although Kitchener eventually admitted that 10,000 natives were
armed by the British during the hostilities, he was also at great pains
to distance himself from his previous support of Taylor's activities.
Many other British troops also believed there was an unwritten 'no
prisoners' order.

Morant himself wrote, the evening before he died:

It really ain't the place nor time
To reel off rhyming diction—
But yet we'll write a final rhyme
Whilst waiting cru-ci-fi-xion!
. . .
But we bequeath a parting tip
For sound advice of such men,
Who come across in transport ship
To polish off the Dutchmen!
If you encounter any Boers
You really must not loot 'em!
And if you wish to leave these shores,
For pity's sake, DON'T SHOOT 'EM!!
And if you'd earn a D.S.O.,
Why every British sinner
Should know the proper way to go is:
'Ask The Boer To Dinner!'

Morant's last words are often claimed to have been, 'Shoot straight you
bastards, don't make a mess of it.' A letter written by a prison warder
who witnessed the execution, however, states they were 'Be sure and
make a good job of it.'

CONCLUSION

Edwin Henry Murrant or Harry Harbord Morant, whoever he was, was a skilful horseman, a very competent writer of sentimental verse and an extraordinarily brave soldier. He was also an unreliable friend, a liar and a man who rarely paid his debts or honoured his commitments. He was not Australian. He committed acts that can be considered war crimes, possibly in a spirit of revenge.

In order to hasten the end of the guerrilla war, British Intelligence secretly constructed a case against Captain Arthur Taylor in order to stop his brutal killing and illegal profiteering activities in the Spelonken district. For various reasons, including a fear of Lord Kitchener's real involvement being revealed, the case failed to produce the desired result. Morant and Handcock, in refusing to testify against Taylor, become the sacrificial scapegoats.

The much-vilified Lieutenant Handcock did kill a fellow trooper and quite probably a civilian missionary. In each case he followed a direct order from his immediate superior officer. He deserves his name to be on the honour roll of those who enlisted and served as much as any other man who enlisted and served.

Handcock and Morant should, by any reasonable sense of British military honour, have been pardoned for any crimes committed in wartime, due to their heroic action in defending a threatened British garrison, which included the men who were their accusers and gaolers, on the night of 23 January 1902.

Colonel J. St Claire, who observed the court proceedings, summed up the official British army position in a confidential report to the War Office:

> I agree generally with the views expressed by the Court of Inquiry . . . The idea that no prisoners were to be taken in the Spelonken area appears to have been started by the late Captain Hunt & after his death continued by orders given personally by Captain Taylor . . . Lieut Morant acquiesced in the illegal execution of the wounded Boer Visser & took a personal part in the massacre of the 8 surrendered Boers on 23 August . . . After the murder of Van Buuren the officers seem to have exercised a reign of terror in the District, which hindered their men from reporting their illegal acts & even prevented their objecting to assist in the crime.

The first published account of the incidents surrounding the case appeared as early as 1902, the same year Morant and Handcock were executed. It was a little book titled *Bushman and Buccaneer: A Memoir of Harry Morant—His 'Ventures and Verses*, written by Australian journalist Frank Fox under the pen name Frank Renar, with a cover drawing by Norman Lindsay. Fox wrote for *The Bulletin* and edited the *Lone Hand* magazine and later worked on British papers as a political and military commentator, served with distinction in World War I and was knighted.

In 1907 the other man originally sentenced to death, Lieutenant George Witton, published his account of the affair, *Scapegoats of the Empire*.

The South African Wars were neglected and almost forgotten for a time once World War I began and it was decades later, in 1959, after two world wars, that Rayne Kruger's book *Goodbye Dolly Gray* aroused some interest and re-opened some debate.

Prior to the reawakened interest in the case in Australia, brought about by the Bruce Beresford film in 1980, there was *Breaker Morant, A Horseman Who Made History*, by Frederic Cutlack in 1962; *The Breaker: A Novel*, by Kit Denton in 1973; and *In Search of Breaker Morant*, by Margaret Carnegie and Frank Shields in 1979.

Bruce Beresford's film *Breaker Morant* was actually based on a play by Kenneth Ross, who successfully sued Angus & Robertson, the publisher of Denton's novel, for publicising that book as the source material for the film.

Since that time more books have been written, all attempting to uncover the truth behind the only execution by British firing squad of British soldiers in the Second South African War: *Breaker Morant and the Bushveldt Carbineers* by Arthur Davey (1987); *The Bushveldt Carbineers and the Pietersburg Light Horse* by William Woolmore (2002); *Shoot Straight, You Bastards* by Nick Bleszynski (2003); *Breaker Morant: The Final Roundup* by Joel West and Roger Roper (2016); and *Ready, Aim, Fire: Major James Francis Thomas, The Fourth Victim in the Execution of Lieutenant Harry 'Breaker' Morant* by James Unkles (2019).

In 2009, James William Unkles, a naval reserve commander and barrister, sent petitions for pardons for Morant, Handcock and Witton to both the queen and the Petitions Committee of the Australian parliament. In November 2010, the UK Ministry of Defence replied: 'After detailed historical and legal consideration, the Secretary of State has concluded that no new primary evidence has come to light which supports the petition to overturn the original courts-martial verdicts and sentences.'

In 2012, the Australian Attorney-General's Department announced that it would not seek a pardon for Morant from the British government, as 'a pardon for a Commonwealth offence would generally only be granted where the offender is both morally and technically innocent of the offence'.

AFTERWORD

> 'Let the jury consider their verdict,' the King said, for about the twentieth time that day.
> 'No, no!' said the Queen. 'Sentence first—verdict afterwards.'
> *Alice's Adventures in Wonderland*, Lewis Carroll, 1865

Understanding our culture and society, in order to make what we call 'human progress', is like rowing a boat. We advance by looking backward while moving forward. If we don't understand where we are coming from we can only move forward in ignorance and repeat the mistakes of the past.

The truth about past events is always somewhere in the background circumstances in which they occurred. If you study the politics and mercenary motivations of those involved, the social conventions, religious beliefs and nationalistic agendas of the time, you will stumble upon the truth eventually. It's all there, somewhere in the past.

We choose to ignore or misunderstand the past at our peril. If you apply a whole new set of rules to history you risk drifting into some sort of parallel universe, where nothing really makes sense, a wonderland of your own creation where, in effect, you can easily falsify the past.

The reason I chose to use quotations from Lewis Carroll throughout this collection, apart from the fact that they make me laugh a lot, is quite simple. The worlds Alice encountered down the rabbit hole and through the looking-glass, and the world in which the elusive snark was hunted, are worlds in which real history does not exist: they are worlds full of furphies.

Finally, here is one last example of this, from our not-so-distant past. Well, from the early twentieth century, which is a century ago admittedly but doesn't seem that long ago to someone my age. It's a story about how someone who was much loved and very famous could, within a few decades, be best remembered for something that never happened.

Roy Rene was born Henry van der Sluys in Adelaide in 1891. With his irreverent and unique style of comedy, he was the most popular variety act in Australia for the first half of the twentieth century. He shaped the Aussie sense of humour through his stage appearances and the character Mo McCacky, in the radio program *McCacky Moments*.

His material ranged from corny wordplay and slapstick to character comedy. On radio he was always hitting his cheeky 'son' Harry and exclaiming, 'Cop that, young Harry!' Other Mo catch-phrases like 'Strike me lucky!' and 'You beaut!' became part of Aussie vernacular. The radio character of Spencer the Garbage Man, played by actor Harry Avondale, provided Mo with plenty of opportunities for low comedy, olfactory jokes and the catch phrase 'Oh, phewwww!' Another 'running gag' in the radio show consisted of Mo attempting to recite a poem titled 'The Barmaid and the Butcher', but never being allowed to begin.

While Mo's comedy often *suggested* that he was *about* to be vulgar, he never was. By today's standards he was very politically incorrect, but never overtly 'vulgar'. In fact, he was scathing about performers who crossed the line into what was then called 'blue comedy' and was remembered by his wife and children as almost prudish in his private life.

Oddly, however, the most repeated story about his theatre performances is about a very 'crude' routine that he is supposed to have performed with his partner of many years, Nat 'Stiffy' Phillips.

The routine supposedly had Mo visiting an optometrist, played by Phillips, for an eye test. Every time Phillips wrote 'F' on a blackboard, Mo read it as 'K'. The punchline of the routine has Phillips asking, 'How come, every time I write F, you see K?'

Now, the interesting thing about this story is that it is the most common anecdote told about Mo's stage career. Whenever Mo's name comes up in conversation you can bet someone will tell you the story, implying that Mo's comedy was often vulgar and bawdy.

The truth is that there is no evidence that the routine was ever performed in any theatre anywhere in Australia or New Zealand where the two comedians appeared. There is no mention of the sketch in any old theatre program notes and no one who knew the duo can ever recall them doing it, because they never did. It would have been totally 'outside' Mo's style of comedy and unacceptable to theatre managers and Mo's audiences.

The only time Mo was ever in trouble for 'going too far' was in Adelaide in the 1920s, when he made a remark about the city's statues that drew a letter of complaint to the theatre.

The sad thing about this furphy is that it completely distorts the truth about Mo's career and memories of his comedic style by making him remembered for something he never did.

Finally, I maintain that the true stories are often far more interesting than the furphies, anyway!

SELECT BIBLIOGRAPHY

Beaglehole, John Cawte, *The Journals of Captain James Cook*,
   The Hakluyt Society/Australian Academy of the Humanities,
   Cambridge/London, 1968

Beatty, Bill, *This Australia, Strange and Amazing Facts*, Halstead Press,
   Sydney, 1941

Beatty, Bill, *A Treasury of Australian Folk Tales and Traditions*, Ure Smith,
   Sydney, 1960

Bleszynski, Nick, *Shoot Straight, You Bastards!*, Random House,
   Australia, 2003

Brown, Max, *Australian Son*, Georgian House, London, 1948

Cameron-Ash, Margaret, *Lying for the Admiralty: Captain Cook's Endeavour
   Voyage*, Rosenberg, Sydney, 2018

Clarke, William Branwhite, *Remarks on the Sedimentary Formations of New
   South Wales*, Thomas Richards (Govt Printer), Sydney, 1878

Cook, James, *Journal of H.M.S. Endeavour, 1768–1771* [manuscript],
   National Library of Australia

Coulthard-Clark, Chris, *The Encyclopaedia of Australia's Battles*, Allen &
   Unwin, Sydney, 1998, 2001

Curby, Pauline, *Randwick*, Randwick City Council, Sydney, 2009

Curby, Pauline, *Seven Miles from Sydney, a History of Manly*, Manly
   Council, 2001

Cutlack, F.M., *Breaker Morant: A Horseman Who Made History, with a
   Selection of His Bush Ballads*, Ure Smith, Sydney, 1962

Davison, Simpson, *The Discovery and Geognosy of Gold Deposits in
   Australia*, Longman, Green, Longman and Roberts, London, 1860

Dawson, Stuart E., *Ned Kelly and the Myth of a Republic of North-Eastern
   Victoria*, Monash University, Melbourne, 2018

Hargraves, Edward Hammond, *Australia and its Goldfields*, Ingram & Co, London, 1855

Hawkesworth, John, *An Account of the Voyages Undertaken by the Order of His Present Majesty for Making Discoveries in the Southern Hemisphere— in the* Dolphin, Swallow *and* Endeavour, Strahan and Cadell, London, 1773

Hetherington, John, *Norman Lindsay: The Embattled Olympian*, Oxford University Press, Melbourne, 1973

Hoy, Anthony, 'James Francis Thomas—The Man Who Defended Breaker Morant', *The Bulletin*, 4 April 2000

Jones, Ian, *Ned Kelly: A Short Life*, Lothian, Melbourne, 1995

Kennedy, Leo and Looby, Mic, *Black Snake*, Affirm Press, Melbourne, 2019

Lyte, Charles, *Sir Joseph Banks*, Reed, Sydney, 1980

Marchant, Leslie, *France Australe*, Artlook, Perth, 1982

Moloney, John, *I Am Ned Kelly*, Penguin, Melbourne, 1982

Morrissey, Doug, *Ned Kelly: A Lawless Life*, Connorcourt Publishing, Ballarat, 2015

Mossman and Banister, *Australia Visited and Revisited: A Narrative of Recent Travels and Old Experiences in Victoria and New South Wales*, Addey & Co., London, 1853

O'Keeffe, Dennis, *Waltzing Matilda: The Secret History of Australia's Favourite Song*, Allen & Unwin, Sydney, 2011

Quinion, Michael, *Port Out, Starboard Home and Other Language Myths*, Penguin, London, 2004

Reece, Bob, *Exiles from Erin: Convict Lives in Ireland and Australia*, Palgrave Macmillan, London, 1991

Robson, John, *Captain Cook's War and Peace, the Royal Navy years, 1755–1768*, Seaforth Publishing, Barnsley, 2009

Rolfe, Patricia, *The Journalistic Javelin*, Wildcat Press, Sydney, 1979

Scott and MacFarlane, 'Ned Kelly—Stock Thief, Bank Robber, Murderer— Psychopath', *Psychiatry, Psychology and Law*, vol. 21, issue 5, pp. 716–746, 2014

Tholas-Disset and Ritzenhoff (eds), *Humor, Entertainment, and Popular Culture During World War I*, Palgrave Macmillan, NewYork, 2015

Wharton, Captain W. (ed.), *Captain Cook's Journal During His First Voyage Round the World*, Elliot Stock, London, 1893

Witton, George, *Scapegoats of the Empire*, D.W. Paterson, Melbourne, 1907; Angus & Robertson, Sydney, 1982

ACKNOWLEDGEMENTS

Thanks to the following:

Rebecca Kaiser for her good-humoured support and encouragement.
Tom Bailey-Smith for smoothly managing the process.
Susin Chow for her perceptive copyediting and suggestions.
Jillian Dellit for research, suggestions and proofreading.
Pauline Curby for her help and permission to use her research.
All at Allen & Unwin.